Contents

Intelligence for an Age of Terror

GREGORY F. TREVERTON

RAND Corporation

CAMBRIDGE UNIVERSITY PRESS
Cambridge, New York, Melbourne, Madrid, Cape Town, Singapore, São Paulo, Delhi

Cambridge University Press
32 Avenue of the Americas, New York, NY 10013-2473, USA

www.cambridge.org
Information on this title: www.cambridge.org/9780521518451

First published 2009

Printed in the United States of America

A catalog record for this publication is available from the British Library

Library of Congress Cataloging in Publication data

Treverton, Gregory F.
Intelligence for an age of terror / Gregory F. Treverton.
p.   cm.
Includes bibliographical references and index.
ISBN 978-0-521-51845-1 (hardback)
1. Intelligence service – United States.   2. Terrorism – Government
policy – United States.   I. Title.
JK468.I6T723   2009
363.325′1630973 – dc22   2008047224

ISBN   978-0-521-51845-1 hardback

Intelligence for an Age of Terror

During the Cold War, U.S. intelligence was concerned primarily with states; nonstate actors like terrorists were secondary. Now, the priorities are reversed – and the challenge is enormous. States had an address, and they were hierarchical and bureaucratic; thus, they came with a "story." Terrorists do not. States were "over there," but terrorists are there and here. Therefore, they put pressure on intelligence at home, not just abroad. They also force intelligence and law enforcement – the Central Intelligence Agency (CIA) and the Federal Bureau of Investigation (FBI) – to work together in new ways, and, if those 700,000 police officers in the United States are to be the "eyes and ears" in the fight against terrorism, new means of sharing not only information but also analysis across the federal system are imperative. The strength of this book is that it underscores the extent of the change and ranges broadly across data collection and analysis, both foreign and domestic, and it presents the issues of value that arise as new targets require the collection of more information at home.

Gregory F. Treverton is director of the RAND Corporation's Center for Global Risk and Security. Earlier, he directed RAND's Intelligence Policy Center and its International Security and Defense Policy Center and was associate dean of the Pardee RAND Graduate School. His recent work has focused on terrorism, intelligence, and law enforcement, with a special interest in new forms of public–private partnership. Dr. Treverton has served in government for the first Senate Select Committee on Intelligence, handling Europe for the National Security Council (NSC); most recently, he served as vice chair of the National Intelligence Estimates (NIEs). He holds a B.A. summa cum laude from Princeton University and a master's degree in public policy and a Ph.D. in economics and politics, both from Harvard University. His books include *Reshaping National Intelligence for an Age of Information* (Cambridge University Press, 2001) and *New Challenges, New Tools for Defense Decisionmaking* (2003).

Preface

This book very much stands alone, but it also takes up where my 2001 book, *Reshaping National Intelligence for an Age of Information,* left off. At the beginning of the last chapter of that earlier book, completed before September 11, I observed that the book had been mostly about how intelligence should reshape in continued fair weather for globalization. What, I asked, might turn that weather fouler? The first excursion I considered was a major terrorist attack on the United States (the other, haunting from the perspective of 2009, was a global economic collapse). This is hardly prescient – a stream of blue-ribbon panels had predicted an attack, sometime.

I imagined that an attack would make intelligence more important, which has turned out to be the case and thus became a reason for this book. (The other prediction I made was that military instruments would not turn out to be very relevant, and so military budgets would decline. On that score, I was either wrong or premature – depending on whether the war in Iraq is regarded as central to or a diversion from the fight against terror.) It struck me then, and continues to strike me now, that for all our talk about terrorism and other transnational threats as the preeminent targets of intelligence, the implications of that shift run much deeper than is usually realized. That became a second reason for doing this book.

As usual, the book accreted as much as it was written, as I drew on and adapted work done for other purposes. In the process, I incurred intellectual debts to a large number of colleagues, not all of whom I name here. My old friend Philip Bobbitt and I have come to many similar conclusions about the market state and about intelligence in an age of terror, sometimes by different routes, and I am always stimulated by talking with or reading him. John Parachini, who directs RAND's Intelligence Policy Center, has been a sparring partner for ideas throughout. RAND has provided support of a more tangible sort, first to assess the 2004 intelligence act and outline the next steps, then to work on drafting this book.

After September 11th, I had the opportunity to build up RAND's analytic support for the FBI – first in a review of the Bureau's internal security in the wake of the Robert Hanssen spy case and a blue-ribbon panel report, and most recently in a congressionally mandated assessment of the pros and cons of establishing a domestic intelligence service separated from law enforcement, a project of which the FBI was not the sponsor but in which it did have a keen interest. The work has been for me a fascinating introduction to a very different organizational culture than traditional intelligence, one I've come to admire in many respects. Even better, Bruce Ciske of the Bureau has been my informal guide throughout that introduction – a distinct professional and personal pleasure.

My chapter on analysis draws on work commissioned by the then–Assistant Director of Central Intelligence for Analysis and Production, Mark Lowenthal, and his deputy, Bill Nolte. I am grateful to them for that chance to snoop around the analysis shops in the intelligence community, and to my then–RAND colleague in that venture, Bryan Gabbard. I'm also grateful to Roger George and Jim Bruce, longtime colleagues, the latter now at RAND, whose edited volume on analysis gave me the chance to think more about "politicization."

The chapter on analysis and the sections on learning organizations draw on a chapter commissioned by the CIA for a book on the psychology of intelligence analysis. The editor of that book, Dr. Richard Rees, worked over my chapter harder and more creatively than any editor ever has – all to my benefit. Alas, the book's fate is a kind of parable for the challenges U.S. intelligence faces. Cleared as unclassified, the CIA still decided not to publish the book – because an "official" publication by the CIA was thought to sanction comments that were critical, albeit intended as constructive criticism. The result was thus the oddity of an unclassified book that is available only on the CIA's highly classified computer system.

Finally, I have had the good fortune for the past several years to be a sometime visiting professor at the Swedish National Defence College. Only the Swedes would invite a foreigner to develop an intelligence program at their national defense college, but they have, happily. It has given me opportunity and incentive to think comparatively across a range of issues from the nature of the target and how to deal with "complexities," to how to engage both new customers and private citizens in jointly producing useful intelligence. I thank my colleagues there, especially Wilhelm Agrell, Lars Nicander, Jan Leijonhielm, and Magnus Ranstorp.

I owe debts of other sorts to two other people, to whom I dedicate this book. The late Richard E. Neustadt, my friend, mentor, and colleague, first introduced me to the particularities of the political "tribe" when I was a graduate student. The example of his graceful prose left a lifelong appreciation for the power of a four-word sentence. The other is my wife, Karen – partner, friend, and more throughout the writing of this book and the rest of life's adventures. Needless to say, none of these good people should be held responsible for any shortcomings that remain. Those are mine alone.

Pacific Palisades, California   January 6, 2009

Acronyms

Symbol	Definition*
AAR	after-action review
ACS	Automated Case Support (FBI)
AFL–CIO	American Federation of Labor and Congress of Industrial Organizations
ATTF	Anti-Terrorism Task Force (U.S. attorneys)
AUMF	authorization for use of military force
BfV	Bundesamt für Verfassungsschutz, or Federal Office for the Protection of the Constitution (Germany)
CALL	Center for Army Lessons Learned
CAPPS II	Computer-Assisted Passenger Prescreening System II
CBM	confidence-building measure
CBP	Customs and Border Protection
CBRN	chemical, biological, radiological, or nuclear
CD	Counterintelligence Division (FBI)
CENTCOM	Central Command
CIA	Central Intelligence Agency
CID	Criminal Investigative Division (FBI)
CMS	Community Management Staff
COINTELPRO	Counterintelligence Program (FBI)
COPS	Community Oriented Policing Services
CSIS	Canadian Security and Intelligence Service

*All institutions are in the United States unless otherwise specified.

CTC	Counterterrorism Center (CIA)
CTD	Counterterrorism Division (FBI)
CTR	Currency Transaction Report
DARPA	Defense Advanced Research Projects Agency
DCI	Director of Central Intelligence
DDNI	Deputy Director of National Intelligence
DEA	Drug Enforcement Administration
DHS	Department of Homeland Security
DI	Directorate of Intelligence
DIA	Defense Intelligence Agency
DIAC	Defense Intelligence Agency Center
DMPI	designated mean points of impact
DNI	Director of National Intelligence
DST	Direction de la Surveillance du Territoire, or Territorial Surveillance Directorate (France)
DTA	Detainee Treatment Act
EAD	Executive Assistant Director (FBI)
EC	electronic communication (FBI)
ECPA	Electronic Communications Privacy Act
FAA	Federal Aviation Administration
FBI	Federal Bureau of Investigation
FIA	Future Imagery Architecture
FIG	Field Intelligence Group (FBI)
FISA	Foreign Intelligence Surveillance Act
FISC	Foreign Intelligence Surveillance Court
FNLA	National Front for the Liberation of Angola
FRA	Defence Radio Establishment (Sweden)
FutureMAP	Future Markets Applied to Prediction
HUMINT	human intelligence
ICDO	Integrated Concepts Development Office
IFOR	Intervention Force (United Nations)
IG	Inspector General
IMINT	imagery intelligence
INR	State Department Bureau of Intelligence and Research
INS	Immigration and Naturalization Service
IRA	Irish Republican Army
IRS	Internal Revenue Service

ISAC	Information Sharing and Analysis Center
ISE	Information-Sharing Environment
ISI	Inter-Service Intelligence (Pakistan)
ISR	intelligence, surveillance, and reconnaissance
IT	information technology
JMIC	Joint Military Intelligence College
JMIP	Joint Military Intelligence Program
JTFCT	Joint Task Force Counterterrorism (DIA)
JTTF	Joint Terrorism Task Force
LEA	law enforcement agency
MASINT	measurement and signatures intelligence
MATRIX	Multistate Antiterrorism Information Exchange
MLE	military liaison element
MPLA	Popular Movement for the Liberation of Angola
NATO	North Atlantic Treaty Organization
NCIX	National Counterintelligence Executive
NCTC	National Counterterrorism Center
NED	National Endowment for Democracy
NGA	National Geospatial Intelligence Agency
NGO	non-governmental organization
NIC	National Intelligence Council
NIC-C	National Intelligence Coordination Center
NIE	National Intelligence Estimate
NIO	National Intelligence Officer
NIP	National Intelligence Program
NIPF	National Intelligence Priorities Framework
NOC	non-official cover
NRO	National Reconnaissance Office
NSA	National Security Agency
NSB	National Security Branch
NSC	National Security Council
NSL	National Security Letter
NYPD	New York Police Department
ODNI	Office of the Director of National Intelligence
OIPR	Office of Intelligence Policy and Review (Justice Department)
OSINT	open-source intelligence
PA&E	policy analysis and evaluation

PACOM	Pacific Command
PDB	President's Daily Brief
PNR	passenger name records
RCMP	Royal Canadian Mounted Police
RCMP-SS	Royal Canadian Mounted Police Security Service
RDM	robust decision making
RFU	Radical Fundamentalist Unit (FBI)
SAC	Special Agent in Charge (FBI)
SAG	Strategic Assessments Group (CIA)
SAR	suspicious activity reporting
SCC	Sector Coordinating Council
SCI	secret compartmented intelligence
SIGINT	signals intelligence
SIS	Senior Intelligence Service
SOCOM	Special Operations Command
SOUTHCOM	Southern Command
SSA	Social Security Administration
STEP	Science and Technology Experts Program
TIA	Total (Terrorism) Information Awareness
TIARA	Tactical Intelligence and Related Activities
TIDE	Terrorist Identities Datamart Environment
TLAM	Tomahawk Land Attack Missile
TSA	Transportation Security Administration
TSC	Terrorist Screening Center
TSDB	Terrorist Screening Database
TSP	Terrorist Surveillance Program
TTIC	Terrorist Threat Integration Center
UAV	unmanned aerial vehicle
UBLU	Usama Bin Laden Unit (FBI)
UN	United Nations
UNITA	National Union for the Total Independence of Angola
WMD	weapons of mass destruction

Intelligence for an Age of Terror

1

Introduction

National-intelligence services, in the United States and elsewhere, had not digested the implications of the end of the Cold War when the first wave of terrorist attacks struck: September 11, 2001, in the United States; March 11, 2004, in Spain; and July 7, 2005, in Britain – dubbed "9/11," "3/11," and "7/7." They had not absorbed the effect of one major change when they were hit by yet another. Thus, intelligence is being reshaped under this onrush of events. Especially in the United States, it is also being reshaped under the looming shadow of acrimony about emotional issues at the edge of intelligence, issues with epithets like "Guantanamo" and "Abu Ghraib" and "torture." These epithets with their implications for intelligence are considered in Chapter 9. The onset of an age of terror has highlighted the role of intelligence services in detecting and preventing possible terrorist acts. At the same time, a series of investigations, especially in the United States and Britain, has focused attention on the performance of those intelligence services.[1] If and when the next major attack comes, recriminations about why it was not prevented will make the post–September 11 debate look decorous.

This book begins with where intelligence has been – the legacy of institutions and operating practices inherited from the Cold War – but its purpose is to describe where intelligence needs to go. The required reshaping is dramatic. In the United States, the process began with the Terrorism Prevention and Intelligence Reform Act of 2004; however, that law was the bare beginning of the reshaping, hardly the end. It is intriguing that all the countries that took intelligence seriously during the Cold War face some version of the same challenges: they have

1

Table 1.1. *Intelligence: From the Cold War to an Age of Terror*

	Old: Cold War	New: Age of Terror
Target	States, primarily the Soviet Union	Transnational actors, also some states
"Boundedness"	Relatively bounded: Soviet Union ponderous	Much less bounded: terrorists patient but new groups and attack modes
"Story" about Target	Story: states are geographic, hierarchical, bureaucratic	Not much story: nonstates come in many sizes and shapes
Information	Too little: dominated by secret sources	Too much: broader range of sources, although secrets still matter
Interaction with Target	Relatively little: Soviet Union would do what it would do	Intense: terrorists as the ultimate asymmetric threat

considerable capacity but a capacity that is primarily military in character, so they are asking how that capacity should be reshaped. In an age of terror, they all face the need to collect more information about their inhabitants: How can they do so without trampling on privacy and civil liberties? The challenges vary in scope and circumstances, but they are kindred across countries. This book draws comparisons across nations to illuminate issues, especially arrangements for domestic intelligence.

With the end of the Cold War and, a decade later, the onset of Muslim extremist terrorism, the task of intelligence changed dramatically. Table 1.1 summarizes the major differences.

These changes frame all subsequent chapters, with a number of themes common throughout. One theme is risk. Intelligence always has been a hedge against risk but now, as the nature of the threat has changed, so has the nature of the risk. Terrorists who are willing to die for their cause as suicide bombers, for example, cannot be deterred from acting in any way similar to the way that states could. Thus, there is even more pressure on intelligence, which now has to be not merely good enough to structure deterrent threats. Rather, it also needs to reach deeply into small groups – their proclivities and capabilities – to provide an understanding that can lead to preventive action. As the Irish Republican Army (IRA) stated after that group's bombing of a Brighton hotel in 1984 failed to kill Prime Minister Margaret Thatcher, "Today we were unlucky, but remember we only have to be lucky once. You will have to be lucky always."[2]

A second theme is the corresponding expansion in the consumers of intelligence. National intelligence used to be designed primarily for a relatively small set of political and military leaders of states. Now, in principle, it could be of use to a huge number of consumers, from police officers on the beat to private-sector managers of major infrastructure. Intelligence has moved, according to the catchphrase, from the "need to know" to the "need to share" – a catchphrase that captures the diagnosis but badly poses the remedy.

A third theme is the increased number of needs for – and, therefore, types of – intelligence across a variety of time horizons from immediate warning to longer term understanding. Much of the Cold War intelligence was puzzle-solving, looking for additional pieces to fill out a mosaic of understanding whose broad shape was a given.[3] Those puzzles – for example, "How many warheads does a Soviet missile carry?" – could be solved with certainty if we only had access to information that, in principle, was available. Puzzle-solving is inductive. Mysteries are different; no evidence can settle them definitively because they are typically about people, not things. They are contingent; that is, mystery-framing is deductive – the analysis begins where the evidence ends.

There were mysteries during the Cold War, but the age of terror seems especially rife with them. For instance, many of another nation's military capabilities could be treated as a puzzle during the Cold War and assessed by counting tanks, divisions, and rockets. Now, however, even the capabilities of terrorists are a mystery: those capabilities *depend*, not least, on us. Given the lethality of even a single suicide bomber, what can be counted is not of much use to count.

A final overarching theme is boundaries – of both law and organization. During the Cold War, democratic societies drew boundaries – with varying degrees of sharpness – between intelligence and law enforcement, between home and abroad, and between public and private. The first two boundaries, in particular, were drawn to protect the privacy and civil liberties of a nation's citizens. In the circumstances of the Cold War, those boundaries made sense. However, they set up nations to fail against a terrorist foe who respects none of those boundaries. Now, the balance between security and privacy is being struck anew and, in the process, the organizational distinctions – such as between intelligence and law enforcement – are being erased.

CHANGED TARGETS AND A MISMATCHED LEGACY

As an intelligence challenge, transnational targets such as terrorists differ from traditional state targets in a number of ways, which are summarized in Table 1.1. Chapter 2 describes the shift in more detail. Transnational targets are not new; intelligence has long been active against organized crime and drug traffickers but as a secondary activity. Although state targets of intelligence will remain – Iran, North Korea, China, and Russia, for example – the shift to terrorists as a primary target is momentous. First, while the current Islamic extremist terrorists hardly act quickly but instead carefully plan their attacks over years, transnational targets are less bounded than state-centric targets. There will be discontinuities in targets and attack modes, and new groups will emerge unpredictably.

Second, intelligence ultimately is storytelling. It is helping policy makers build or adjust stories in light of new or additional information or arguments. However, the new transnational targets deprive both intelligence and policy of a shared story that would facilitate analysis and communication. We knew what states were like, even very different states such as the Soviet Union: they were geographical, hierarchical, and bureaucratic. There is no comparable story for nonstates, which come in many sizes and shapes.

Third, given that U.S. foes were closed societies, Cold War intelligence (including analysis) gave pride of place to secrets – that is, information gathered by human and technical means that intelligence "owned." Terrorists are hardly open, but an avalanche of open data is relevant to them: witness the September 11 hijackers whose real addresses were available in California motor-vehicle records. During the Cold War, the problem was too little information; now, the problem is too much. Then, intelligence's secrets were deemed reliable; now, the torrents on the Web are a stew of fact, fancy, and disinformation.

Finally, and perhaps most portentous, terrorists shape themselves around us; that was hardly the case for the Soviet Union. As former

U.S. Secretary of Defense Harold Brown quipped about the U.S.–Soviet nuclear competition, "When we build, they build. When we cut, they build."[4] Although various countries – especially the United States – hoped that their policies would influence Moscow, as a first approximation, intelligence analysts could presume that they would not. The Soviet Union would do what it would do. The challenge, in the first instance, was figuring out its likely course, not calibrating the influence that other nations might have over that course.

The terrorist target, however, is utterly different. It is the ultimate asymmetric threat, shaping its capabilities to our vulnerabilities. The September 11 suicide bombers did not come up with their attack plan because they were airline buffs. They knew that fuel-filled jets in flight were a vulnerable asset, that defensive passenger-clearance procedures were weak, and that the scheme obviated the need to face a more effective defense against procuring or importing ordnance. By the same token, the London, Madrid, and other bombers conducted sufficient tactical reconnaissance to shape their plans to the vulnerabilities of their targets. To a great extent, we shape the threat to us; it reflects our vulnerable assets and weak defenses. As military planners would state, it is impossible to understand red – that is, potential foes – without knowing a lot about blue – ourselves – that is, our own proclivities and vulnerabilities.

That fact has awkward implications for intelligence, especially foreign intelligence that in many countries has been enjoined from examining the home front and, less formally, has worried that getting too close to "policy" is to risk becoming politicized. Moreover, to the extent that intelligence now becomes the net assessment of red against blue, that too has been the province of the military, not civilian, agencies.

The Cold War legacy of intelligence is mismatched to the changed threat. That legacy, the subject of Chapter 3, consists of three parts. The first is the boundaries that were drawn. In an important sense, it should not be surprising that cooperation between the Central Intelligence Agency (CIA) and the Federal Bureau of Investigation (FBI) before September 11 was ragged at best. Americans wanted it that way. Out of concern for civil liberties, they decided that the two agencies should not be too close. The FBI and the CIA sit astride the fundamental boundaries of the Cold War – boundaries between intelligence and law enforcement, between foreign and domestic, and between public and private. The distinctions run deep. The boundaries were reinforced by the second legacy: the institutional legacy.

The institutional legacy, on the collection side, was an organization of "stovepipes" by source. The clandestine service, or directorate of operations, of the CIA was primarily responsible for espionage, or human intelligence (HUMINT); the National Security Agency (NSA) for signals intelligence (SIGINT); and the National Geospatial Intelligence Agency (NGA) for pictures and other imagery intelligence (IMINT). There was, perhaps, a certain logic to that organization during the Cold War. With one overwhelming target – the Soviet Union – the various "INTs" were asked, in effect, what they could contribute to understanding the puzzle of the Soviet Union.

For its part, analysis was organized primarily by agency, not by issue or problem. The directorate of intelligence of the CIA was first among equals, but the Defense Intelligence Agency (DIA) was just as large in numbers, and the much smaller State Department Bureau of Intelligence and Research (INR) tended to punch well above its weight in interagency discussions. The military services each had their own intelligence arm, primarily addressing the foreign threats that their service's weaponry would confront; the joint combatant commands also had their intelligence units, heavily tactical in orientation. In Washington, there were smaller analytic units in departments ranging from Energy to Commerce, which were explicitly departmental, serving the needs of local consumers.

If organizing intelligence by source on the collection side and by agency on the analysis side made a certain sense during the Cold War, it cannot be the right way to organize now. On the collection side, if the terrorist target is more of a mystery than a puzzle, then the Cold War's implicit competition among the INTs for puzzle pieces needs to give way to explicit cooperation across those INTs in framing the mysteries. Now, moreover, it is not just that there are more targets but also more consumers and more information – although the information is varied in reliability and little of it is owned by intelligence as were the secret sources during the Cold War.

The final Cold War legacy was a product of the boundaries. Domestic intelligence was a stepchild in the system. Unlike most of its major because the CIA had withheld their names from TIPOFF, the basic terrorist watch list. Neither did the FBI have any reason to look for them – for instance, by conducting a basic Internet search for their names or by querying its informants in Southern California – because the last the FBI knew from the CIA was that the two terrorists were overseas. No agency told the Federal Aviation Administration (FAA) to be looking for the two, apparently because the FAA was not in the law enforcement business. The airlines were not informed because they were private, not public. So, on the morning of September 11, four sets of terrorists succeeded in boarding U.S. commercial jetliners, and three managed to strike their target: the World Trade Center towers in Manhattan and the Pentagon in the nation's capital.

In the United States, the 2004 Act made a start at reshaping intelligence. The Act – and more so the Senate version of the bill that was modified in conference with the House of Representatives – proposed national intelligence centers under the authority of the new Director of National Intelligence (DNI) and organized around issues or missions. The centers, with the National Counterterrorism Center (NCTC) as the prototype, would both deploy and use the information, technology, and staff resources of the existing agencies: the CIA, DIA, NSA, and others. They would be intelligence's version of the military's "unified combatant commands" and would look to the agencies to acquire the technological systems, train the people, and execute the operations planned by the national intelligence centers. So far, in addition to the NCTC, the National Counterproliferation Center is the only other center to be established, although the DNI has named "mission" managers for North Korea, Iran, and Cuba–Venezuela.

The FBI, under Director Robert Mueller, was facing enormous pressure, and there was considerable talk of creating a new domestic-intelligence agency separate from the Bureau. Mueller, however, moved rapidly to turn the Bureau from almost pure concentration on law enforcement to prevention and intelligence. Both Congress and the postmortem commissions decided to give the FBI time to see if the change could be made enduring. The FBI adopted the Weapons of Mass Destruction (WMD) Commission's recommendation to create not only a Directorate of Intelligence (DI) within the FBI but also a National Security Branch (NSB), incorporating intelligence and the FBI's Counterterrorism Division (CTD) and Counterintelligence Division (CD).

Yet, the 2004 Act marked only the beginning of the change; Chapter 5 lays out the agenda ahead. The main challenge is also the reason for having a DNI in the first place – to better manage the entire set of U.S. intelligence agencies so that the nation gets the most from the $40-plus billion it spends annually on intelligence. John Negroponte, the first DNI, took over control of managing and delivering the "crown-jewel" analysis – the President's Daily Brief (PDB) – which had been the CIA's product. However, the nation did not need a DNI to deliver the PDB; for that, the former Director of Central Intelligence (DCI) was fine.

Rather, the DNI needs to be a major player in programmatic decisions – of which there was not much evidence in the DNI's first several years – a need more pressing as the distinction between "national" and "tactical" systems blurs, meaning that the intelligence agencies and the Pentagon share systems and compete for priority. This will require a much greater analytic capacity than what the DNI inherited if he is to be compelling inside the executive branch and with Congress.

At present, U.S. collection produces too much data and too little information, and the strategic-management task requires driving trade-offs not only across the stovepipes but also within them. U.S. collection techniques, especially for imagery, are fairly well understood by targets. Also, the Cold War espionage practices will not work against terrorist targets because, alas, Al Qaeda operatives do not go to embassy cocktail parties. The sheer volume of the data, or "take," from collection, just from intelligence's own secret sources, threatens to overwhelm the processing of it. The challenge is to be less passive and quicker in innovation. For signals, that means getting closer to targets. For imagery, it means smaller platforms, increased use of stealth, and employing more of the spectrum. For espionage, it means more diversity in spymasters and moving out of official cover. However, it also means being patient.

Meeting these challenges amounts to changing the agencies of the intelligence community to adaptive-learning organizations. The need applies with particular force to intelligence's most precious asset, its people. New recruits, across the community, are very different. They are fearless and computer-savvy – used to communicating, searching,

and reaching out. They will not tolerate the information environments – compartmentalized, slow, and source-driven – that current intelligence provides. Neither will they long be satisfied with work
assignments that amount to, as one put it, "a few square miles of Iraq."
They seek new challenges in "portfolio careers." To get and keep
them – a great opportunity – intelligence will have to change the way
it structures careers throughout the career cycle – from mentoring to
lateral entry at senior levels. New personnel practices and new forms
of training can also build jointness in a legacy of the stovepiped intelligence community. Training is similarly stovepiped and scattered; too
much of it was oriented toward credentials rather than doing better on
the job, and it was not integral to careers. There were no focal points
for tool-building and lesson-learning. In all these respects, the DNI
also has an opportunity.

The third major agenda item is domestic intelligence. If, thus far,
the United States and its leaders have opted not to create a domestic-
intelligence agency separate from law enforcement, the question of
whether to do so will remain on the agenda. Another major terrorist
attack would drive it immediately to the top. On this score, although
international comparisons cannot settle the question for the United
States, they are particularly apt because almost all of America's principal partners in the age of terror have chosen to separate domestic
intelligence and law enforcement into distinct government agencies.
For the United States, the choice is ultimately whether the considerable transition costs – costs driven home by the experience of the
Department of Homeland Security (DHS) – are justified by potential
improvements in domestic intelligence, especially in the value of what
is collected and the value added by analysis.

A critical part of the agenda is intelligence analysis, the subject of
Chapter 6. The postmortems in the United States, more so than in
Britain, were scathing in regard to analysis – for instance, the WMD
Commission on intelligence before the Iraq war: "This failure was in
large part the result of analytical shortcomings; intelligence analysts
were too wedded to their assumptions about Saddam's intentions."[5]
The Senate Select Committee on Intelligence was equally scathing
about the October 2002 National Intelligence Estimate (NIE), concluding: "Most of the major key judgments...either overstated, or
were not supported by, the underlying intelligence reporting. A series

of failures, particularly in analytic tradecraft, led to the mischaracterization of the intelligence."[6]

There are no easy solutions to improving analysis; legislation or reorganization or exhortation cannot produce more creativity. The shortcomings run deep into organizational culture; for instance, most intelligence analysis in the U.S. government has made little use of either machines or formal methods. Thus, there is no substitute for a rich variety of pilot projects and experiments, many of which involve dramatic departures from current practice. For instance, psychologists tell us that harried people are not likely to be creative; creativity requires some "down" time for reflection. However, intelligence analysts are now frantic all the time; therefore, creating special units enjoined from immediate production but encouraged to think makes sense yet cuts against the organizational grain – not to mention the political imperative of wringing any possible waste from the system!

Improving analysis requires putting consumers at the center of the process. Ultimately, analysis is not information nor is it elegant papers reflecting deep judgment. Rather, it is improved understanding by the people who have to make a decision. Intelligence, and especially analysis, will not be truly reshaped until it changes how it considers its *products*. When I oversaw the National Intelligence Council (NIC) estimates, I realized that the NIEs were not our real product. Rather, it was National Intelligence Officers (NIOs) – that is, not paper but people, experts in a position to attend meetings and offer judgment. A starting point for the reshaping would be recognizing that *analysis* should be plural, encompassing many consumers with many different needs for intelligence.

MANY CONSUMERS, TOO MANY SECRETS

The mushrooming of consumers compounds the challenge of communication between intelligence and its consumers – the subject of Chapter 7. Communication was already difficult at the federal level before September 11. The specific concern in the WMD debate was *politicization*: the risk that intelligence would be under pressure – usually more implicit than explicit – to produce assessments that suited the preferences of national administrations. Yet, protection against politicization needs to be balanced against its opposite: intelligence that is not relevant to any policy question at issue. At the NIC, I thought almost all the work we did was interesting, but I distinguished "interesting" from "interesting *and* useful" – that is, an answer to a question that the policy world was asking in some form. Perhaps the more subtle danger for the future, as in the run-up to the Iraq war, is that government leaders will feel impelled to use intelligence to justify their policies, which puts intelligence in an unwanted and public position.

Now, the consumer "tribe" has become vastly larger and more heterogeneous – including 700,000 law enforcement officers in 18,000 government jurisdictions, not to mention the private-sector managers of "public" infrastructure, such as information, banking, and transportation. The federal agencies call reaching out to them "information-sharing," which is the wrong approach on many grounds. It implies that agencies own their information, to be shared only as they see fit, and that the challenge is primarily technical; that is, if only the pipes were big enough to let the information flow all the way to the cop on the beat, all would be well.[7] The problem is not technology. Technology can help, but the challenge is one of policy, not hardware.

In fact, the heart of the issue is how intelligence does its business. Existing business practices, with each intelligence agency controlling the information it produces, make it difficult to share across U.S. intelligence, let alone getting information to state and local authorities. The core of the policy problem begins with intelligence, with existing security procedures designed to limit information to those with a "need to know," not share it. Yet, fresh analytic insights are likely to arise precisely from those who come to the information with a fresh perspective, who have *no* need to know. The fundamental challenge is in reshaping how the U.S. government thinks of information and how information should be used and controlled.

The latest season of inquiry, unusual in the last half-century, has been more about intelligence's analysts than its operators.[8] From the Bay of Pigs in the 1960s to the Iran–Contra Affair in the 1980s, the customary focus of allegations of failure was bungled covert operations, not analysis (not that today's analysts have relished their season!). Achieving significant results with small secret projects became increasingly unlikely between the 1950s and the 1990s. Early targets of

U.S. covert action sought and almost pleaded not to be regarded as enemies of the United States. However, for Nicaragua's Sandinistas or Iran's Khomeini – not to mention Al Qaeda's bin Laden – the United States was more useful as an enemy than as a friend. Cuba's Castro bridged the two periods, with America-as-foe becoming the best thing he had going for him. As the scale of operations grew, so did the likelihood that they would become public. They become "overt covert"; in the most visible example, U.S. support to the *mujahideen* contesting Soviet occupation of Afghanistan after 1979 was a very open secret, one entailing a half billion dollars a year.

If covert action cannot be kept secret, then why not do it openly? In the past two decades, that question came to acquire a "yes" answer – the biggest change in "covert" action and the theme of Chapter 8. The United States, operating through its own aid agencies and through the government-funded National Endowment for Democracy (NED), provided aid to democratic groups and processes around the world, and it had lots of company from other countries and from non-governmental organizations (NGOs). Indeed, the operation that led to Slobodan Milosevic's fall from power in Serbia in 2000 was almost a carbon copy, accomplished overtly, of what the United States earlier had accomplished covertly (e.g., in Chile).

The other major change is more recent, driven by the age of terror; the jury is still out. CIA covert operators and military Special Operations Forces have been thrown together. In Afghanistan and later in Iraq, the results were impressive, and the operations were secret only in their tactical details. More broadly, however, these developments raise thorny questions of authorization and accountability. When the CIA acts, it requires a presidential "finding" sent to Congress; yet, the military can be authorized simply through the chain of command from the president as commander in chief.

Like it or not, intelligence in democracies is becoming more the subject of political debate, which is the proposition at the core of Chapter 9. For the United States, that partly reflects the passion surrounding issues at the edge of intelligence, such as torture. However, it also reflects changes as the center of intelligence's business: the change in targets and the consequent need to expand surveillance at home. That, too, is driving the debate as its stretches democratic oversight of intelligence – attested to by controversies over the boundaries of SIGINT collected at home in countries from the United States to Sweden.

For oversight as well, the Cold War solutions may no longer suffice. After the investigations of the 1970s, the U.S. Congress passed the Foreign Intelligence Surveillance Act (FISA) to provide judicial oversight of domestic surveillance for national-security rather than law enforcement purposes. A secret court reviewed applications from the Justice Department and the FBI. However, after September 11, the Bush administration argued that it could not target named individuals with specific warrants before the fact; rather, it needed to scan wide swathes of communication, searching for connections of interest. It may be that oversight will have to move from judicial approval before the fact to some form of continuing legal or congressional review as surveillance proceeds.

The change in intelligence's targets also raises ethical issues that slide into prudential questions in a democracy. These are also illuminated by a comparative perspective, suggesting how different practices and experiences are reflections of the different national ways of dealing with intelligence – which, in turn, reflect different political cultures with different relationships between governments and people and different ways of defining power. In Europe, for instance, Britain and France still consider themselves as global powers and are quite different from countries such as Germany and the Netherlands, which do not.

The campaign against terrorism is not only mixing military force and intelligence in new ways; it also is straining the limits of both – from the limits of preemption to the use of covert action away from the battlefield. Intelligence is expanding dramatically in both expense and breadth of activity, some of which is controversial, especially at home. At the same time that intelligence is seeking and being given new powers, technology is providing new opportunities to survey large quantities of information about individuals. The irony is that intelligence will be more effective the less terrorists understand of its scope and methods – which constrains the scope of the public debate but cannot be allowed to constrain it too much.

2

The Changed Target

The change in targets for intelligence is dramatic. To be sure, for all the emphasis on terrorists and other nonstate (or transnational) targets, the change is hardly absolute. Intelligence dealt with nonstates before, and nation-states – such as North Korea, Iran, and China – still loom large in the work of U.S. intelligence. While some of those state targets, such as North Korea, are familiar in the sense that they resemble the secretive Soviet Union, others present different and unfamiliar – if not entirely new – challenges.

This chapter defines the change in targets, focusing on transnational targets such as terrorists. The change is widely acknowledged, yet its implications run far deeper than are usually recognized. The change goes to the heart of how intelligence does its business – from collection to analysis to dissemination, to use the labels that are increasingly less apt. Before turning to transnational targets, some discussion of remaining state targets is appropriate because those also cover a range. The chapter then details the challenges of transnational targets, concluding by illustrating some of the implications of that change with the issue of possible acquisition of WMD by terrorists.

THE RANGE OF STATE TARGETS

States will not only remain targets for intelligence; they will also remain, for all the competition from transnational actors – ranging from NGOs to international business, to drug lords and terrorists – the key actors in the international system. Thus, they will remain an important target for intelligence. Those state targets also cover a

Table 2.1. *Range of State Targets*

Closed	Mixed	Open
Soviet Union then, North Korea now	China, Iran now	U.S. allies; much of the world
Basic data on capabilities secret: focus on puzzles	Puzzles about capabilities remain; mysteries important too	Most capabilities transparent; mysteries critical
Secret sources dominate collection; too little information	Secret sources valuable; open sources as well	Secrets less valuable; too much information is a problem

range, roughly from closed to open. In fact, the range is a continuum, and Table 2.1 identifies three positions of interest along that continuum: closed, mixed, and open. To be sure, even the most open states keep some secrets, a reminder that openness is relative. The secrets kept by otherwise open societies – for instance, "What capabilities and plans does Israel have for military strikes on nuclear facilities in its neighborhood?" – drive intelligence leftward in Table 2.1. For those questions, information is in short supply, and secret sources become more important.

Questions about states came and come with considerable shape. States are geographic; they come with an address. As important, they come with considerable "story" attached. I have realized that, ultimately, intelligence is storytelling. It is helping those who will take action construct and adjust the stories in their head that will guide their decisions. Absent some story, new information about a topic is just a factoid. The story provides a pigeonhole and context for the new information. To be sure, if the story in their head becomes too hardened, too impervious to adjustment in light of new information, the new information may simply be discarded if it does not conform to the story. This is also called mindset or "groupthink" and it is the root of most of what are called intelligence failures, which is a major subject of Chapter 6.

We know what states are like, even those states as different from the United States as the Soviet Union – or North Korea: they are hierarchical and bureaucratic. Because their purposes are broadly similar – that is, protecting and seeking to assure decent living conditions for (at least some of) their citizens – their internal institutions share similarities. The devil may be in the details, for instance, in understanding the differences in the workings and influence of the Japanese Diet by comparison to the U.S. Congress, but at least "legislature" provides a shared starting point for the discussion. As a result, the fact that states come with stories attached not only facilitates the task of analyzing them, it also "greases" the conversation between intelligence and policy about the results of that analysis.

Most intelligence questions about states fell and fall into the frequently used distinction between *puzzles* and *mysteries*. Puzzles are questions that could be answered with certainty if only with access to information that, in principle, is available. Dave Snowden, in his business-related writing about the philosophy of information, calls them *known problems*, for which there is a unique relationship between causes and effects.[1] The challenge is to correctly categorize the problem, obtain the necessary data to solve it, and apply accepted formulas. Military-targeting issues are puzzles; so are many issues about a state's capabilities: "How many nuclear devices does North Korea have?"

Much of Cold War intelligence was puzzle-solving – that is, looking for additional pieces to fill out a mosaic of understanding whose broad shape was a given. Because so much that was open about the United States and other democracies was secret about the Soviet Union – basic economic and military statistics, for instance – the United States and its allies spent billions of dollars on exotic collection systems to solve those puzzles.

Because those puzzles were secret, by definition, solving them relied heavily on secret intelligence sources: espionage (HUMINT) and what came to be called "technical collection" by "national technical means" – primarily satellites taking pictures and other imagery (IMINT), or satellites, ground stations, and other platforms intercepting signals from those states (SIGINT).

Those secret sources, especially HUMINT, were nicely matched to puzzle-solving. HUMINT, by nature, is a target-of-opportunity business. Spies in place may not be invited to a critical decision meeting or they may attend but not be able to get the information to their handler quickly lest their cover be blown. As a result, spies may or may not be able to provide useful information about fast-moving plans or intentions. For most puzzles, however, the puzzle piece that is not available today will still be welcome tomorrow. Therefore, if a spy cannot steal that secret puzzle piece today, the piece will still be valuable if it can be transmitted tomorrow. The result is an apparent paradox: while spying is often conceived of as a means of obtaining an inside look at an adversary's intentions (and sometimes is), it is more reliably valuable at solving puzzles. It is little surprise, then, that most espionage targets are puzzles: military plans, weapons designs, and industrial processes.

In contrast to puzzles, no evidence can definitively solve mysteries because, typically, they are about people, not things. They are contingent. Snowden labels these *knowable problems*, which involve contingent relationships between a limited set of causes and effects. In this realm, analytic techniques can be used to predict outcomes, at least probabilistically. We cannot know the answer, but we can know – in the case of intelligence, usually from recent history and perhaps some theory – which factors are important to monitor and something of how they interact to produce the answer. Russia's inflation rate for this year is a mystery; so is whether Israel might strike Iranian nuclear facilities. While Soviet capabilities were treated primarily as a puzzle, those of terrorist groups are a mystery because they depend until the very last moment on the actions and vulnerabilities of their foes – more on that later.

For puzzles, the product is *the* answer: North Korea has X nuclear weapons; Soviet missiles have Y warheads. To be sure, the answer may not be definitive; it may remain a best estimate. If this is true, however, it is not because of inherent uncertainty. Rather, it is because information available in principle is unavailable in fact. The answer is as close as we can come with the information at hand. The infamous October 2002 NIE about whether Iraq had WMD sought to solve a puzzle: Iraq either had or did not have WMD programs, with relevant proscribed materials to match. The NIE was rightly criticized on a number of grounds, which are discussed in Chapter 7. Yet, although its answer – a resounding "Yes, Saddam has them" – was dead wrong, in fact, it was probably the only answer that could have been offered given the evidence and argument at hand.[2]

For mysteries, the product is a best forecast, perhaps in the form of a probability with key factors identified as well as how they bear on the estimate. If analysts do not and cannot know what Russia's inflation rate will be this year, they do know – from Russia's experience as well as that of other countries – which factors will be important in determining that rate and, at least roughly, how they will combine to produce it. So, the answer can be conveyed by laying out those determinants along with quantitative or qualitative assessments of where they stand and how they are moving. Doing so can lead to a best forecast, along with some bounds of uncertainty. To sharpen both the forecast and the bounds, sensitivity analyses (e.g., using scenarios or a variety of quantitative methods) could test the effects of different levels of determinants on outcomes.

Most of the states at the closed end of the continuum are steeply hierarchical, led by small Leninist Party cadres or individuals. For them, preserving the leadership's position – also known as *regime survival* – is paramount. In principle, such states could be more nimble and thus more unpredictable than more open states with more deliberative and thus cumbersome processes of governance. However, this assumes that the authoritarian leaders could bring their cadres – and, to the extent it matters, their people – with them in sharp changes of course. Rather, the inertia in such systems is often underappreciated. The most dramatic change of course that the Soviet Union made was to collapse – hardly what Mikhail Gorbachev intended.[3] The North Korean leader, Kim Jong-il, performed a nifty tap dance in keeping the international community off guard about his nuclear intentions, but it was a tap dance on a very small dance floor.

Two of the states of most interest in the mixed category raise the importance of story – or its absence – in somewhat similar ways. For Iran, the overarching U.S. story is unremitting hostility toward that country's theocratic leadership, hostility that dates back to the takeover of the U.S. embassy in 1979. Pure enmity hardly makes for empathy; instead, it makes it too easy to turn foes into caricatures of pure evil. That is what occurred with Iran under the Ayatollah Khomeini, and it occurred with Al Qaeda after the attacks of September 11, 2001. Serious efforts to understand the foe almost became politically incorrect for American society if not for its intelligence. Iran's president, Mahmoud Ahmadinejad, was frequently portrayed as a madman in popular commentaries. His 2005 statement, which was first translated as "the occupying regime [in Israel] must be wiped off the map," immediately became characterized as a call to destroy the state of Israel, if not a call to genocide.[4]

From this perspective, Ahmadinejad may have been his own worst enemy. However, the more significant point is that the United States was slow to try to understand Iran on its own terms. In fact, Ahmadinejad, whose title was "president," actually was not that powerful. He was less like a president in American terms and more like a French prime minister, whose writ did not run far beyond administering the government's budget and overseeing its civil service. In addition, because the United States had so constricted its connections – of both government and private business – into Iran, it had little wherewithal for understanding the country even if it was moved to try. As in other cases of émigré populations in the United States, the counterpart of too little contact with Iranians in Iran may have been too much influence from émigré Iranians in the United States – thus injecting into the national discussion the combination of enmity and wishful thinking characteristic of those who feel exiled from their homeland.

The difficulty was compounded because although Iran remained a state, it was a theocratic state and thus a new creature for twentieth- and twenty-first–century Americans, inside and outside intelligence. We have no story about such governments. For example, the fusion of church and state, rather than their separation, provides an unfamiliar context for parsing the relationship between Ahmadinejad, the country's titular president, and its supreme leader, a cleric. As a result, the United States first exaggerated Ahmadinejad's importance and then insulted him when he visited the United Nations in New York in 2007. The lack of story made it all but impossible to fathom the evidence that many younger Iranians seemed to be among the most pro-American people in the world. Lacking context, it was easy for Americans to be tempted to believe regime change was around the corner.

For China, too, there was and is no story. How are we to understand "Leninist capitalism": booming, frontier capitalism presided over by a tight Communist Party? The combination seems one that cannot endure. China's future is a mystery. China's communist leaders may have a vision, even a plan for that future, but whether that plan is implemented in anything like the form they now intend will depend on thousands of bumps, small and large, in the road along the way. The plan will be adjusted – or thrown entirely off course. All intelligence can do in the present is frame that mystery of China's future in a way that helps to see America's interest more clearly and perhaps provide more steadiness to policy along the way, as the twists and turns in China's course sometimes befuddle and sometimes anger Americans.

If parsing the theocratic state of Iran is a new challenge for Americans, framing the China mystery was and is especially sharp because it is a mystery that the United States has not confronted in a long time. China is both a possible military competitor *and* an economic partner of the United States. This is a combination we have not seen in a long time. Perhaps pre–World War II Germany is the most recent kindred mystery, combining economic interest and military concern, but it paled in economic importance then by comparison to China now. Moreover, from the time Hitler took power, the meaning of Germany's military growth became increasingly less mysterious; that Germany's rising power would pose a threat to U.S. interests became increasingly plain.

Not so for China. Taiwan remains a major flashpoint and driver of Chinese military planning. In other respects, however, China's military rise is simply the by-product of its economic growth. Whether China will become a military competitor of the United States only on paper or whether its military power will become a threat remains to be seen. That, too, is a mystery, one wrapped within the larger China mystery. Therefore, it is not surprising that U.S. discussion of China veers sharply between competitor and partner. Indeed, listening to conversations about China in Washington and Los Angeles makes one wonder whether the same country is being discussed! In Washington, the language is of military and competitor, while in Los Angeles, it is of economic and partner, the need to be there.

LOOKING AT TRANSNATIONAL ISSUES: HOW ARE THEY DIFFERENT?

As an intelligence challenge, transnational targets such as terrorists differ from traditional state targets in a number of ways. Table 2.2 elaborates on those differences.

Transnational targets are not new for intelligence, for it has long been active against organized crime and drug traffickers. What *is* new is twofold: (1) the importance of transnational threats, especially

Table 2.2. *From Cold War Targets to Age of Terror Targets*

	Old: Cold War	New: Era of Terror
Target	States, primarily the Soviet Union	Transnational actors, also some states
Objects of Scrutiny	Mostly big, rich, and central	Many small, even single individuals, and peripheral
"Story" about Target	Story: states are geographic, hierarchical, bureaucratic	Not much story: nonstates come in many sizes and shapes
Location of Target	Mostly "over there," abroad	Abroad and at home
Consumers	Limited in number: primarily federal, political military officials	Enormous numbers in principle: including state, local, and private
"Boundedness"	Relatively bounded: Soviet Union ponderous	Much less bounded: terrorists patient but new groups and attack modes
Information	Too little: dominated by secret sources	Too much: broader range of sources, although secrets still matter
Interaction with Target	Relatively little: Soviet Union would do what it would do	Intense: terrorists as the ultimate asymmetric threat
Form of Intelligence Product	"Answer" for puzzles; best estimate with excursions for mysteries	Perhaps "sensemaking" for complexities
Primacy of Intelligence	Important, not primary: deterrence not intelligence-rich	Primary: prevention depends on intelligence

but not only terrorism; and (2) the range of transnational threats of concern. In the past, organized crime and drug traffickers were a secondary activity for intelligence; now, some of the transnational threats, such as terrorism, are the primary activity.

Moreover, the range of current and prospective transnational targets is broad. If "threat" is conceived broadly, then threats can be thought of as covering a range. At one end are those *threats that come with threateners* attached, people who mean us harm.[5] At the other end are developments that can be thought of as *threats without threateners*. If they are a threat, the threat results from the cumulative effect

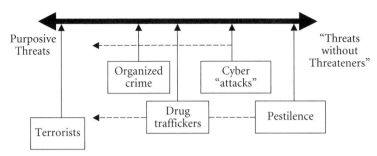

Figure 2.1. From purposive threats to "threats without threateners."

of actions taken for other reasons, not from an intent that is purposive and hostile. They might also be called *systemic threats*. Those who burn the Amazon rain forests or try to migrate here or spread pandemics here do not necessarily wish Americans harm; they simply want to survive or get rich. *Their* self-interest becomes a threat to *us*. Figure 2.1 displays the continuum.

It is interesting that the main transnational targets for intelligence in the past – organized crime and drug traffickers – fell somewhere in the middle of that continuum. The activities of both created national-security concerns, but the danger the traffickers posed to the nation was a by-product of their main purpose, which was to enrich themselves. Also in the middle of that continuum, energy imports are commerce, but the products are so crucial to national economies as to invoke security concerns – sometimes stunningly misposed. Those concerns have waxed and waned with price and supply, and they have been reconfigured recently not only by much higher prices but also by the resulting new winners and new losers and by the changes in the nature of global energy trade. Moreover, as both trade and investment become global, economic transactions driven by commerce – with no threat intended – may come to look menacing, as it was recently with China's proposed purchase of UNOCAL or with a Dubai-based company's interest in taking over U.S. ports.

What is striking now is that the ends of the continuum are more important; they are primary, not secondary. At the "they-mean-us-harm" end, terrorism by Islamic extremists does not pose the existential threat to the United States that the Soviet Union and its nuclear weapons did, but it is more than an inconvenience – and it frightens

Americans well beyond its actual harm so far. For instance, immediately after the September 11 attacks, polls asking how concerned respondents were about more terrorist attacks in the United States recorded 49 percent as worrying a "great deal" and 38 percent worrying "somewhat." Two years later, those concerned a "great deal" had fallen to 25 percent but those "somewhat" concerned had increased to 46 percent.[6]

In fact, the loss of life on September 11 was off the charts of Americans' historical experience with terrorism. In the five years after 2001, the annual numbers of fatalities of Americans from terrorism, worldwide, were all less than 100 – and typically barely into double digits. The total for 2005 was fifty-six, which may have resulted as much from a change in counting rules as from an actual increase in fatalities.[7] That total compares with an average during the same five years of 62 people killed annually by lightning, 63 from tornadoes, 692 in bicycle accidents, and an incredible 41,616 in motor-vehicle–related accidents.

One reason for the fear is that people find it difficult to deal with low-probability occurrences, especially those with devastating consequences. A generation ago, researchers compared the assessments of experts on nuclear power with those of nonspecialist citizens. Two groups of citizens ranked the risk posed by nuclear power as number one in a list of thirty activities and technologies; the third group ranked it number eight. By contrast, the experts ranked it number twenty.[8] For nuclear weapons and nuclear war, the gap was even wider. The citizens may have been right and the experts wrong – fortunately, we had no proof during the Cold War for nuclear weapons. Working every day on the issue may have desensitized the experts or they may have reduced their own cognitive dissonance by subconsciously downgrading their own assessments of the risk. In any event, the difference was striking; on issues such as nuclear power, in which evidence is available, the experts' views tended to correlate with the evidence (e.g., numbers of fatalities).

When I spoke about the terrorist threat, especially in the first years after 2001, I was often asked what people could do to protect their family and home. I usually responded by giving the analyst's answer, what I labeled "the RAND answer." Anyone's probability of being killed by a terrorist today was essentially zero and would be the same tomorrow, barring a major discontinuity. So, they should do nothing. It is not surprising that the answer was hardly satisfying, and I did not regard it as such. I came to realize what studies of other risks indicated, that terrorism is especially frightening because it seems random.[9] We have the sense that we can do something about other things that might kill: we can diet, or not smoke, or drink less alcohol. The sense is partly illusion, but terrorism seems entirely random. However, it is not random – choosing to live outside of major cities would reduce a person's already vanishingly low probability of being killed by a terrorist – but so it seems.[10]

At the other end of the continuum, global warming seems increasingly serious as a global threat – if not directly to the United States, then to countries and regions in whose stability the United States has important stakes. (Global pandemics are a direct threat to the United States.) Like terrorism, global warming runs beyond the mystery category because we are not sure of the factors that produce it or, especially, how they combine. Moreover, effects may cascade in discontinuous ways. Like bridges that are not maintained, there may be little visible effect for years, but all of a sudden there is a catastrophic effect. The best that intelligence can do may be to provide "if–then" assessments; for example, if warming has given physical effects in particular places, then it will exacerbate given sources of social and political tension.[11]

The changed threat also requires more seamless connections across what had been thought of as separate disciplines: early warning and crisis management. Crime and drug trafficking are clearly located in the middle of the threat spectrum. What is striking, however, about a pestilence that appears in the United States is that it might be either a purposive terrorist tactic or an "innocent" contagion due to greater global connectedness and the multiplicity of previously unknown pathogens. A cyber "attack" might be a determined attack by a hostile group or "simply" a set of smart young people seeing how far they can go.

The difference is not likely to be immediately clear, which is why both disease and cyber attacks are shown in Figure 2.1 with a dotted line, indicating that better situation awareness might take them quickly from the "they-mean-us-no-harm" category to the purposive-threateners' category. Or, the "crisis" might arise rapidly and at home if, for instance, a local newspaper published pictures of the Koran being desecrated.

Objects of Scrutiny

To overstate for effect, the targets of Cold War intelligence were big, rich, and central. That is, the overarching concern about the Soviet Union was the Red Army: "How big and sophisticated a force could the Soviet economy sustain?" When the Cold War froze into stalemate in Europe, to be sure, other more peripheral parts of the world became more important in the East–West competition: witness Angola, Afghanistan, or especially Vietnam. However, Europe remained the main game and the main prize. Intelligence was also interested in individuals during the Cold War, but they were mostly easily identified: the leaders of major governments or factions.

Now, by contrast, many of the objects of scrutiny for intelligence are small, poor, and peripheral. In an age of terror, a single individual or small group can do enormous damage; the September 11 hijackers proved that decisively. In the era of the Worldwide Web, a single French banker can also do enormous damage, although fortunately his damage was mere money. The bank trader lost Société Générale more than $7 billion before being discovered in early 2008, making very risky and very large bets while covering them with his understanding of the "seams" in the bank's oversight system. These small objects of scrutiny do not identify themselves; rather, they may arise unpredictably. Many (but not all) of the September 11 hijackers had been on the radar screens of U.S. or other intelligence; later, however, homegrown would-be terrorists in Britain came as more of a surprise.

Similarly, the places to which intelligence has to turn its scrutiny have changed. Many of them are poor and peripheral, such as Afghanistan. We now know enough about terrorists to know that they are not generally poor, but we also know that poor countries are not only fertile ground for recruiting terrorists but also can be co-opted by terrorist groups as bases and safe havens. After the fall of the Soviet Union, if U.S. interest in peripheral places was mostly discretionary, driven by simple suffering or the interests of allies, it is no longer. The U.S. government and its intelligence agencies need to pay attention to poor, peripheral places that might be part of the threat of terrorism.

No "Story"

Although state targets of intelligence will remain – Iran, North Korea, China, and Russia, for example – the shift to terrorists and other transnational developments as primary targets is momentous. If states – even states very different than the United States – came with some "story" attached, transnational targets, especially terrorist groups, do not. These new targets deprive intelligence and policy of a shared story that would facilitate analysis and communication. If we knew that states were geographical, hierarchical, and bureaucratic, there is no comparable story for nonstates, which come in many sizes and shapes.

Al Qaeda is an example: more than five years after September 11, it was unclear whether the organization was a hierarchy, a network, a terrorism venture capitalist, or an ideological inspiration. There is no doubt that it contained elements of all four, as well as other character-istics in different measures, but that hardly amounted to a story. As a result, interpreting additional information as well as communicating those assessments was difficult. The "hierarchy" and "network" views made it difficult to conceptualize the March 2004 Madrid bombers, who seemed to have little to do with Al Qaeda "Central." In turn, once the "inspiration" view of Al Qaeda became accepted, it made for very different interpretations of the extent to which Al Qaeda Central had been able to reconstitute itself five years and more after September 11.

Disease has some story attached. We know what diseases are and something about how they spread – for example, smallpox. Yet, for all we know, a smallpox outbreak in the United States could be either a purposive terrorist tactic from a group that obtained the few remain-ing smallpox pathogens or an "innocent" contagion due to greater global connectedness and the possible leak of previously unknown pathogens. As with problems of cyber security, the difference is by no means likely to be clear. Today, an opponent can wage a "war with-out fingerprints"; as a result, not only might it be unknown who is attacking but also that we are being attacked in the first place. Talk about the absence of story!

Location of the Target

Transnational targets not only come without a story, by definition, they also come without an address. They are, after all, transnational: they are both "over there" (abroad) and "here" (at home). By contrast, although early in the Cold War the United States worried about communists at home (some of the abuses stemming from that concern are discussed in Chapter 3), for the most part, the intelligence challenge of communism could be divided into foreign intelligence abroad and counterintelligence at home. The task at home was mostly tracking white-collar spymasters from the communist countries as they tried to recruit spies in the United States. Dividing the task in that way enabled the distinctions, or "oppositions," that are the subject of Chapter 3: intelligence versus law enforcement, foreign versus domestic, public versus private. Those distinctions were reflected in organizations and their operating concepts. They made great sense during the Cold War, especially in safeguarding American civil liberties. However, transnational threats, especially terrorists, respect none of the distinctions. The oppositions set up the country to fail on September 11, which is the starting point of Chapter 3.

The fact that transnational targets are "here" as well as "over there" impels nations to reconsider what has been regarded as domestic intelligence. Not only do they face the necessity of collecting more information about their citizens and residents – and doing so with minimal damage to civil liberties – they also need to rethink the boundaries that the distinctions established. Terrorists are criminals but may commit only one crime, and then it will be too late. Terrorist groups have much in common with international crime organizations except for one critical difference: criminals want to live to steal another day; they are not candidates for suicide bombers.

More, and More Diverse, Consumers

Not only did consumers during the Cold War share with intelligence a story about states – territorial and usually hierarchical, with histories, traditions, bureaucracies, and standard operating procedures – they also were relatively few in number. Most consumers were located at the apex of the national-security decision-making establishments and most were political–military officials. Busy and distracted, they were not always an easy target for intelligence to serve. They were, however, an identifiable and familiar target. When the Cold War ended, intelligence looked for new consumers and, at first, found them in domestic agencies such as the Department of Commerce, which wanted staff work as much as intelligence analysis.

Then, after the attacks of September 11, intelligence's consumers mushroomed, this time including state and local officials and private managers of infrastructure. Transnational issues thus involve a much wider variety of consumers, extending to agencies outside the traditional national-security establishment and outside the federal government. There are eighteen thousand relevant government jurisdictions at the state and local levels in the United States, consisting of more than 600,000 police officers; nationwide, there are three times as many private-security as public police officers. Virtually none of them have security clearances to see any classified federal information, much less the secret compartmented intelligence (SCI) that is intelligence's preeminent stock-in-trade. Both the FBI and the DHS have made efforts since September 11 to clear state and local officials, but the numbers – although significant – remain small. The FBI has provided clearances to approximately two thousand state and local officials per year, mostly at the secret level.[12]

The lack of a story for transnational targets such as terrorists, or the presence of tentative, competing stories about them often based only on short histories, is also compounded by the different organizational cultures involved. As discussed in Chapter 3, traditional intelligence and law enforcement are different enterprises. Even the meaning of *intelligence* differs between the two. State and local officials are unfamiliar with the products of national-intelligence agencies and are prone to imagine (or hope) that there is magic behind the green door of classification, if only the feds will open it.

Moreover, who is the "key" consumer is far less clear. An airport security officer or a public health doctor may have a more urgent "need to know" about a threat than the president of the United States because he or she may be in a more immediate position to thwart it.

At the same time, most new transnational consumers have little familiarity with intelligence and how to interpret it. For this reason too, the challenge of connecting with the consumer is greater in the transnational than in the state-to-state arena.

Less "Bounded"

States, for the most part, are clearly "delineated," having known borders and capitals and doing much that is openly observable. Moreover, states act within the context of formal and customary rules (e.g., established military doctrines), which gives predictability to many of their actions. By contrast, transnational actors are amorphous, fluid, and hidden, presenting intelligence with major challenges simply in describing their structures and boundaries. Because such actors are also far less constrained by formal rules than their state counterparts, they can engage in a wider variety of tactics on a regular basis, adding immensely to the challenge of forecasting their behavior.

The relative lack of constraints is obvious in the case of the Islamic extremist terrorists. It is also the case for organized crime and drug trafficking, actions that by definition put their perpetrators on the other side of the law. The political scientist, James Rosenau, referred to the transnational actors as "sovereignty-free."[13] For him, they confront an "autonomy dilemma" parallel to the "security dilemma" that states face. Yet, free of sovereignty, transnational actors are also free of many of the obligations and constraints of sovereign states. Even the transnational actors that most of us are likely to label "good" may be in a position to buy considerable freedom of action, for better or worse. Indeed, the scale of some private activities literally outstrips government: the approximately $800 million that the Bill and Melinda Gates Foundation contributes every year for global health approaches the annual budget of the World Health Organization and is comparable to the funds given to fight infectious disease by the U.S. Agency for International Development.

While the current Islamic extremist terrorists hardly act quickly but instead carefully plan their attacks over years, transnational targets as well are in another sense less bounded than state-centric targets. There will be discontinuities in targets and attack modes, and new groups will emerge unpredictably. Intelligence had a decade to explore the impact of Gorbachev's accession on the Soviet system; however, in the case of Al Qaeda, for example, events unfolded at a stunning pace after September 11, 2001.

Moreover, the transnational arena involves networked actors subject to what students of the emerging science of networks refer to as "cascades," making them more vulnerable to sudden change than state-to-state systems. Some networks, such as electric power grids, are tightly coupled systems. Small changes within the network accumulate until the network reaches a "tipping point," after which dramatic domino-like sequences ensue, such as the collapse of the network – that is, the failure of the electric power grid. As an example from beyond terrorism, in the Asian financial meltdown of 1997, a relatively small crisis involving the Thai currency quickly enveloped much of Asia as networked financial markets produced cascading effects.[14]

Broader and Lower Quality Information Base

Given closed foes, Cold War intelligence gave pride of place to secrets – that is, information gathered by human and technical means that intelligence owned. Terrorists are hardly open, but an avalanche of open data is relevant to them: witness the September 11 hijackers whose real addresses were available in California motor-vehicle records. During the Cold War, the problem was too little (good) information; now, it is too much (unreliable) information. Then, intelligence's secrets were deemed reliable; now, the plethora on the Web is a stew of fact, fancy, and disinformation.

Because of the unbounded and high-profile nature of transnational threats, intelligence must wade through an ocean of information that contrasts sharply with the more limited information that was available on closed societies such as the Soviet Union. Much of the information is, at best, of uncertain reliability. Moreover, when compared to a state with a long history, much less contextual information is available that can be used to evaluate the reliability of new information. For these reasons, the problem of separating "signals" from "noise" is more acute in the transnational domain.

That lack of context – the lack, in other words, of a story – means that information-gathering against terrorists necessarily involves "mining" or other processing of large quantities of information. After the September 11 attacks, with the names of the hijackers known, the government could quickly pick up their trail through motor-vehicle records, addresses, credit cards, and the like. However, that was after the fact; before the fact, names of interest may yet be unknown or following them is bedeviled by aliases or different transliterations of the same Arabic name.

Whatever the legal debate over the NSA's post–September 11 Terrorist Surveillance Program (TSP) – a debate discussed in Chapter 9 – the program vividly illustrates the challenge of dealing with the presence of a vast amount of information and the absence of much context for processing it.[15] In the wake of September 11, the U.S. government worried about new plots and new cells, but it had few specific leads. Rather, it trolled through large numbers of telephone calls, almost all international, where there was reason to believe one of the participants had links to Al Qaeda – for instance, because a call came from a region of Afghanistan or Pakistan where Al Qaeda was thought to operate.

Interaction with the Target

While various countries, especially the United States, hoped that their policies would influence Moscow, intelligence agencies could presume that as a first approximation, those efforts at influence would fail; recall Harold Brown's statement about the U.S.–Soviet nuclear competition: the Soviet Union would do what it would do. The challenge, in the first instance, was figuring out its likely course, not calibrating influence that other nations might have over that course.

The terrorist target, however, is utterly different. It is the ultimate asymmetric threat, shaping its capabilities to our vulnerabilities. The September 11 suicide bombers did not come up with their attack plan because they were airline buffs. They had done enough tactical reconnaissance to know that fuel-filled jets in flight were a vulnerable asset and that defensive passenger-clearance procedures were weak. They could get box-cutters through airport security, and the scheme obviated the need to face a more effective defense against procuring or importing ordnance. Similarly, the London, Madrid, and other bombers did enough tactical reconnaissance to shape their plans to the vulnerabilities of their targets.

To a great extent, we shape the threat to us; it reflects our vulnerable assets and weak defenses. In that sense, the capabilities of terrorists are a mystery, not a puzzle, because those capabilities depend on their continuing adaptation to the vulnerabilities of their targets, not on counts of missiles, guns, or even cells. For instance, Al Qaeda–linked plotters in 2006 planned to blow up airplanes over the Atlantic with liquid explosives smuggled onto planes as sport drinks or other permitted carryons. They had adapted to the airport security procedures then in effect, knowing that drinks were permitted as carryons and that most detectors in place could not identify explosives.

As military planners would describe it, it is impossible to understand red, potential foes without knowing a lot about blue, ourselves. In contrast to states such as the Soviet Union, transnational actors such as terrorists have a more intense relationship with the dominant actor in the international system, the United States. Their tactics are often predicated on our policies and defensive measures, making their behavior less determinate and predictable. Our understanding of transnational actors' proclivities will lead us to take actions that – to a greater extent than would be the case with more structured, internally driven state actors – will prompt adaptive behavior on their part. That process of adaptation can turn the predictions of intelligence into "self-negating prophecies" – and that is if the intelligence is sufficient to make accurate predictions.

This interaction between "us" and "them" has awkward implications for intelligence, especially foreign intelligence that has in many countries been enjoined from examining the home front and, less formally, worried that getting too close to "policy" is to risk becoming politicized. The task for intelligence now cuts directly across the foreign–domestic distinction. Moreover, to the extent that intelligence now becomes the net assessment of red against blue, that too is something that has been the province of the military, not civilian, agencies.

"Sensemaking" of "Complexities"

Transnational targets involve both puzzles and mysteries, but they also invoke what might be thought of as *mysteries-plus*, what Snowden calls "complexities." Where Al Qaeda leaders hid out along the Pakistan–Afghanistan border was a puzzle, albeit one whose solution might have altered rapidly as the leaders shuttled among hideouts.

When, where, and how Al Qaeda might attack the United States may be thought of as a mystery. It can be so conceived to the extent that we believe we have some understanding of the nature of Al Qaeda and its links to affiliates, of its strategy, proclivities, and so on – to the extent, in other words, that there is now at least the beginnings of a story about Al Qaeda.

Yet, the mystery conception seems not quite apt as a way to frame the challenge of understanding Islamic extremist terrorism and other transnational targets. Because the terrorism comes with relatively little relevant history and context and because it is so unbounded, it involves a wide array of causes and effects that can interact in a variety of contingent ways. Large numbers of relatively small actors respond to a shifting set of situational factors. Moreover, because interactions reflect unique circumstances, they do not necessarily repeat in any established pattern and therefore are not amenable to predictive analysis in the same way as mysteries. The September 11 terrorists in 2001 and the Fort Dix plotters in 2006-7 both had connections to Al Qaeda; however, the links were very different, and the first did not provide any sense of pattern for the second.[16]

To be sure, the distinction between transnational and traditional intelligence problems should not be overstated: there are state-to-state problems, such as battlefield situations or crisis diplomacy, in which situationally driven interactions among numerous players can also produce a wide variety of outcomes.

These complexities in understanding transnational issues require combinations of regional and functional expertise. In addressing puzzles or even mysteries, a country's political or economic analysts often can work in relative isolation from analysts with other specializations, but that is not as much the case for terrorism and other transnational issues. Assessing, for instance, the risk of dangerous weapons proliferating across the globe draws on specialists in science and technology, illicit transfers, money laundering, politics, and network behavior – to name only a few – to track and comprehend the activities of weapons networks. To a much greater extent than in traditional areas, transnational analysis is a team or even networked activity (because specialists will be located in many agencies). This has potential benefits in terms of avoiding mental biases (i.e., mixing different perspectives) as well as potential risks in the form of groupthink and "lock-in."

The challenge of dealing with complexities still lies ahead for the most part. The goal is to convey a sense of emerging patterns with an eye to reinforcing or disrupting, respectively, positive or adverse patterns. Communicating that sense may be difficult in a discrete paper or stream of electrons. Rather, it may be best accomplished with the active participation of policy officials – for instance, using computer power to *fly through* a wide range of variables and scenarios, looking for patterns.[17] Such processes run into two familiar obstacles: (1) the canonical separation of intelligence from policy; and (2) the fact that policy officials, in particular, are always hard-pressed for time. Because the product is a sharpened sense, the problem is not one simply of communication; the sense needs to develop out of shared analytical work.

The product is what might be called *organizational sensemaking*, as developed particularly by the noted organization theorist, Karl Weick.[18] Sensemaking is the process through which organizations – not individuals – comprehend the complex environment with which they must contend. It is a continuous, iterative, largely informal effort to understand, or "make sense," of what is going on in the external environment that is relevant to the organization's goals and needs. In essence, it is the collective intuition of an organization. Through conversations at all levels, organizations construct ongoing interpretations of reality by comparing new events to past patterns – or, in the case of anomalies, by developing stories to account for them. Weick argued that the fluid sensemaking process has clear advantages as a framework for organizational action over "decision making" because the latter often locks the organization into polishing and defending formal decisions that may no longer be appropriate in fast-changing situations.

The methodology for sensemaking – creating a unified, explanatory, consensual understanding about the world that leads to principled, consistent action – requires forms of analysis and interactions with consumers that are not yet developed, well known, or widely used. Because it requires common understanding, it probably requires a more interactive intelligence process than products; therefore, there is a premium on ways to facilitate that interaction. After all, the real need is not good analysis on a piece of paper; too often in intelligence, paper goods (or streams of electrons) are treated as ends in

themselves. Rather, the need is for improved understanding by officials who will decide or act (although that understanding may begin
with a piece of paper) and deeper research by teams of analysts.

It is difficult to spell out sensemaking in practice because it is not
yet fully developed or implemented; it remains largely a theoretical
construct. However, let us return again to the questions of when,
where, and how Al Qaeda and its kin might next strike the United
States. Viewed from a sensemaking perspective, the challenge would
entail a continuing conversation between intelligence and policy, a
conversation conducted in the knowledge that the sensemaking process could fail (or succeed) dramatically at any moment. The conversation would be as informal as possible, aiming to sustain open-mind-
edness about a wide variety of terrorist organizations and connections,
motives, and attack modes. It would test new information against
a variety of hypotheses – in the absence of high confidence about
which factors mattered and how they were connected – and create
new ones as necessary. The product would be a sharpened sense for
possibilities and probabilities against the understanding that a high
degree of uncertainty was ineradicable. The WMD illustration later in
this chapter tries to sharpen the sense for sensemaking.

Importance of Intelligence

The last major difference between transnational targets, especially
terrorists, and state targets such as the Soviet Union may be the most
important. If *prevention* is the name of the game, the pressure on
intelligence is extraordinary. In his 2002 national-security strategy,
President Bush was speaking of Iraq but was graphic about the need
to prevent attacks, by preemptive action if need be: "We must be
prepared to stop rogue states and their terrorist clients before they
can threaten or use weapons of mass destruction against the United
States and our allies and friends.... To forestall or prevent such hostile acts by our adversaries, the United States will, if necessary, act
preemptively."[19]

Or, as he stated more colorfully in his speech to the nation on
March 19, 2002: "We will meet that threat now, with our Army, Air
Force, Navy, Coast Guard, and Marines, so that we do not have to
meet it later with armies of fire fighters and police and doctors on the

streets of our cities."[20] He had foreshadowed the new strategy in his speech at West Point in June 2002: "By confronting evil and lawless regimes, we do not create a problem, we reveal a problem. And we will lead the world in opposing it [sic]."[21]

In contrast, the dominant strategy of the Cold War – deterrence – was not so sensitive to the specifics of intelligence. It rested on the assumption that for all its differences in goals and ideology, the Soviet Union was like us – modern, rational (in our terms), and not self-destructive. The strategy perceived Soviet intentions as hostile but rational. Thus, once Moscow had nuclear weapons, the way to ensure that it did not use them was deterrence, which came to be associated with second-strike retaliation: as long as the United States (and its allies) had the capacity to wreak unacceptable damage on the Soviet Union after a Soviet nuclear first strike, that first strike would never come and the promise of U.S. retaliation would never be tested.

Two of the four main themes of debate about Cold War deterrence did not involve intelligence, and the one theme that did was highly technical. The first was: How much is enough? That is, how much second-strike destruction would be enough to deter any Soviet first strike? The second was the question that animated U.S.–European discussions during the Cold War: If NATO judged itself dangerously inferior to the Warsaw Pact in conventional forces along the central front in Europe, how could it credibly invoke some possibility of using nuclear weapons first if a Pact conventional attack in Europe were succeeding? Trying to answer that question sometimes led to torturous reasoning and tortured policy, but those policy issues did not much depend on intelligence.[22]

The logic of deterrence did raise one intelligence issue – a technical issue invoked by the awful, paradoxical aphorism about deterrence: offense is defense and defense is offense; killing people is good, killing weapons is bad. By this logic, if the Soviet Union had high confidence that it could defend against a retaliatory strike – by some combination of killing U.S. missiles in a first strike and then killing the residual missiles en route to the Soviet Union – it might be tempted by a first strike. The challenge for intelligence came down especially to assessing critical puzzles: "How many independent warheads did Moscow have, with what accuracy, and thus how much of a threat did the Soviet Union pose to U.S. missile forces for retaliation?"

The fourth issue might have involved intelligence but for the most part did not. That issue was Soviet *intentions* and *perceptions*: "How much risk of nuclear war was the Soviet leadership willing to take, and how much did it see the nuclear standoff in terms akin to those of the United States?" To be sure, all of the issues were hotly debated, and intelligence bore on them. However, they were mysteries at least, and therefore intelligence was not very decisive. The only exception was one episode during the Reagan military build-up during the 1980s when Moscow, imprisoned in its own paranoia, was convinced that the United States was preparing a nuclear first strike. Fortunately, the KGB's chief officer in London had volunteered to spy for Britain. He alerted British officials to Moscow's concern, and Britain shared this intelligence with the United States. Senior American leaders, including President Reagan, were aghast and took pains to reassure their Soviet counterparts.[23]

In contrast to deterrence, prevention – whether by preemption, disruption, or simply defending vulnerabilities – requires enormous precision in intelligence. Consider military preemption against enemies' dangerous weapons, like WMD. America's capacity for intelligence, surveillance, and reconnaissance (ISR) is unparalleled, in a world class by itself. It is also improving rapidly. However, its shortcomings are virtual descriptions of the features of our foes' WMD programs. Existing ISR is not good at detecting objects that are hidden under foliage, concealed, or especially underground; neither is it good at locating objects precisely by intercepting their signals. Would-be proliferators conceal their facilities or change the pattern of activities at weapons sites, as India did before its 1998 explosion of a nuclear weapon. With respect to the puzzle of North Korean nuclear weapons, the best that U.S. intelligence could do in the 2000s was a "guesstimate" that the country had some but with no judgment about location sufficient to permit a preemptive strike.

If terrorist threats are to be prevented by disrupting them or by closing the vulnerabilities they seek to exploit, then immense pressure is placed on intelligence to understand threats well enough, soon enough. It means moving back up the chain from possible terrorist acts to groups and their proclivities, if not their intentions. It requires an understanding of mysteries or complexities that is as fine-grained as the Cold War understanding of the puzzle of Soviet missile capabilities. In one respect, however, deterrence and prevention are alike: in both cases, the goal is nothing – no attack. This raises the question of metrics: for deterrence, metrics for policy more than for intelligence; for prevention, metrics for intelligence more than for policy because prevention is so intelligence-intensive. If there is no attack, did policy and intelligence succeed, was the country merely lucky, or was the threat exaggerated from the beginning?

"We're All Bayesians Now"

I recently met a former colleague, a former Soviet (now Russian) specialist, in the halls of the CIA, and we had a conversation about methods of intelligence analysis. At one point, he quipped: "We're all Bayesians now." The quip stayed with me. *Bayesian* derives from a famous theorem discovered by an English preacher, Thomas Bayes, and published in 1763. It has come to describe both an inclination and a process to update subjective probabilities in light of new evidence. In an important sense, almost all intelligence analysis is and always has been Bayesian, for even with regard to puzzles, finding *the* piece that will solve the puzzle with certainty is rare. However, the uncertainty and unboundedness of transnational targets, especially terrorists, underscore the need for both a Bayesian attitude and more formal approaches to making that approach concrete.

The basic idea is easiest to capture with a puzzle. Suppose I hand you a coin. You assume that it is a fair coin and that if you toss it, heads and tails are equally likely outcomes. Therefore, your initial estimate is that it is a fair coin. However, suppose you begin tossing it; if you get heads three times in a row, you might begin to suspect the coin is not fair. You probably would not reject that assumption altogether because you know that the chances are one in eight that a fair coin would yield three straight heads. Rather, you would adjust your initial certainty that the coin is fair and begin to entertain the thought that it might not be. If additional tosses produced still more imbalances toward heads, you would move toward the judgment that the coin is unfair.

In a Bayesian sense, Defense Secretary Donald Rumsfeld's famous quote about United Nations (UN) inspections searching for WMD in the run-up to the 2003 Iraq war was dead wrong: "The absence of evidence is not necessarily the evidence of absence."[24] What he meant was that just because UN inspectors had not found evidence of active WMD programs did not prove that Iraq had no such programs. Of course, that was right. Yet, in a Bayesian sense, each day that the UN inspectors did not find evidence of WMD should have shifted the odds in the direction of Iraq not having them. The way the puzzle was framed – "Does Saddam Hussein have WMD?" – meant that it could have been solved definitively in only one direction: "Yes, he does." Otherwise, Rumsfeld could have continued to repeat the same argument until every square inch of Iraq had been searched. In a Bayesian sense, however, he would have been wrong not to entertain more and more strongly the possibility that Iraq, in fact, had no WMD programs or stockpiles.

The Bayesian approach is easiest to grasp for puzzles because of the direct relationship between new puzzle pieces of information and more confidence about the puzzle's solution. However, as an approach – a way of thinking – it is probably even more important for mysteries and complexities because it not only underscores the inherent uncertainty but also forces hard conversation – in a sensemaking process – about precisely what a new piece of evidence (or logic) means and how much difference it makes.

Traditional warning is a Bayesian process, although it is not always perceived that way. Warning seeks to turn a mystery – "Are they going to attack?" – into a puzzle by identifying indicators along the path to war and then monitoring them. The logic of warning can be extended to other intelligence problems – for instance, the possibility that a terrorist group is indeed planning an attack or that a suspected terrorist group is seeking a chemical, biological, radiological, or nuclear (CBRN) weapon. For some of those issues, the paths might be more numerous and, thus, the collection problem more difficult.

In one sense, the warning (or the CBRN) problem is no different than many more familiar intelligence challenges: it requires intelligence from several sources to be laid atop one another, perhaps in short order – what has come to be called "multi-INT" in intelligence jargon. In the case of warning, very few indicators are "unique" signifiers – that is, actions that *only* (or virtually only) bespeak an attack, not other and legitimate purposes. In the Cold War, troops needed to leave their garrisons to train; therefore, indicators that troops had left their garrisons were suggestive but hardly definitive. Rather, the warning became serious if more indicators began to flash. Likewise, intelligence cannot follow every suspicious group, so it would have to combine some information about groups with the Bayesian-path analysis. There would have to be a hint or tip that a particular group might be terrorists to trigger a monitoring of its activities along paths to attack or especially to lethal weapons.

The analogy of terrorism with warning can be extended, as will be discussed, because in both cases, policy measures may sharpen the Bayesian updating of probabilities by making actions more unique or more visible. In the Cold War, the North Atlantic Treaty Organization (NATO) and the Warsaw Pact negotiated confidence-building measures (CBMs) that, for instance, required prenotification of training and maneuvers above a certain size. As a result, if intelligence collection detected out-of-garrison activity that had not been prenotified, the indication would become more unique precisely because the CBM was in effect.

Paths to Warning. The first step in this Bayesian analysis, for warning or for terrorism threats, is asking, "What information is important?[25] What should be collected?" For warning, it begins with paths to attack. "What would a potential adversary need to do to pose a threat of attack?" This path would run all the way back to intelligence about military capabilities because they would structure a potential adversary's possibilities for attack. Then, against those capabilities, the challenge would be to develop indicators that could be detected on the path to war. This is true for terrorism as well as for traditional warning.

In traditional warning, however, the set of indicators usually would be bounded, if perhaps not small in number, and some of the indicators might be fairly clear-cut. In the Cold War central-front example, if indicators had detected significant Warsaw Pact movements out of garrison, not prenotified, in a Bayesian sense, that movement would have raised the probability of attack from very low to quite high. In contrast, indicators for terrorists will be less bounded and less decisive.

The difficulty is that even when a group is identified as potential terrorists, the paths to attack – and, thus, the possible set of indicators along those paths – would be very large and also would include many that were not definitively linked to a terrorist attack. The paths would include reconnaissance of targets, purchase of explosives or other weaponry, travel for reconnaissance or training, exercises or rehearsal, and so on. Even trying to anticipate more specific attacks, such as those with CBRN weapons, would still be made difficult by the numbers of CBRN weapons and paths to buy, steal, or develop them. Biological weapons, for instance, include four groups: aerobic bacteria, anaerobic bacteria, viruses, and biological toxins. Again, other intelligence sources might provide hints for which particular agents have been of interest to terrorist groups,[26] which might lead to selecting, for example, anthrax, botulinum toxin, ricin, and several others as weapons of first concern along biological-weapons paths.

Just as traditional warning would want to ensure as many paths to war as possible had been identified, in principle, the Bayesian approach to terrorism would seek to identify as many paths to terrorism – or CBRN terrorism – as possible. Again, separate intelligence, perhaps from another source, about recent attempted attacks or the proclivities of groups would help to pare the number of paths. Those paths might be divided into phases, such as surveilling and selecting targets; acquiring training; purchasing (or stealing or making) equipment; making weapons; staging and practicing; and so on. For at least some CBRN attacks, it might be worth elaborating the possible paths in advance – admittedly, an extensive process. For that purpose, the paths might again be divided into phases: developing the concept, acquiring the materials, building a weapon, and deploying it.

Uniqueness. Because most steps along all the paths to a terrorist attack will have possible purposes other than an attack, looking for steps and therefore indicators that rank higher in "uniqueness" is critical. Carefully inspecting a building can be terrorist surveillance, but it can also be simply tourism or curiosity. For reasons of uniqueness, traditional warning was difficult to extend to more political and economic issues. Many political indicators, for instance, might be relevant to foreseeing a coup or other sudden change of government but would be, at best, ambiguously related to that warning – they were not, in the sense of Bayesian analysis, very unique. If a step or indicator has few applications other than a terrorist attack, it is highly unique; by contrast, if it has many applications, it is less unique. Uniqueness tends to trump simple importance because a step that is important but not very unique is of limited use to intelligence. For instance, acquiring laboratory equipment is important in almost any path to producing biological weapons, yet that action ranks low in uniqueness. Possible purchasers of laboratory equipment range from students to hobbyists to an enormous range of legitimate businesses. Therefore, giving much attention to that action in the absence of other indications that a group is potentially terrorists would be a simple waste of time.

Computers are also important in building a nuclear weapon but hardly unique. In contrast, buying or stealing enough fissile material to make a nuclear weapon is very unique – it bespeaks an interest in building such a weapon. In this manner, asking about uniqueness gives intelligence a way to determine which items along a path deserve focus.

Visibility. For indicators, visibility is also critical. Something that cannot be monitored by intelligence is not very useful as an indicator. The decision by an opponent's general staff to launch preparations for an attack would be wonderful warning but is not likely to be very visible. For that reason, espionage, which may or may not be available on any given day, generally cannot be counted on for warning; it is a target-of-opportunity business. Is there some way a particular indicator manifests itself so it could be searched for or recognized? The answers will differ across phases and tasks. Much of terrorist planning, for instance, will be invisible to intelligence until long after the fact, left in terrorist staging areas, or available only with luck – such as seizing a computer in a cave in Afghanistan. By contrast, recruitments may be more visible, along with some kinds of training. In the biological-weapons example, acquiring laboratory equipment is important but not very unique. Moreover, it is also generally not very visible. If, by contrast, a group suspected of terrorism recruited a biologist, that action might be more unique *and* more visible.

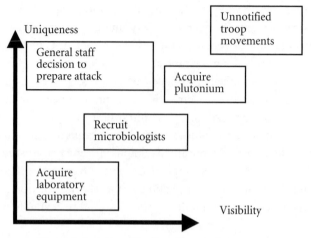

Figure 2.2. A Bayesian intelligence framework.

Thus, the two key characteristics of potential indicators are as follows:

- *Uniqueness*: How indicative is the indicator of terrorism? Or are there many other explanations for the indication that are not related to terrorism?
- *Visibility*: How much does a step, phase, or task on the path to terrorism lend itself to being monitored by intelligence?

In a Bayesian approach, the intelligence problem becomes an assessment of conditional probabilities. That is, against a prior suspicion that a group might engage in terrorism, does each available indicator increase or diminish that suspicion? Each additional observation made with respect to an individual or group provides additional information – like additional flips of the coin – permitting analysts to sharpen their assessment of whether that person or group is more likely to engage in terrorism.

The two characteristics provide the basis for an intelligence framework, as suggested by Figure 2.2.

Ideally, intelligence would focus on indicators that were both very indicative of terrorism as opposed to another more benign activity and very visible. Alas, the world frustrates the convenience of intelligence; therefore, few potential indicators fall in the upper right portion of Figure 2.2 – such as large, unnotified troop movements on the central front during the Cold War. Most indicators will be like acquiring laboratory equipment in the bioweapons example – perhaps important but not useful for intelligence because they are low in uniqueness and visibility. Thus, it is shown in Figure 2.2 near the origin on both axes. By contrast, acquiring a microbiologist is more detectable and more unique, although surely not high on either characteristic.

Still, if the objective of an intelligence strategy is to detect terrorist attacks, especially those including CBRN weapons, it should concentrate on the indicators along the paths that rate higher along each dimension shown – that is, those that fall farthest from the origin. For instance, for terrorist paths to nuclear weapons, acquiring plutonium is quite unique and also detectable by intelligence. It is shown in the upper right-hand corner in Figure 2.2. These judgments could then help target further surveillance or other intelligence collection.

Both uniqueness and visibility depend on the context, and policies can increase both, especially visibility. In terms of context, if the framework were applied not to an industrial society, like the United States or Britain, but instead to a poor region of the world with only a limited industrial base, even the acquisition of laboratory equipment might acquire some uniqueness. On analogous reasoning about uniqueness, after September 11 when NSA began trolling through large numbers of telephone calls, it concentrated on those parts of the world known to harbor terrorists, such as the Afghanistan–Pakistan border. Similarly, large purchases of fertilizer might carry more uniqueness in a large city than in a rural agricultural area – although they might not be very visible in either locale.

Similar considerations can also apply to visibility: transactions that are buried among thousands or millions of others in rich countries – thus obscuring the signal with enormous noise – might stand out more in poorer countries. That might be true whether the activity were observed in surveillance or detected by SIGINT, and it might apply to a wide range of indicators from simple international travel – which is much rarer to and from poor regions – to possession of materials that could be used to produce weapons.

Cold War CBMs, a policy instrument, increased uniqueness more than visibility. Large troop movements would have been visible in any case, but CBM limitations on out-of-garrison activity implied that any activity over the limit was – on the face of it – threatening. Policies can also make some of the steps along paths to terrorism more visible. For instance, in 2007, the U.S. Nuclear Regulatory Commission tightened procedures for licenses to acquire radioactive materials after U.S. Government Accountability Office investigators, posing as West Virginia businesspeople, obtained a license in twenty-eight days using nothing more sophisticated than a telephone, a fax machine, and a rented post office box. The move sought to make acquiring radioactive materials more transparent.

A similar intent lay behind the expansion of suspicious activity reporting (SAR) requirements in the United States after September 11. However, that was widely perceived as simply amassing reports to no real advantage, and private businesspeople began asking for more clarity in what was required to be reported. In effect, possible paths to terrorist acts were not specified clearly enough; therefore, what was a fruitful indicator remained ambiguous.

Part of this strategy might also be to collect and analyze combinations of observations that, taken alone, might not raise a flag but, taken jointly, could be alarming. For instance, in some circumstances, buying large quantities of fertilizer might be suspicious but not strongly so. If, however, that action were combined with other purchases relevant to building a bomb, such as triggering mechanisms and renting a closed panel truck, then the combination could be alarming in the sense of sharply raising the Bayesian probability of an attack – perhaps raising it more than the sum of the three actions had they occurred independently.

In another example, if a suspect person or group acquired a milling machine, it could be an indicator of their possibly pursuing radiological weapons. Several paths to such weapons require a milling machine to grind radiological materials into a fine powder that then could be dispersed efficiently. However, because milling machines are also common in industry, observing the purchase of only a milling machine would only slightly increase the suspicion that a radiological weapon was being developed.

By contrast, observing the purchases of a milling machine and shielding equipment might increase suspicion. Shielding equipment is more unique, so its purchase alone would increase the suspicion more than the purchase of only a milling machine. However, there is synergy between the two, so observing the two purchases together might increase the suspicion more than the sum of the two observed separately. For illustration, if the effect was a 3 percent increase in the belief for a milling machine alone and a 35 percent increase for the shielding equipment alone, the two together would result in a 45 percent increase in the suspicion of a radiological weapon being developed.

Particular observations or combinations would also suggest what to look for next – again, a key reason for employing the Bayesian intelligence strategy. Take as an the example the task of assessing the probability that a person or group is developing a type of radiological device, or "dirty bomb." If the observations revealed the presence of radiological materials or a Geiger counter, that fact would suggest that shielding equipment should also be present because the two items are often collocated. The logic would move from one action to the next along a particular path.[27] If a group were observed investigating sources of radiological materials, that observation would affect the suspicion that the group was interested in acquiring radiological materials – which, in turn, would affect the suspicion about whether the group is developing a radiological weapon.

In an information-rich environment, it is necessary to have a method to determine which resources should be explored next to maximize leverage in updating suspicions. Bayesian networks provide a systematic method for updating the suspicion that a particular set of observations indicates a person or group is planning a terrorist attack. The approach permits intelligence to identify which observations have the most leverage by exploring how different combinations of evidence bear on the assessment of whether, for instance, a terrorist act is being planned or a CBRN weapon is being developed.

The CBRN problem is like other transnational "complexities" in that it requires a wide variety of experts – in this case, ranging across the set of possible attacks, weapons, and paths to them – along with people who have some sense for visibility, what intelligence can detect. The point is then to use the framework as a logic structure for how observations affect prior beliefs or suspicions. For example, if shielding equipment already has been observed, what should collection focus on next to provide the greatest leverage in determining whether a radiological weapon is being developed?

To be sure, the process is complicated, and it lacks the time urgency that is likely to be characteristic of sensemaking with regard to other intelligence challenges of dealing with terrorist complexities.

Elaborating paths in detail would justify the cost for only the most lethal of potential terrorist threats, such as those with CBRN weapons. That elaboration of paths would be applied to a particular group only if there were reason to believe it was engaged in planning terrorism. However, these examples suggest something about the nature of the process that will be required for many transnational issues – Bayesian, iterative, involving a varied set of experts, and conducted in the awareness that uncertainty cannot be resolved entirely, only reduced.

3

The Cold War Legacy

When I gave lectures in the early years after September 11, I was often asked, "Why didn't the FBI and the CIA cooperate better before September 11?" My answer was then and would still be now, "Because we, the American people, didn't want them to." We feared that the concentration of police and intelligence power would infringe on the privacy and liberties of our citizens. Especially after the congressional investigations of the 1970s, we had decided as a people that – out of concern for privacy and civil liberties – the two agencies should not be too close. By the latter stages of the Cold War, when early concern about communists linked to Moscow in our midst turned out to be exaggerated (to put it gently), raggedy cooperation between the two agencies was good enough. However, it set us up to fail on September 11, 2001.

That is the first sense in which the Cold War legacy of intelligence was and is mismatched to the transnational threat that the United States and its allies now face. The FBI and the CIA sit astride the fundamental boundaries, or "distinctions," of the Cold War – boundaries between intelligence and law enforcement, between foreign and domestic, and between public and private. The nation said that just as law enforcement was one thing and intelligence another, so too it distinguished sharply between home and abroad and between the public and the private sectors. The distinctions run very deep.

The boundaries were reinforced by the second of the Cold War legacies: the institutional legacy. The lion's share of what the United States spends on intelligence went and still goes for collection. Satellites and other sophisticated collection platforms are expensive, while analysts are inexpensive by comparison. Collection came to be organized in what government officials call "stovepipes," and, as important, the stovepipes were denominated by *source*. The clandestine service, or directorate of operations, of the CIA was primarily responsible for HUMINT; the NSA for SIGINT; and the NGA for pictures and other IMINT.

For its part, analysis was organized primarily by *agency*, not by issue or problem. The CIA's Directorate of Intelligence was first among equals, but the DIA was just as big, and the much smaller INR tended to punch well above its weight in interagency discussions. The military services each had its own intelligence arm, primarily addressing the foreign threats that its service's weaponry would confront, and the joint combatant commands also had their intelligence units, heavily tactical in orientation. In Washington, there were smaller analytic units in departments ranging from Energy to Commerce. Those were explicitly departmental, serving the needs of local consumers.

The ways that both collection and analysis were structured made sense during the Cold War. On the collection side, with one overarching target – the Soviet Union and its allies, a target that was mostly treated as a puzzle – the structure asked the stovepipes, in effect, "What can you add to our understanding of the target? What puzzle pieces can you add to solving the Soviet puzzle?"

On the analytic side as well, the work of the intelligence organizations was highly focused on the Soviet Union. In that circumstance, organizing by agency made sense. It permitted a combination of competition, with analysts from different agencies looking at essentially the same information from somewhat different perspectives, professional backgrounds, and specialization – for example, DIA analysts naturally focused more on military dimensions of problems that cut across the military and the political. The organization by agency meant that all the analytic organizations, except the CIA, worked *for* a set of consumers and therefore could tailor their work to the needs of those consumers.

The final Cold War legacy was the product of the boundaries. Domestic intelligence was a stepchild in the system. Unlike most of its major partners, the United States had not created a domestic-intelligence service. Rather, the domestic-intelligence function continued to be performed by the FBI, where it was twice circumscribed.

It was part of an FBI that first and foremost was a law enforcement organization, which occasioned the post–September 11 quip about trying to understand the FBI pre–September 11 through intelligence. Intelligence may have been important but surely was not central. Second, the domestic-intelligence function was limited by the boundary between intelligence and law enforcement, a "wall" that also extended inside the FBI and inhibited cooperation among intelligence and law enforcement officials, even those working on similar issues.

The set of institutions, practices, and conceptions that built up during the "hot war" and the long ensuing Cold War may have served the United States well enough then – although that is a debated point, to put it gently.[1] However, they set up the nation to fail on September 11, 2001, and they continue to set us up to fail. The mismatch is most visible in the campaign against terrorism; therefore, that is the focus of this chapter. However, the legacy ran well beyond terrorism and non-state actors – it also affected how we designed military power and how we perceived its use. The long Cold War against an opponent whose only asset was military might suffuse our approach to intelligence, just as it colored our view of the world. It militarized U.S. foreign policy and gave pride of place to technology over statecraft.

It is important to emphasize that this mismatched legacy was not entirely inflicted on the United States. The visible mismatches in the campaign against terrorism we mostly inflicted on ourselves. They were inflicted on us in the ways that usually get the most attention from an observer: powerful personalities, like the CIA and the FBI directors who were not on speaking terms when I first went to Washington in the 1970s and bureaucratic fights over turf. There was also the sharp distinction in organizational culture that is explored in this chapter. Yet, in the end, those mismatches were also done in the name of privacy and civil liberties and were, on the whole, a sensible response to the threat the nation then faced.[2] If the price of ragged cooperation between the CIA and the FBI during the Cold War was an occasional botched handoff of a spy that moved into or out of the United States, it was not too high a price.

The price became too high on September 11, and the nation is rethinking the set of organizational distinctions and procedural restraints that it developed during the Cold War. Then, the country came – haltingly but in the end firmly – to a striking of the balance between security and privacy. September 11 demonstrated that the nation faces a very different threat, one that compels a rethinking of the balance, which is and will be as halting as the Cold War process. Moreover, the balance that was struck combines organizational distinctions with constitutional protections and restraints on official discretion. As a result, the rethinking involves how government organizations relate to one another, to the Constitution, and to the country's citizens.

BUILDING THE LEGACY OF BOUNDARIES

By the mid-1970s, if the period still seemed one of high Cold War, at least the communist threat on the home front had faded. In that context, the nation's first-ever investigations of intelligence looked for abuses of the rights of Americans and found them, especially in a curious mixing of intelligence, or counterintelligence, and law enforcement at the FBI during J. Edgar Hoover's long tenure as director.[3] The justification and ostensible target of these "counterintelligence programs" (COINTELPROs) was the operations of hostile foreign intelligence services and their possible involvement in (especially) protests against the war in Vietnam.[4] However, most of COINTELPRO's specific targets were American citizens in civil rights and antiwar groups. People such as the Reverend Martin Luther King, Jr., were not only surveilled but also harassed – and worse.

In reaction to the revelations, the nation judged that if the communist threat at home had ever justified intrusive surveillance of Americans, it did so no longer. The domestic-intelligence activities of the FBI were sharply restrained, and the "wall" separating intelligence from law enforcement was built higher. A compromise between presidential discretion and civil liberties resulted in the 1978 passage of the FISA and the creation of the Foreign Intelligence Surveillance Court (FISC), a court operating in secret to grant covert wiretapping and other surveillance authority for intelligence – as opposed to law enforcement – purposes.[5] Before the FISC, presidents had claimed the right of searches for national-security purposes with no warrants whatsoever – a claim to which President George W. Bush returned after September 11.

The wall between intelligence and law enforcement had effects all across both domains, and the FISA made the divide explicit. If the FBI or other officials sought wiretaps or other surveillance for criminal cases, they had to submit Title III affidavits to federal courts, indicating the "probable cause" that the location or communication line being bugged had been or was being used to commit crimes. If, by contrast, the purpose of the surveillance was national security, with no reasonable case that a crime had yet been committed, then the chain of procedure was the one defined in the FISA: from the FBI to the Department of Justice to the FISC.

Espionage is a difficult conviction to make because the foreign power handling an American spy is hardly likely to cooperate. In those circumstances, most convictions occur when spies confess, which means that probable cause would be too high a standard even for criminal cases of espionage, especially in the early stages. For terrorism intelligence, it would be a crippling standard because only one crime might ultimately be committed, and then it would be too late. As Chapter 2 emphasizes, the goal of investigation against terrorism has to be to prevent terrorism, not prosecute it.

The FISA and the FISC were relegated as Cold War footnotes as long as their primary purpose was to sanction surveillance on foreign installations in the United States or on Americans suspected of spying for foreign powers. That task of keeping track of "white-collar" spies was consigned to the CD of the FBI, a type of service within a service, proud of its own work but not a path to rapid ascent in what was preeminently a law enforcement agency. The FISA and domestic intelligence became prominent in the post–September 11 debate about whether more could – and should – have been done to prevent the attacks, and then again five years later, when it transpired that President Bush had ordered the NSA to sharply increase interceptions of communications in the wake of September 11, including communications of Americans with those suspected of terrorist connections. The administration had not used the FISA process to authorize the wiretaps. Its main argument for why it had not was that the FISA process was too cumbersome; however, the music behind the words was a reversion to the historical argument that presidents had an inherent right to resort to warrantless surveillance when national security was at stake.[6]

If, until September 11, the investigations of the 1970s were the final act in striking the Cold War balance between security and liberty, they rested on a longer history of postwar institution building. Now, the rebalancing means not just reshuffling intelligence and law enforcement organizations and refashioning their cultures, it also means rethinking basic categories of threat and response.

Law enforcement and intelligence are different worlds, with different missions, operating codes, and standards. The differences were driven home to me in the Clinton administration in the mid-1990s. Iraqi intelligence was suspected of being behind a plot to kill the first President Bush during a post-presidential visit to Kuwait. The plot to plant a bomb never came anywhere close to the former president, but the Clinton administration still confronted the issue of whether to retaliate in some fashion. It put together a team that combined CIA intelligence analysts with FBI and Justice Department law enforcement officers. Watching the two interact was fascinating because the disciplines are so different. In the end, the Clinton administration decided that the case for involvement by Iraqi intelligence was strong enough to call for cruise-missile strikes against Iraq.

Intelligence, what John Le Carré refers to as "pure intelligence," is oriented toward the future and toward policy – that is, it seeks to inform the making of policy.[7] Living in a blizzard of uncertainty where the "truth" will never be known for certain, intelligence seeks to understand new information in light of its existing understanding of complex situations. Thus, its standard is "good enough for government work." In the Iraqi case, that meant good enough for what our Pentagon colleagues called "TLAM therapy" – that is, retaliation against Iraq by strikes with U.S. cruise missiles, specifically Tomahawk Land Attack Missiles (TLAMs).

Because intelligence strives above all to protect sources and methods, its officials want desperately to stay out of the chain of evidence so they will not have to testify in court. Protecting sources and methods is intelligence's highest calling. By contrast, in the military, for instance, if officers have to cut corners with classified documents in order to get the job done, they do so. As a result, during the period when I was at the NIC, I sometimes had difficulty getting senior military officers through the CIA polygraph (i.e., lie detector). They simply came from a different culture than that of pure intelligence; so does law enforcement.

By contrast to intelligence, law enforcement is oriented not forward but rather toward response; it is after the fact. Its business is not policy but rather prosecution, and its method is cases. Law enforcement strives to put "bad guys" in jail. Its standard is high, good enough for a court of law – or, in the Iraqi case, good enough for the court of international public opinion. Law enforcement knows that if it is to make a case, it must be prepared to reveal something of how it knows what it knows; at least, it is aware that it will face that choice.

Traditional law enforcement has no real history of analysis in the intelligence sense of the term; indeed, the meaning of the word *intelligence* is different for law enforcement, in which it means "tips" to finding and convicting evildoers more than looking for patterns to frame future decisions. To be sure, "intelligence-led policing," which was developed in England in the 1990s, was given an urgency by September 11. It rejects the reactive nature of traditional law enforcement, seeking instead to identify and manage emerging criminal problems. It seeks, in short, to prevent the next crime, not just prosecute the last one. Yet, it is first and foremost a collection strategy, one that emphasizes awareness of the local domain; in that, it has much in common with what is called *community policing.*[8] Law enforcement and policing also traditionally have been defined in geographical units. These definitions are increasingly mismatched to threats such as terrorism that respect no geographical boundaries.

Different cultures compounded the effect of the wall. For instance, FBI agents have Top Secret clearances, but few are cleared into the SCI that is the woof and warp of intelligence. Therefore, when faced by unfamiliar FBI counterparts in meetings, CIA officers would be genuinely uncertain about how much they could say. For different reasons – those related to the fear of compromising criminal cases in progress – FBI agents would be similarly reticent. The safest course was to say nothing. If the conversation turned to matters domestic, then the CIA officials would also be uncertain about how much they should *hear.*

Cooperation between the two was probably best in the Counterterrorism Center (CTC), under the DCI before the 2004 Act but primarily a CIA organization, and the limits even there were suggested by the handling of the terrorist watch list (discussed later in this chapter). Because CTC was an intelligence organization, it was and is oriented abroad. It was also heavily operational, seeking to disrupt terrorist networks – again abroad. To the extent that law enforcement could be a tool in accomplishing that foreign task, it was welcome – although CIA agents would be careful to stay out of the chain of evidence. Working on operations abroad through the CTC was terrain on which cooperation between the two agencies was easier than it could be in following terrorists in and out of the United States.

A second distinction, foreign versus domestic, magnified the intelligence–law enforcement disconnect. American institutions and practices both during and prior to the Cold War drew a sharp distinction between home and abroad. The FBI had conducted wartime espionage and counterespionage in Latin America and, in December 1944, Hoover had proposed that the FBI run worldwide intelligence operations similar to its Latin American operations.[9] The proposal had some support outside the FBI, at the U.S. State Department in particular. However, President Harry Truman worried openly that giving the intelligence mandate to the FBI would risk creating a "Gestapo-like" organization; therefore, foreign operations went first to the Central Intelligence Group (i.e., the CIA predecessor) and then to the CIA. Both agencies, however, were barred from law enforcement and domestic operations.

Relations between the two agencies were ragged from the start. When I went to Washington to work on the first-ever investigations of intelligence in the 1970s, the directors of the CIA and the FBI literally did not speak to one another. Their relationship improved over time, mostly because it could not get worse! The National Security Act of 1947 was clear in proscribing the police function for the CIA. The NSA, created later, was and is also barred from law enforcement and domestic spying; therefore, if the trail of conversations or signals that the NSA was monitoring became "domestic" – that is, involved a U.S. person, corporation, or even resident alien – then the trail had to end. That was what led to the FISA. Once enacted, the data from FISA-authorized domestic wiretaps went to the FBI, not the NSA, which is why the flap erupted in 2005 over the post–September 11 NSA operations involving telephone conversations of U.S. citizens.

The FBI was required to provide information to the DCI but only if that information was "essential to the national security" and only "upon the written request" of the DCI.[10] The FBI also was responsible for protecting material before federal grand juries and, although sharing was possible, in practice information came to be shared only with a court order. Both sets of provisions were an invitation to the FBI to hoard information, not share it. Holding back was the careful thing to do lest providing information somehow contaminated a prosecution in progress.

A third distinction is public versus private. During the Cold War, national security was a government – and, largely, a *federal* government – monopoly. To be sure, private companies and citizens played a role but, for most citizens, fighting the Cold War simply meant paying their taxes. That does not seem likely to be true in the same degree for the campaign against terrorism and for homeland security. Across the country, there are three times as many "police" – security guards and the like – in the private sector as in governments. Civilians' lives will be affected – ranging from the inconvenience of waiting in long lines at airports to more difficult questions about how much security will make use of prescreening, national databanks, and biometrics.

THE INSTITUTIONAL LEGACY: TYRANNY OF THE "STOVEPIPES"

That institutional legacy, on the collection side, was an organization of stovepipes by source. Figure 3.1 illustrates that organization: the CIA clandestine service, or directorate of operations, primarily responsible for HUMINT; the NSA for SIGINT; and the NGA for pictures and other IMINT. Quaintly, intelligence referred and still refers to everything else – from newspapers to the entire Web to "gray" materials that might be private but not secret – as "open source" and sometimes

Figure 3.1. Intelligence collection stovepipes by source.

labels those sources as a separate "INT," OSINT. Intelligence analysts have their hands full coping with the materials coming to their
workstations from the secret INTs: HUMINT, SIGINT, and IMINT.
As a result, while I was at the NIC, we used to joke that sometimes
outsiders did better than intelligence insiders because they were not
denied access to OSINT!

Soon after I left the NIC for RAND in 1996, I was talking with
my colleague and squash partner, David Chu. Chu had been director of the Pentagon's policy-analysis shop, policy analysis and evaluation (PA&E) for the entire twelve years of the Reagan and first
Bush administrations. Chu later served the administration of the second President Bush as undersecretary of defense. He fought many
bureaucratic battles but never made them personal. In all those years,
as far as I can tell, his grace and good spirit meant that he never made
a permanent enemy – the rarest of rarities in modern-day Washington.

On that occasion in 1996, I suggested that the then-DCI and his
staff had not scrubbed the budgets of the major collector stovepipes,
particularly the National Reconnaissance Office (NRO) and the NSA,
very hard because the money resided in the Pentagon budget. We
assumed, I ventured, that Chu and his colleagues were giving those
budgets and programs a hard look. To my surprise, Chu responded
that he thought the DCI had done the analysis! PA&E had not. I concluded, alas, that for better or worse, the stovepipe managers had been
left with considerable autonomy.

The stovepipes were also baronies, all the more so because the
barons presided over arcane technical arts not easily grasped by mere
budgeters or even by analysts. Through the years, various efforts
sought to draw on NIOs or other intelligence analysts to provide guidance to the big collectors. During my own time at the NIC, we asked
the NIOs to finish every NIE or other major project with a postmortem on collection: "Where in the process would more or different information – information that, in principle, could have been collected – have made a difference? If they wanted more, on what issues
would they be prepared to have less, given that collection capabilities
were limited?"

That process – which amounted to modestly reallocating collection capabilities that already existed – was difficult enough, especially
for NIOs who came from outside intelligence and thus were relative

newcomers to the collection disciplines. Trying to extend the process in some form to influence what new collection capabilities might be created ran into a more formidable obstacle. Because systems begun today would enter service years from now, it was not obvious that the needs or tastes of current consumers, such as NIOs, should drive those systems. However, if not them, then who and how?

As a result, over time, those baronies had become encrusted in their own world. The numbers are classified, but as long as a decade ago, the mismatch between money and result in the stovepipes was marked. In one instance, intelligence virtuosity with satellite collection platforms turned NRO over time into a satellite designer and operator. Thus, there was little surprise that intelligence did not come quickly to other platforms for technical collection, especially the unmanned aerial vehicles (UAVs, or "drones" in another era) that figured so prominently in post–September 11 operations in Afghanistan and Iraq. That same virtuosity also led to the situation in which the majority of SIGINT data came from ground stations, but the lion's share of the money went to satellite collection. Past virtuosity made for present slowness in understanding that SIGINT now has to get close to the signals that it targets before they disappear into encryption or huge fiber-optic lines.

For its part, analysis was organized primarily by agency, not by issue or problem. Although the directorate of intelligence of the CIA was first among equals, the DIA was just as big in numbers. The INR was a major player in interagency discussions – for instance, those leading to NIEs. The analytic arms of the military services – the Office of Naval Intelligence, the National Ground Intelligence Center, and so on – were less visible in interagency discussions because their focus had been the foreign threats that their service's weaponry would confront. The joint combatant commands – Pacific Command (PACOM) and Southern Command (SOUTHCOM), for instance – also had their own intelligence units. While those commands were heavily tactical in orientation, they could be important players if an assessment concerned the risks of war in their area.

In Washington, there were smaller analytic units in departments ranging from Energy to Commerce. The larger of those, such as those at Energy, actually did some intelligence analysis, while the smaller units, such as those at Commerce, were basically information brokers, conveying and tailoring raw data or the assessments of other agencies to their own customers. All those units were explicitly departmental, serving the needs of local consumers.

There was, perhaps, a certain logic to the organization of both collection and analysis during the Cold War. With one overwhelming target, the Soviet Union, the various "INTs" were asked, in effect, what they could contribute to understanding the puzzle of the Soviet Union. Which additional puzzle pieces could they contribute? Puzzle pieces from one INT would redirect the search from another. For instance, if IMINT located a new Soviet production facility of interest, that imagery might be able to identify its general purpose by its configuration in comparison to other such facilities observed earlier. That would then be a spur for SIGINT to try and locate communications traffic to that facility – and, with any luck, including telephone traffic that might indicate not only what was being produced but also for what part of the Soviet establishment and when. Or, the process might begin with an open-source account of some mysterious factory opening – and so on.

For analysis, the logic was not so different. With a clearly identified target, the target of analysis was also obvious. The organization by agency made possible a combination of specialization and competition against the clearly identified target. The CIA and the DIA could develop specializations with, for instance, the former concentrating on technology – especially weapons technology – with the latter giving more attention to military organizations and orders of battle. Yet, the two overlapped enough so that there could be and were intense debates about issues such as the specific qualities of major Soviet weapons, especially nuclear-tipped missiles. Those debates were fought in the continuing series of NIEs about Soviet conventional and nuclear forces. The most celebrated of those debates, in 1969, concerned whether a new and large Soviet missile, the SS-9, carried warheads that could be targeted separately.[11] If it did, it threatened the syllogism of deterrence (discussed in Chapter 2), raising the risk of a "disarming" first strike by the Soviet Union against U.S. missile forces for retaliation.

The organization of intelligence by agency, along with the relatively contained set of consumers – primarily political and military officials at the top of the U.S. government – meant that all the agencies except the CIA knew for whom they worked: DIA found its customers at the Pentagon, INR at the State Department, and so on. Working for everyone, the CIA risked working for no one. Its most natural partner was the National Security Council (NSC) and especially the NSC staff, which was for much of the Cold War a small organization with a large mandate and, therefore, an equally large need for help.

Yet, if that organization made sense during the Cold War, it makes no sense for an age of terror. The transnational target outlined in Chapter 2 is much less well defined. Indeed, policy and intelligence are engaged in a joint effort to create a story or stories to comprehend that threat. Meanwhile, the number of consumers has mushroomed and their nature has dramatically diversified – from political–military officials to cops on the beat and private-sector managers of major infrastructure. Moreover, information is also mushrooming, and most of that information – in contrast to the Cold War – is not "produced" or "owned" by intelligence agencies.

In those circumstances, the way to organize cannot be by stovepipe and agency; rather, it has to be by problem or issue. Figure 3.2 suggests such an organization, using one critical functional issue – terrorism – and one key problem country – North Korea – as examples. The logic is to put consumers, sources, and analysts together – virtually in preference to physically – because today's pressing problem may not be tomorrow's and, once government organizations have buildings, they are literally set in concrete.

As Chapter 5 discusses in more detail, this logic was embraced, albeit rather tepidly, by the 2004 Act creating the DNI. It is reflected

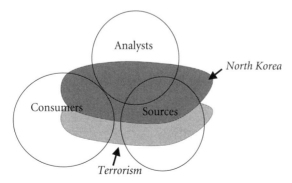

Figure 3.2. Intelligence organized by issue, not source or agency.

in the idea of intelligence "centers" as the basic work units of intelligence. So far, however, as Chapter 5 discusses, the idea has been resisted by the main agencies; thus, the centers are few – by 2008, only two and in areas where the DCI had already created CIA-dominated centers, counterterrorism and counterproliferation. In other areas, the DNI created mission managers intended to provide focus to both collection and analysis on key countries: North Korea, Iran, and Cuba–Venezuela.

THE FBI AND THE PRIMACY OF LAW ENFORCEMENT

If the ragged cooperation between the CIA and the FBI is testimony to the limited cooperation across intelligence and law enforcement as well as across foreign and domestic, other aspects of the September 11 failure – especially the Phoenix memorandum and the Moussaoui case – speak to the third main Cold War legacy: the mission and practices of the FBI. The Bureau was preeminently a law enforcement organization; almost immediately after September 11, Director Robert Mueller began driving a sea change in the FBI mission to prevention and intelligence. The Bureau was and is dominated by special agents, and those agents naturally were attracted to where there were "collars" to be made – that is, criminals to be caught – which is not terrorism because terrorists ultimately might commit but one crime. Accordingly, the FBI viewed the world through the lens of the *case* and *case file*. If information was not relevant to making a case, it was not of much account. Therefore, the post–September 11 investigations were full of reports of terrorism training manuals and similar materials that went untranslated for years because they were not directly relevant to a particular case.

The Moussaoui misadventure illustrates some of the features of the FBI organizational culture, even though it was played out not in the center of the organization, law enforcement. Rather, it was in counterterrorism, which was before September 11 if not exactly a backwater, then surely not an area in which there were many collars to be made. In this instance, an FBI special agent in the Phoenix field office sent an electronic communication (EC) to FBI headquarters and to the New York field office on July 10, 2001.[12] The EC warned about potential dangers from Al Qaeda–affiliated individuals training at

U.S. flight schools. The memorandum was sent to the Usama Bin Laden Unit (UBLU) and the Radical Fundamentalist Unit (RFU) within the Bureau's counterterrorist organization. Headquarters personnel, however, decided that no follow-up was needed, and no managers actually took part in this decision or even saw the memorandum before the September 11 attacks. The CIA was made aware of the Phoenix special agent's concerns about flight schools, but it offered no feedback despite the information that the CIA possessed about terrorists' interest in using aircraft as weapons.

Neither did the FBI officials who saw the Phoenix EC at headquarters ever connect those concerns with the body of information already in the FBI's possession about terrorists' interest in obtaining training at U.S. flight schools. The full contents of the "Phoenix Memo" were not initially made public, but it is stunning that so little was made of it, especially because it drew attention to certain information *already in the FBI's possession* suggesting a specific reason to be alarmed about a particular foreign student at an aviation university in the United States.[13] Another of then–Secretary of Defense Rumsfeld's famous quotations was his typology of intelligence questions: *known knowns*, what we know we know; *known unknowns*, what we know we do not know; and, most important for him, *unknown unknowns*, what we do not know we do not know.[14] Yet, the episode – like the September 11 use of planes as bombs – is a reminder of the importance of *unknown knowns*: what we do not know (or do not remember) we know.

The foreign student was Zacarias Moussaoui – Zakaria Mustapha Soubra in the Phoenix memorandum – the suspected "twentieth hijacker," who was arrested on August 16, 2001, in Minneapolis for a visa violation. FBI agents at the field office suspected him of terrorism and, with increasing desperation, sought to search his laptop computer but were denied permission by FBI headquarters. To get permission, FBI field offices had to go through the usual FISA procedure, requesting it through headquarters and the Department of Justice's Office of Intelligence Policy and Review (OIPR), with formal requests approved in secret by the FISC. Reportedly, of twelve thousand requests, the FISC turned down just one Justice Department request for authority.[15] All of the 1,228 requests submitted in 2002 were eventually approved,[16] which raises the concern that the FISA bar may be set too low.

The Moussaoui case, however, suggested that in practice, if not in law, the FBI and the Justice Department may have set the bar too high, at least before September 11. In that event, headquarters and FBI lawyers briefed orally by the agent handling the case believed that there was not enough evidence for a FISA search.[17] In the process, the standard apparently applied was that there had to be "probable cause" (i.e., substantial basis) that Moussaoui was an "agent of a foreign power," which in turn was interpreted to mean that he was linked to an already "recognized" terrorist organization – which Moussaoui was not because his link to Al Qaeda was as yet unknown.

In fact, the standard applied was more demanding than the law at the time, which required probable cause that the targeted person was an "agent of a foreign power," which in turn was defined as "any person who ... knowingly aids or abets any person in the conduct of [certain] activities." Those activities include "international terrorism," and one definition of "foreign power" includes groups that engage in "international terrorism."[18] Moreover, those making decisions in the Moussaoui case never saw the now-famous EC from the Phoenix field office, which arrived at headquarters in late July. The warnings in that communication about suspicious activity at U.S. flight schools would have buttressed concerns about Moussaoui's own flying lessons.

The Moussaoui case can be seen as a testament to sloppy procedures, poor information technology, tensions between FBI field offices and headquarters, excessive caution or simple ignorance about complicated points of law, or all of those in some combination. It also may be that previous tensions between the FBI and the FISC had a "chilling effect" and made for more caution, which was alleged in the letter from Special Agent Coleen Rowley to FBI Director Mueller, dated May 21, 2002.[19] In any event, the case surely bespeaks considerable – perhaps excessive – caution on the part of the FBI and the Justice Department in venturing FISA requests onto new terrain. Foreign spies were one thing; foreign "students," even those with worrisome connections, were quite another.

The Moussaoui case underscores what Senator Richard Shelby (R-AL) labeled the "tyranny of the case file."[20] That culture, if not tyranny, can hardly be overstated. Because the FBI was then and still is, to a considerable extent, a law enforcement organization, its agents were trained and acculturated, rewarded, and promoted within an institutional culture whose primary purpose was to capture and prosecute criminals. Within the Bureau, information was stored, retrieved, and simply *understood* principally through the conceptual prism of a "case" – a discrete bundle of information that is constructed to prove elements of crimes against specific potential defendants in a court of law.

The culture and case-file mindset meant that information the FBI collected either was or was not relevant to the case at hand. If it was relevant, it often disappeared into federal grand juries. Before the Patriot Act of November 2001, it took a court order to share that information with anyone, including CIA analysts – who, of course, usually would not know what information was there and thus might be requested. If the information collected was not relevant to the case at hand, it often was simply discarded.

For instance, the FBI knew that convicted terrorist Abdul Hakim Murad had been involved in an extremist Islamic plot to blow up twelve U.S.–owned airliners over the Pacific Ocean and crash an aircraft into CIA headquarters.[21] Murad was not charged with a crime in connection with the CIA crash plot, apparently because that plot was merely at the "discussion" stage when he was apprehended. Because the CIA crash plot did not appear in the indictment, however, the FBI effectively forgot about it, and Murad's case file essentially ignored it. FBI agents interviewed by the joint congressional investigation confirmed that Murad's only significance to them was specifically in connection with the crimes for which he was charged: "The other aspects of the plot were not part of the criminal case and therefore not considered relevant."[22]

Convinced that the only information that really matters was information directly related to the criminal investigation at hand, the FBI thus ignored this early warning sign that terrorists had begun planning to crash aircraft into symbols of U.S. power. As a result, rather than being stored in a form that would have permitted information to be assessed and reassessed in light of a broader set of information about terrorist plans and intentions over time, the Murad datapoint was simply forgotten. Like all the other tidbits of information that might have alerted a sophisticated analyst to terrorists' interest in using airplanes to attack building targets in the United States, this episode disappeared into the depths of an old case file and slipped out of the FBI's usable institutional memory. It became an unknown known.

Given the tyranny of the case file, suppose – as a senior FBI counterterrorism agent posed it to me – the FBI had done better at connecting the dots about flying lessons in the summer of 2001. His account is self-serving but with merit. What could the FBI have done? No crime had yet been committed because taking flying lessons is not a crime, not even for Middle Easterners and not even if they are uninterested in landings and takeoffs. Suppose, then, that the FBI had started knocking on doors of flight schools asking to interview Middle Eastern students – all without a crime or case. How far would it have gotten, at a time when Justice was suing local police departments over racial profiling? The question is a haunting reminder of the force of the Cold War distinctions and of the law enforcement mission of the FBI.

BARONS, AGENTS, AND FURNITURE

After I left government (for a third time), I had the opportunity to lead a RAND Corporation project that, at the urging of Congress, reviewed the internal-security procedures at the Bureau in the wake of a Soviet spy, Robert Hanssen, in the FBI and of a blue-ribbon panel chaired by former FBI (and CIA) director, Judge William Webster, to recommend reforms.[23] I had known the FBI before September 11 but it was from the perspective of intelligence, not law enforcement, which at that time was the FBI's preeminent mission. In those days, the analogy with place-kickers in the National Football League was apt: they, like intelligence officers at the FBI, were important in substance but not very high in the organization's pecking order.

So, this opportunity was a fascinating exposure to a very different organizational culture. My first day of conducting interviews at the Bureau drove home just how different it was. I was interviewing the officer in charge of the FBI's asset and informant database, sensitive information. She was an agent, impressive and vocal about how much she hated being at FBI headquarters. She wanted to be back out on the streets catching bad guys. Later in the day, I complimented her to another agent who had been her boss at the Washington field office. His response was a reminder of just how different this culture was.

"Oh, yes," he said, "she's terrific. She's the best fugitive tracker in the Bureau. And she can put the entire contents of her sidearm through a target the size of a donut." This was not the kind of compliment one was likely to receive at the RAND Corporation!

I mused about why the FBI was the most headquarters-phobic government organization I had ever encountered, easily surpassing even the military on that dimension. It finally hit me: bad guys did not get collared at headquarters – or so we profoundly hoped! – but rather only in the field. As long as the FBI was preeminently in the law enforcement business, literally nothing of value was accomplished at headquarters. Intelligence is different in that sense because although collection abroad is critical, most analysis happens if not at headquarters, then in Washington, policy officials are briefed there, and so on. For intelligence, much of value occurs at headquarters, and something of value happens at headquarters even for the military in planning, training, and the like.

The old FBI was not just headquarters-phobic, it was also – not surprisingly – radically decentralized. The Special Agents in Charge (SACs) of field offices were barons in their domain. As Maureen Baginski, who came from NSA to become the FBI's Executive Associate Director (EAD) for Intelligence, said: "I'd known barons abroad – the CIA station chiefs in foreign countries – but the experience of barons at home was a new one for me." As an example of just how decentralized it was, many agents in the New York field office distrusted the Bureau's workhorse information system, the Automated Case Support (ACS) system, and simply refused to upload material to it.

In the words of the Webster blue-ribbon panel, several agents believed "that it is possible to ascertain user passwords by employing ACS system tools" and that the system's features have "resulted in a number of horror stories about exposure of confidential files on ACS." Therefore, "personnel charged with investigating espionage allegations generally do not upload case file information into ACS ... [and] do not even solicit help with leads on ACS because on one occasion, when a lead was sent to a field office, new agents who covered the lead – unaware of the unit's avoidance of ACS [and how ACS file restrictions operate] – uploaded information without restricting it."[24]

That culture is powerful and it pervades the entire organization, reflected at every level and in every area. It contributed to the autonomous, decentralized authority and traditions of the field offices, which also are sharper in the FBI than in any other government organization I have known. Before September 11, money was allocated and careers were made through criminal investigations, not long-term analysis or other work. "Intelligence" in the Bureau's practice was tips to finding and catching evildoers; it was not the assembling of a broad mosaic of understanding. Producing clear, evidence-based narratives that would indict criminals was prized; drawing "iffy" inferences based on fragmentary information in order to support decision making was not. Given a choice between more agents on the street and better technology, the culture opted for the former, resulting in the FBI's famously backward technology. It is, in the words of one investigator, "where the [IBM] 360s went to die" – or, as an FBI agent told me, "We took the dirt-road alternative to the information superhighway a generation ago."

In my work after September 11, reinforcing security at the FBI amounted to changing its organizational culture, and September 11 required yet another culture change. The culture was one in which security, other than physical security, was not a top priority. Although the distinctions have softened over time, still the gap between special agents and "support" is yawning. As Baginski said to me on one occasion: "I've been told that there are two kinds of people at the Bureau. There are agents, and there is furniture. I may have a fancy title, but I'm still furniture." Activities, like intelligence, that were not primarily performed by agents have been given less priority and fewer resources, never mind whether those other activities are filing, or doing science, or analyzing intelligence. Stated more crudely, if you did not carry a gun at the Bureau, as agents do, you were a second-class citizen. Technical security was not fully appreciated or supported. Personnel security was seen as an administrative function. The combination of emphasis on law enforcement and the role of agents argued against compartmentalizing information. "Need to know" was not applied in the same sense that it is meant to be applied elsewhere in the government. Even when there existed reasons to do so, the information-technology (IT) systems in place meant that there was not always the means to do so.

Indeed, reinforcing security was a change in culture within a change in culture because the shift toward counterterrorism was changing the FBI's mission and, with it, its culture. In the long run, that change in mission made the approach of the Webster Commission, which essentially applied an intelligence-agency template for security to the FBI, all the more appropriate. Yet, in the short term, the Bureau was and is being tugged in two directions, characterized by insiders in the early 2000s as "Webster" and "9–11." While the former argues for being more careful with and compartmentalizing information, the latter creates enormous pressure to get on with the job and to share information widely in doing so. Even so, there are good reasons in law enforcement to restrict access to certain types of information. There needs to be a comprehensive and deliberate approach to information management that enables the work and work processes of the FBI.

TERRORISM AND PREEMPTIVE PROSECUTION

In many respects, counterterrorism bridges the two classic Bureau missions – criminal law enforcement and counterintelligence – reflected in the work of the Criminal Investigative Division (CID) and the CD. CID informants, for instance, are themselves criminals who are likely to commit unauthorized crimes. Thus, the premium in handling them is to get their tips, then move them quickly out of the chain of evidence by running an FBI operation. By contrast, while CD assets may commit crimes, many of them are "white-collar spies," who may provide valuable intelligence throughout a considerable period of working for the Bureau. Persons of interest to the CTD might be either; that is, they might provide valuable intelligence even as they commit unauthorized crimes, such as running guns or laundering money.

In that sense, countering terrorism, especially at home, has much in common with operations against drug traffickers and organized crime. The intelligence task for all three puts a premium on unraveling networks, which often span countries and continents. The main difference, it is often observed, is that criminals want to live for their cause (i.e., money), not die for it. They want to live to steal another day. Some terrorists, by contrast, are prepared to die for their cause.

That fact drives the intelligence task back to prevention, or preemption. That, in turn, produces another major difference between fighting terrorists and fighting crime: because potential terrorists, especially homegrown terrorists, must be stopped before they strike, the decision to roll up the operation has to come much earlier. Indeed, drug dealers and other criminals need to be allowed to commit their crimes so that they can be prosecuted. However, the consequences are usually modest; a drug shipment, for instance, might be seized *after* it was sold and the crime thus committed.

Terrorists, however, cannot be allowed to strike and therefore need to be found and stopped before they do. Combating them becomes what might be called preemptive prosecution and, like other preemptive strikes, it is risky. It means relying on often unreliable informants to infiltrate insular communities, and it means making arrests before anything close to a terrorist attack actually happens. The process sometimes will end with a prosecution but often without a conviction – there is a slender record of U.S. convictions of terrorists since September 11. The process is a messy and unsatisfying ordeal, but it may be the best that can be done.

The Fort Dix case of 2007 is an illustration.[25] The principal informant, Mahmoud Omar, a legal immigrant from Egypt, had been convicted of bank fraud and served time. In 2002, the government tried and failed to deport him, and two years later it tried again. The same year the government made a third try, 2006, the FBI put Omar on the payroll, and the immigration case quietly went away. He infiltrated a group of friends in Cherry Hill, New Jersey, who the government suspected of harboring terrorist intentions. For sixteen months, Omar earned thousands of dollars recording hundreds of conversations. According to court documents, he drove one man to do surveillance of possible targets and he offered to help buy illegal weapons for the group. Finally, in 2007, Omar handed over the men, thereafter known as the "Fort Dix Six."

In May 2006, when the U.S. attorney announced the arrests on the steps of the courthouse in Camden, New Jersey, he called the Fort Dix case "the model for the post–September 11 era." He meant that as a compliment. Eight different law enforcement agencies had cooperated, all of them following up on the tip of a concerned citizen. The investigation had run for a long time, eighteen months. Six suspects were in jail: five charged with conspiring to kill soldiers at the Fort Dix military base in southern New Jersey and the sixth facing weapons charges. No one had gotten hurt. "This," said the attorney, "is what we've been talking about developing since [September 11]."

The first tip had indeed come from a citizen, a store clerk at a Circuit City store where three of those arrested – brothers – went to get an 8-mm video converted to a DVD. The clerk thought nothing was out of the ordinary as he copied the video until he noticed bearded men in camouflage shooting guns and shouting in a foreign language. After thinking about it overnight, he then called the police.

The police took the tip seriously and reviewed the tape. They were struck by the words *jihad* and *Allahu Akbar* (which means "God is great"); however, those words are ambiguous because they are used by many devout and law-abiding Muslims the way Christians might say, "Praise God" or "God bless." The men in the video plainly liked guns, but was it what the government has termed a "militia-like" training?

As terrorism domesticates, the profile of a would-be terrorist is becoming increasingly less obvious. Most homegrown terrorism plots are the work of "unremarkable men," as a 2007 report on radicalization by the New York Police Department (NYPD) stated it, or "a group of guys," as U.S. intelligence officials call them. In those circumstances, intelligence has to be attentive to minor behaviors. For instance, one month before the July 7, 2005, London transit bombings, two of the suicide bombers went whitewater rafting together. A decade earlier, the Circuit City tape might have been ignored as just "guys with guns"; in 2006, it was not.

Enter the informant, Omar. Just as America's spies are foreigners, not U.S. officials, informants also are not undercover FBI agents – quite the contrary. The FBI has very few agents who can pass as young Muslim extremists. Therefore, most informants are people who, like Omar, need something badly enough that the government has a handle on them. Usually, they need money or a way to reduce their prison sentences or to avoid deportation. Many have criminal records; the Justice Department's Inspector General (IG) reported in 2005 that 10 percent of a sampling of informants had committed new, unauthorized crimes while working for the FBI.

Omar was hired by the FBI to ingratiate himself with the men in the Circuit City video, and he did his job persistently if not always gracefully, returning repeatedly to a shop owned by the family of one of those ultimately arrested. The family had immigrated to the United States from Jordan. The three brothers who were arrested were illegal immigrants from the former Yugoslavia, who looked and sounded like Americans.

Omar recorded more than 100 hours of his conversations with those later arrested, but still the amount of information is minimal. Most of the conversations were the tedious chatter of young men, more about fishing or Fords than *jihad*. The most damning statements seem to have come from one man when he was alone with Omar, allegedly saying, "If you want to do anything here, there is Fort Dix and I don't want to exaggerate, and I assure you that you can hit an American base very easily.... When you go to a military base, you need mortars and RPGs." The language is ominous but could also be interpreted as a response to Omar. At another point, the man said, "I am at your services as you have more experience than me in military bases and in life," while at another time he is more assertive. As he and Omar traveled to Fort Dix and other military bases to conduct surveillance, he said, "My intent is to hit a heavy concentration of soldiers."

Informants are almost by definition not entirely reliable, so they are closely monitored. However, tape recorders and other recording devices not only can be turned off, they also malfunction often. Moreover, on one occasion, Omar gave his handler false information in order to protect a friend. Informants – and the baggage that often comes with them – are not new. What is new is the heavy reliance on informants in terrorism cases. In drug cases, after all, no one usually gets arrested until someone actually has drugs. Terrorism cases are more difficult. If an informant or source comes back with a kilo of cocaine, the case is quite clear; in a terrorism case, if he outlines what the group is planning, it is only his word.

Therefore, again and again, accused terrorists have argued that they were entrapped. They did so in the Fort Dix case, although entrapment is notoriously difficult to prove. Harder evidence is in short supply. The father of one of those arrested owned a pizzeria and had a map of the base and clearance to deliver there. The map found its way into the group's hands. Court documents do not contain evidence of a specific date or a detailed plan. Perhaps the direst charges are that three of those arrested wanted to buy fully automatic guns and went to Omar's apartment to get them. When they did, the police moved in and made the arrests. Meanwhile, Omar, the informant, vanished.

The point is that prosecutions may not be the point; disrupting terrorist plots is. The risks, however, are that innocent people will go to jail on flimsy evidence or, on the flip side, that juries will become so leery of dodgy informants that they will set guilty people free. Over the longer term, the risk is that rumors of entrapment will become so pervasive that they will poison relations between the FBI and other government agencies, as well as their best potential allies – the Muslim communities across the United States.

The question will remain how much the intelligence-agency template for the FBI will need to be adapted to an organization that will retain a powerful law enforcement past and continuing mission and that will be moving toward more emphasis on a counterterrorism mission that crosses intelligence and law enforcement. The new mission is more proactive than the old, more centered on public safety by looking ahead to consequences and planning accordingly.

The agents are a "band of brothers," now including many sisters. That band makes for powerful capacity. As one agent told me, "When you go out the door on an operation, you don't have to look over your shoulder to see if anyone is with you. They are." As with most powerful cultures, however, the pluses and minuses of the FBI culture are the same attributes. Agents easily shared information within the band – perhaps too easily, as was suggested by Robert Hanssen, who not only took advantage of the shortcomings of the ACS but was also allowed access to information he had no need to see. However, FBI agents were not distinguished before September 11 by their willingness to share *outside* the band. The Bureau brought and brings state and local police officers to work with it but does so primarily on its terms, as members of FBI joint-task forces, with clearances to match.

The culture is powerful; it is a source of capacity to act in the public interest. However, changing it, like changing any powerful organizational culture, is difficult and slow. The FBI culture prized – and prizes – action; it favored agents on the street over technology, taking that dirt-road alternative to the information highway. It was and to a considerable but changing extent still is a culture of law enforcement, which puts a premium on sharing information, not closeting it. The "can do" spirit of the organization makes the gap between headquarters and the field more striking than for virtually any other government organization. The question for the future is how much this legacy needs to be changed – and how much it can be changed.

4

The Imperative of Change

If the boundaries served the democratic nations tolerably well during the Cold War – in particular, by safeguarding the privacy of citizens – they set up those nations to fail in an age of terror. Terrorists respected none of those boundaries. They were not "over there" – they were both there and here, with the precise configurations changing and unpredictable. By the mid-2000s, for instance, the terrorist threat to Britain was almost entirely "domestic" – homegrown cells with tentacles reaching abroad, to Pakistan in particular. By contrast, for the United States, the problem was still primarily "over there," although with its tendrils reaching into the United States. Whether that would change remained to be seen – and remained a task for intelligence in an age of terror.

Terrorists targeted not armies but rather private citizens. As a result, the so-called war on terrorism not only hyped the threat but also mislocated it, implying that military instruments, in which the United States reigned supreme, would be primary. While those terrorists might commit crimes, they might commit only one, and then it would be too late. They could not be dealt with as either an intelligence or a law enforcement problem; rather, they had to be treated as both.

By the same token, if organizing intelligence – on the collection side, by source, and on the analysis side, by agency – may have made a certain sense during the Cold War, it cannot be the right way to organize now. On the collection side, if the terrorist target is more of a mystery than a puzzle, then the Cold War's implicit competition among the INTs for puzzle pieces needs to give way to explicit cooperation across those INTs in framing the mysteries. Moreover, it is not just that now there are more targets but also more consumers and more information – although it is information varied in reliability and little of it "owned" by intelligence as were the Cold War secret sources.

In the United States, the 2004 Act made a start at reshaping intelligence. It – and more so the Senate version of the bill that was modified in conference – proposed national intelligence centers under the authority of the new DNI and organized around issues or missions. The national intelligence centers, with the National Counterterrorism Center (NCTC) as the prototype, would both deploy and use the information, technology, and staff resources of the existing agencies – the CIA, DIA, NSA, and others. The centers would be intelligence's version of the military's "unified combatant commands," looking to the agencies to acquire the technological systems, train the people, and execute the operations planned by the centers. So far, in addition to the NCTC, the National Counterproliferation Center is the only other center to have been established, and it does not have the operational role of the NCTC.

At the same time, the FBI, under Director Mueller, was under enormous pressure, and there was considerable talk of creating a new domestic-intelligence agency apart from the Bureau. Mueller, however, moved rapidly to turn the Bureau from almost pure concentration on law enforcement to prevention and intelligence. Both Congress and the postmortem commissions decided to give the FBI time to see if the change could be made enduring. The FBI adopted the WMD Commission's recommendation to create not only a Directorate of Intelligence within the FBI but also the National Security Branch (NSB), incorporating intelligence plus the FBI's Counterterrorism and Counterintelligence Divisions (CTD and CD).

HITTING THE "WALL"

The effect of all the Cold War boundaries was vividly on display in the run-up to September 11.[1] By the spring of 2000, two of the hijackers, Khalid al-Mihdhar and Nawaf al-Hazmi, were living under their own names in San Diego, and the latter even applied for a new visa. The INS had no reason to be concerned because the CIA had withheld the two terrorists names from TIPOFF, the basic terrorist watch list.

Neither did the FBI have any reason to look for them – for instance, by conducting a basic Internet search for their names or by querying its informants in Southern California – because the last it knew from the CIA was that the two terrorists were overseas. No agency told the FAA to be on alert for the two, apparently because it was not in the law enforcement business. The airlines were not informed because they were private, not public.

According to the joint Senate–House investigation of September 11, the CIA's procedures for informing other agencies – FBI, State, NSA, and the then-INS – of suspected terrorists were both restricted and haphazard.[2] By its own guidelines and later by a January 2001 memorandum of understanding, the CIA was supposed to notify at least the FBI and the NSA of all people it suspected to be terrorists. In fact, the CIA seems only to have put people on the watch list if it also had information that they were about to travel to the United States – a more restrictive criterion. Moreover, in the investigation's words, the CIA "apparently neither trained nor encouraged its employees to follow its own rules on watchlisting." The number of names the CIA put on the watch list soared after September 11 – from 1,761 during the three months before September 11 to 4,251 in the three months afterward.

The ragged connections between the CIA and the FBI were graphically illustrated by their misdealings over the Al Qaeda–affiliated terrorists, al-Mihdhar and al-Hazmi. The saga of what the two agencies told one another, and when, was played out in the series of investigations of the September 11 tragedy.[3] The two men attended a terrorist meeting in Kuala Lumpur, Malaysia, in early January 2000. This meeting was known to and surveilled by the CIA, which already knew that al-Mihdhar possessed a multiple-entry visa permitting him to travel to the United States. The NSA had independent information that linked al-Hazmi to Al Qaeda. Neither the CIA nor the NSA, however, saw fit to provide those names for the main watch list, the so-called TIPOFF database.

There was some initial confusion about what the CIA told the FBI regarding al-Mihdhar and al-Hazmi. CIA e-mail traffic reviewed by the joint congressional investigation, however, suggests that the CIA briefed the FBI in general terms. The 9/11 Commission's account indicated that a CIA analyst had passed the surveillance photographs to an FBI analyst working in the *USS Cole* Investigation Unit. The CIA, however, still did not bother to tell the FBI that al-Mihdhar had a multiple-entry visa that would allow him to enter the United States. In early March 2000, the CIA learned that al-Hazmi had arrived in Los Angeles on January 15. Despite having just learned of the presence in this country of an Al Qaeda terrorist, the CIA apparently did not inform other agencies. Indeed, the internal cable transmitting this information contained the notation: "Action Required: None, FYI." This information came hard on the heels of the intelligence community's alarm over possible "millennium plots" by Al Qaeda. Moreover, Al-Hazmi arrived at about the same time the CIA knew that Al Qaeda terrorist, Ahmed Ressam, was also supposed to have arrived in Los Angeles to conduct terrorism operations. Still, however, the CIA refused to notify anyone of al-Hazmi's presence in the country.

By this point, al-Mihdhar and al-Hazmi – both of them terrorists known to the CIA – were living in San Diego under their real names. They signed these names on their rental agreement, both used their real names in taking flight-school training in May 2000, and al-Mihdhar even used his real name to obtain a motor-vehicle identification card from the State of California. In July 2000, al-Hazmi applied to the INS for an extension of his visa, sending in the application using his real name and his current address in San Diego (where he would remain until December 2000). INS had no reason to be concerned because the CIA had not put their names on TIPOFF, and the last the FBI had heard from the CIA the two were overseas.

The CIA's failure to put al-Mihdhar and al-Hazmi on the watch list became even more inexplicable in January 2001, when the CIA discovered that a suspect in the *USS Cole* bombing also had attended the Malaysia meeting. This might have been taken as confirmation that the two terrorists had links to Al Qaeda operational cells, thus making them even more a concern, but the CIA still did not bother to inform TIPOFF. This failure was particularly damaging because al-Mihdhar was overseas at the time; putting his name on the watch list would have enabled INS agents to stop him at the border.

Even when given the opportunity to tell the FBI – in face-to-face meetings – about the presence of the two terrorists in the United States, the CIA refused. The 9/11 Commission report describes the sequence, using only first names for the officials involved: John, CIA official – International Terrorism Operations Section; Dave, CIA analyst; Jane, FBI analyst – FBI's *USS Cole* Investigation Unit; Mary, FBI analyst – detailed to the CIA's Bin Laden Unit.[4] John had given the three surveillance photographs of the Kuala Lumpur meeting to Jane to show to FBI New York agents. She received no more information regarding the photographs.

On June 11, 2001, Dave, Jane, and the *USS Cole* case agents met in New York to discuss information and to share the surveillance photographs of Kuala Lumpur. Because the CIA never disseminated reports on its tracking of al-Mihdhar, Jane was prevented from pulling any information on his visa or travel to the United States. For his part, Dave told investigators that as a CIA analyst, he was not authorized to answer questions from the FBI about the CIA information during the June 11 meeting. Thus, he resisted telling his FBI counterparts what he knew – that al-Mihdhar and al-Hazmi had come to the United States. The FBI agents left the meeting without learning any information that would initiate an investigation on al-Mihdhar.

There was additional contact between the two agencies. For instance, John contacted Mary to review the Kuala Lumpur materials another time. Yet, Dave stated to investigators that NSA reports that contained information on Mihdhar could not be shared with criminal investigators without permission of the Justice Department's OIPR. This stopped Jane from passing information to the FBI agents who were most knowledgeable about Al Qaeda. When Jane drafted a lead on information regarding al-Mihdhar, one agent, who worked on the *USS Cole* case, contacted her after reading the lead with interest. In the words of the 9/11 Commission report: "'Jane' later insisted, however, that because the agent was designated a 'criminal' FBI agent, not an intelligence FBI agent, the wall kept him from participating in any search for al-Mihdhar."[5]

Meanwhile, al-Mihdhar, in Jeddah, Saudi Arabia, applied for a new U.S. visa in June 2001. However, because neither he nor al-Hazmi was on the TIPOFF list, his name did not appear when the State

Department officials who took this application checked his name against their database, which incorporated TIPOFF watch list information. Therefore, al-Mihdhar was given a visa and returned unchallenged to the United States in July.

The CIA finally put al-Hazmi and al-Mihdhar on the watch list in late August 2001, by which point they were already in the United States and in the final stages of preparing for the September 11 attacks; the CIA also added the names of two others who were expected to try and enter the United States. Apparently, the FBI did little with the information and also failed to share it with the INS until the INS had already admitted the other two into the country. Questioned about its failure to follow up on this cable, one FBI official said, "If the cable says, "Don't let them in the country, and they were already in the country, what's the point of bringing this up now?" In any event, the FBI failed to locate Khalid al-Mihdhar and Nawaf al-Hazmi, who hijacked the jet that crashed into the Pentagon on September 11.

The FBI tried to find the two terrorists but was hampered by a combination of its own regulations and the prevailing view that terrorism was a second-order mission, especially in the United States. The Bureau did not shift agents to counterterrorism from its primary law enforcement mission. Neither did it search the Web for information that would have revealed al-Hazmi and al-Mihdhar living under their real names in San Diego. On October 18, the *Los Angeles Times* reported that a simple check of public records and addresses through the California Department of Motor Vehicles would have disclosed the correct location of the two hijackers. A check with credit card companies would have shown airline-ticket purchases and given their correct addresses.[6] (According to testimony before the congressional investigation from an FBI agent in New York, who also conducted such a search after the September 11 attacks, finding al-Mihdhar's address could have been accomplished "within hours.") The Bureau also did not ask for help from Treasury officials in tracking down al-Mihdhar and al-Hazmi through their credit card or banking transactions.

A State Department official testified that the FBI had refused for a decade to provide the INS with access to its National Crime Information Center Database, on the grounds that the INS is not a "law enforcement" organization. Nevertheless, an internal FBI review concluded that "everything was done that could have been done."[7]

Before September 11, the "standard FBI line" – according to one source who spoke to *New Yorker* writer Joe Klein – was that "Osama bin Laden wasn't a serious domestic security threat," presumably because his earlier attacks had been abroad, not at home.[8]

No agency told the FAA to be on the alert for the four men, apparently because it too was not in the law enforcement business. The airlines were not informed because they were private, not public. A European official testified to the effect of these oppositions on the sharing of information with the United States: "Those we have been arresting are people we knew about before [September 11] but never thought were particularly dangerous to us inside our national boundaries."[9] So, the two hijackers flew their plane into the Pentagon on September 11, 2001.

FIRST STEPS AT REFORM

In an unusual move for a blue-ribbon panel, the 9/11 Commission took the reshaping of American intelligence into new territory. Its report was dramatic and made several recommendations – primarily to reshape the organization of U.S. intelligence but also to begin to change the way it does business. Even more unusual for a blue-ribbon panel, the 9/11 Commission did not report and then disappear; rather, it stayed around, hectoring both Congress and the Bush administration to actually make something happen.

The 9/11 victims' families added political clout to the Commission because they were not about to be ignored. Were it not for them, the Commission may not have been established in the first place. Once it was established, the families fought hard for public hearings and for access to President Bush by the Commission, and they helped with the lobbying after the report was released. The result was the December 2004 bill creating a DNI; veteran diplomat, John Negroponte, was appointed the first DNI in February 2005, reportedly after several other candidates had either turned down the job or removed themselves from the running.

The 9/11 Commission made six broad proposals affecting intelligence and therefore is a good benchmark for assessing what has been accomplished to date. The WMD Commission, which reported after the bill had been enacted, extended the agenda of reform. Neither commission called for a domestic-intelligence service separate from the FBI. Both, and especially the 9/11 Commission, underscored an enormous challenge, one that is the work of years, not weeks or months: the need to not only create the technical infrastructure to better share intelligence but also to rethink the web of "need to know" and other security requirements that frustrate sharing. The 9/11 Commission's principal recommendations were to

- create the position of a DNI, located in the White House and possessing what the preexisting DCI did *not* have – real authority over the budgets of the fifteen U.S. intelligence agencies
- institute an NCTC reporting to the DNI, responsible for both joint operational planning *and* joint intelligence
- establish national intelligence centers, organized around discrete issues on the model of the NCTC, under the authority of the DNI
- make the CIA director a position separate from the DNI and charge him or her primarily with building a better espionage capacity for the nation
- set focal points for oversight in both the House and the Senate, for both intelligence and homeland security, in place of the eighty-eight committees and subcommittees of Congress before which DHS officials now appear
- rethink the web of "need to know" and other security procedures that frustrate not just sharing intelligence but also intelligence work as a whole
- *not* create a separate domestic-intelligence service after the model of the British MI-5; instead, it encouraged the FBI to move forward with changing its mission from pure law enforcement to terrorism prevention and building a DI within the existing FBI

The first four recommendations were embodied – albeit in differing degrees – in the December 2004 bill. The measure that received the most press attention – creating a DNI – was the most familiar. The most far-reaching, however, was the 9/11 Commission's proposal to foster coordination by emulating the military in separating the "organize, train, and equip" function from the actual deployment of intelligence personnel. The existing agencies – CIA, FBI, DIA, and NSA – would, like the military services, be responsible for *building* the intelligence forces, but those forces would be *deployed* by the new "national intelligence centers," which would be shaped by issue or function, not as currently by organization or collection source.

Those centers would be intelligence's equivalent of the military's unified commands. In Iraq, for instance, it was Central Command (CENTCOM) that conducted the war; the troops were provided by the military services, which executed operations under CENTCOM's direction. By analogy, the National Counterterrorism Center would be the "unified command" in the war on terrorism, conducting the intelligence analysis and planning operations. The CIA and other agencies would provide the analysts and other personnel and would conduct the required operations – for instance, intelligence-gathering. Issue-oriented centers have existed in the intelligence community since the mid-1980s. Although in form, like the preexisting CTC, these centers worked for the DCI; in fact, they were dominated by the CIA. This proposal moved them to the DNI and, in principle, made them more central as focal points for intelligence and operations.

Predictably, the sticking point in the final congressional negotiations was the exact power of the DNI over the intelligence operations located in the Defense Department, especially the major technical collectors – the NSA, the NGA, and the NRO. Those agencies are responsible for the majority of the national intelligence budget, and no secretary of defense has been eager to cede authority over them to the DCI or the new DNI. By all accounts, Secretary of Defense Rumsfeld in 2004 was no exception.

The Senate passed a bill similar to the 9/11 Commission recommendations; however, the House version, although it created a DNI, endowed that position with less authority than the Senate bill. In conference, the House achieved many of its objectives.[10] Table 4.1 summarizes the key issues of contention, the Senate version, the House version, and the final outcome.

The most important of these eleventh-hour negotiations were the limits on the key powers of the DNI – to move money and people. Exactly how important those limitations will turn out to be is still a work in progress; Negroponte's term as DNI left it unclear whether the limitations were substantial or whether he simply was disinclined to try to stretch them. In principle, the DNIs have considerable programmatic authority: they develop the National Intelligence Program (NIP) and broad personnel policy across (civilians in) all the

Table 4.1. *The Shaping of the DNI's Authority*

Issue	Senate Bill	House Bill	Final Bill
Declassification of budget intelligence top line	Declassify budget top line	Retain classified budget top line	Retain classified budget top line
Budget execution	Intelligence funds do not flow through the Department of Defense to intelligence agencies	Intelligence funds flow through the Department of Defense	Intelligence funds flow through the Department of Defense
Chain-of-command protection	No chain-of-command protection	No need for chain-of-command provision	Specific provision requiring that implementation "respect and not abrogate" existing military chain-of-command statutes
Budget reprogramming	NID can reprogram unlimited amount of funds without approval of department/agency heads	NID unilateral reprogram authority capped at 5% of department budgets	DNI unilateral reprogram authority capped at 5% of department budgets
Personnel transfers	DNI can transfer unlimited number of personnel without the approval of department/agency heads	No unilateral personnel transfer authority	DNI's unilateral transfer authority is limited to 100 personnel for each new national intelligence center created
Personnel management	DNI can prescribe personnel policies and requirements for all personnel within the intelligence community, including military personnel	DNI personnel-policy authorities limited to civilian employees	DNI personnel-policy authorities limited to civilian employees
DNI control over military programs	Gives DNI primary control over all programs of the NSA, NRO, and NGA, including nonnational (JMIP) military programs	Excludes from DNI primary control all military intelligence programs within the JMIP	Excludes from DNI primary control all military intelligence programs within the JMIP

agencies. In that sense, the DNI's authority over the nation's intelligence budget is roughly comparable to that of the secretary of defense over total defense spending.

The limitations on DNI authority are more apparent at the level of *execution* – for instance, the DNI was restricted from moving more than 100 people to any particular new joint intelligence center. Beyond the 100, the DNI, like the DCI before him, has to bargain with the other agency heads. The 5 percent limit also applies to the DNIs' authority to *reprogram* budgeted money without congressional approval. To be sure, 5 percent of a major agency budget is a lot of money, especially in the context of the DNI's programming authority.[11] Still, the task for Negroponte and his successors was and is to turn a hunting license into real authority.

ASSESSING THE MAIN PROVISIONS

The first three recommendations embodied in the December 2004 bill are the heart of the new approach, seeking coordination, or "jointness," at two levels: (1) the strategic, by breaking down the "stovepipes" that made the separate agencies – especially the big collecting agencies – baronies in their own right; and (2) the day-to-day, by using the national intelligence centers to improve the operational management of intelligence. The first three recommendations formed a cluster, one that could not be easily disentangled, and had an either/or quality to them; therefore, half measures in implementation could wind up being worse than nothing at all.

Create a Director of National Intelligence

The DNI is charged with overseeing national intelligence centers on specific subjects of interest across the U.S. government, managing the NIP, and overseeing the agencies that contribute to it. The logic of the idea was to give the DNI what the position of DCI lacked: authority over budgets for intelligence agencies other than the CIA, over hiring and firing senior leaders, and over setting standards for intelligence's personnel and infrastructure.

As usual in government, the proposition that DCIs had lacked authority to manage the entire national-intelligence budget was not quite as clear-cut as the discussion implied. As many wise veterans observed, the earlier authorities of the DCI could have been enough had presidents so desired – and so ordered of their secretaries of defense. In the Carter administration, when intelligence budgets were falling, the DCI, Admiral Stansfield Turner, exercised more control over the entire budget, and he built a serious program-analysis staff to aid him in the effort. Still, the 2004 bill represented an increase in the DCI's explicit authority.

The DNI replaces the DCI. The position is confirmed by the Senate – as were Negroponte and his successor, retired Admiral Mike McConnell – and the DNI testifies before Congress. The DNI is neither a member of the Cabinet nor has Cabinet rank. The 9/11 Commission proposed to embody interagency cooperation by giving the DNI three deputies, each of whom would also have had a second agency responsibility: foreign intelligence (i.e., the head of the CIA), defense intelligence (i.e., the undersecretary of defense for intelligence), and homeland intelligence (the FBI's EAD for intelligence or the undersecretary of homeland security for information analysis and infrastructure protection). The December 2004 bill scrapped that arrangement, calling instead for a principal deputy director and up to four other deputies with portfolios assigned by the DNI.[12]

For the first director, Negroponte, appointing a military person, General Michael Hayden, director of the NSA, as principal deputy DNI was more than a nod to the Pentagon's concerns about the DNI position. The first DNIs created four deputies in addition to the principal deputy – in 2007, for collection; analysis; acquisition; and policy, plans, and requirements. Another critical senior position – program manager for the Information Sharing Environment (ISE) – also reported directly to the DNI.

The Defense Department's more strictly tactical intelligence programs (dubbed Tactical Intelligence and Related Activities, or TIARA, in "budgetese") – those that serve commands or field commanders – always were slated to remain the Pentagon's responsibility. The Senate bill proposed to give the DNI authority over the Joint Military Intelligence Program (JMIP), a set of tactical joint intelligence activities, some of which came from TIARA and some of which were performed by the NSA or the NGA's predecessor organizations. The final bill authorized the DNI to work with the secretary of defense in preparing both TIARA and JMIP budgets, which together total less than a quarter of the total intelligence budget.

Here, as in other areas, the real challenge for the DNI only began with formal authority. As the capabilities of "national" collection systems in the NIP have improved, they have become increasingly important to warfighters for tactical purposes; thus, the distinction between "strategic" and "tactical" has blurred.[13] Day-to-day, the overlap increases the competition for resources if, for instance, the same satellite systems can locate insurgent combat units in Iraq for warfighters as well as help keep tabs on suspicious nuclear facilities in Iran for the benefit of national policy makers. As a result, intelligence and the Pentagon more often share assets; with that sharing, the competition intensifies over whose needs are more important – all the more so because supporting warfighters is an open-ended mission: more is always better.

The risk of duplication also grows as the military seeks intelligence systems integral to operational units, those on which it can count. Understandably, the warfighters will want to control more of the systems they regard as necessary to waging war, even if they began life as "national" systems. Ideally, they would like those systems to be integral to military commands. The challenge for DNIs, working with secretaries of defense, will be to provide the strategic framework for the argument over needs, thereby reducing the risk of needless duplication.

Some creative compromise over authority probably was always going to be required for those analytic agencies that would be important "troops" for the DNI to deploy but that also have special responsibilities to particular departments. The State Department's INR, for instance, numbers only several hundred but often carries weight beyond its size in interagency deliberations. Secretaries of state, however, are bound to regard the INR as *their* intelligence agency. The secretary of defense and the chairman of the Joint Chiefs of Staff are likely to view the DIA similarly.

The law gave the DNI authority to appoint the director of the CIA. For all the other intelligence agency heads, except one, the DNI was given a veto through the requirement that he or she concur in the appointment made by the department head (e.g., defense, state, treasury, and so on) for whom the intelligence agency worked. The exception is the directorship of the DIA, where the law only gave the DNI a mandate to be consulted.

Creating a DNI is hardly a new idea; it is more a hardy perennial.[14] In an assessment of thirty-one studies of or proposals for reforming intelligence between 1948 and 2002, the top three recurring themes were expanding the DCI's authority, creating a DNI, and giving the DCI more tools to manage the intelligence community.[15]

The 9/11 Commission did a clever job of linking the idea of a DNI to the September 11 failure. In fact, that case was relatively weak, for those failures were more of coordination at the working level than of broad strategic direction. The bare fact that September 11 occurred was enough to spur marked improvement in that day-to-day coordination, along with a change in mission at the FBI. Whatever the link or lack thereof, however, the need for better strategic management of the intelligence community is a pressing one. In the WMD Commission's words, the community is "fragmented, loosely managed, and poorly coordinated."[16]

On the collection side, as has been emphasized, U.S. intelligence's legacy from the Cold War is an organization by collection sources, or "stovepipes" – NSA for SIGINT, CIA for espionage, and so on. If, during the Cold War, that amounted to asking all the information-gatherers what they could contribute to solving the overarching puzzle of Soviet behavior, it cannot be the right way to organize U.S. intelligence now – with many threats, not one; a plethora of information, although of widely varying quality; and many customers. Given difficult problems and arcane technology, plus a division of labor that gave control of the purse strings to the Pentagon but ostensible oversight to the DCI, the stovepipe managers have had considerable autonomy.

Moreover, once the retrieval times for gathering the information became short enough to make that information useful to battlefield commanders, the Pentagon incorporated the stovepipes into real operational decision making that has made possible the pinpoint targeting of adversaries from afar. Strategic and tactical blurred, and it became still more difficult for the DCI to affect how technical resources are allocated.

The case for ending the long mismatch between the responsibility of DCIs and their authority was a strong one. The drive to create a DNI was to accomplish that while serving as a counterbalance to the recent tendency of military consumers to dominate U.S. intelligence.

The question that remains to be seen is whether the December 2004 bill really ends that mismatch and creates that counterbalance. DNIs will have a veto over the appointments of the main agency heads, and they will have budgetary initiative and some authority over execution, as shown in Table 4.1.

To enhance the clout of the DNI, the 9/11 Commission recommended that the DNI be located in the Executive Office of the President. The December 2004 bill, however, directly stipulated that the DNI would *not* be in the Executive Office of the President. As always in political Washington, location bespeaks power and betrays perspective. A DNI housed in the CIA headquarters would have made clear that the CIA director was a subordinate but would have risked that the DNI would become a captive of the CIA, viewed as such. At the other extreme, a DNI housed with only a few subordinates at the Old Executive Office Building, next to the White House, would have been close to power but risked looking like drug czars in previous administrations – long on title but short on troops. The first DNIs, Negroponte and McConnell, appointed in 2007, split the difference, although for reasons that had more to do with available space: they moved the DNI headquarters first to the Defense Intelligence Agency Center (DIAC) at Bolling Air Force Base in southeast Washington, then to permanent quarters at Liberty Crossing in McLean, next to NCTC, but the NIC and other offices remained at CIA headquarters.

The 9/11 Commission and the Senate bill endorsed making public the top lines of the U.S. intelligence budget, a move that is long overdue. Detailed numbers would have remained secret, but the overall budget allocations and the apportionment among agencies could have been safely disclosed without harm to intelligence's "sources and methods." Indeed, keeping them classified when they are bandied about in the press only makes it look like the government has something to hide. It became a shame that America lagged behind Britain – the land of official secrets – which makes its top-line budget numbers known. It was well past time to end that shame.[17] When the Democrats took over Congress in 2006, they moved to require at least the top line to be made public. DNI McConnell complied in October 2007, making public that the budget for fiscal year 2007 was $43.5 billion.[18]

The main reason there was no DNI despite nearly fifty years of calls for one is that none of the most critical officials wanted the change.[19]

For their part, DCIs had not wanted to trade their CIA troops for the uncertain prospects of an intelligence overlord. Secretaries of defense – and their congressional overseers – had been loath to lose control of critical information-gathering agencies. When in the 1970s the White House proposed to give control of the big technical collectors to the DCI, Secretary of Defense Rumsfeld (then as later) is said to have replied: "If they're in my budgets, I'll run them."[20]

The growing importance of those big intelligence collectors in the scheme of military transformation, if anything, probably increased the defense establishment's opposition to giving control to the DNI. It took the shock of September 11 and the pull of the victims' families, the artful connecting by the 9/11 Commission of that failure with the need for a DNI, and continued lobbying by the Commission members to make the December 2004 bill happen.

Create an NCTC

The NCTC is responsible for both joint operational planning and joint intelligence.[21] The Terrorist Threat Integration Center (TTIC), created in 2003, became the NCTC, or at least half of it. It became, in effect, the NCTC's intelligence analysts. The bill left it to the NCTC to work out exactly what the planning task, labeled "strategic operational planning," would entail and how it would work. The NCTC, like the TTIC before it, was to absorb analytic talent then residing in the CIA's CTC, the FBI's CTD, and in the DIA's Joint Task Force Counterterrorism (JTFCT).

The TTIC was created to "connect the dots" of intelligence, both foreign and domestic, in warning of terrorist threats to the homeland. As it turned out, the personnel actually transferred to the NCTC were relatively few. Many more were collocated by those agencies at the NCTC. In effect, the TTIC, now the NCTC, was to become – on the intelligence side – the center of a confederation, with several hundred officials from the CIA's CTC and the FBI's CTD, plus smaller numbers from other agencies located at NCTC headquarters at Liberty Crossing near Tyson's Corner, Virginia, not far from CIA headquarters. The NCTC became a kind of government terrorism "campus."

On the strategic operational planning side, the NCTC drew on a limited inheritance. The CIA's CTC, for instance, from the start was located with the CIA's clandestine operators, the Directorate of Operations, and was more engaged in providing operational support to intelligence operations abroad than it was in pure analysis. The NCTC, however, as framed by the bill, was neither to execute operations – those would be left to the agencies – nor to make policy, which would be left to the president and the NSC. It was to assign responsibilities for operations to lead agencies but not direct the execution of those operations.

The head of the NCTC is appointed by the president and confirmed by the Senate. The DNI oversees the NCTC's operations and budget, and the director of the NCTC reports to the DNI on intelligence and intelligence operations. The NCTC director, however, reports to the president with regard to counterterrorism operations other than those in intelligence. This dual reporting is probably necessary if the NCTC is to play a real role in planning the government's counterterrorism operations, including those undertaken by the Pentagon. However, it runs the risk of further weakening the DNI position by dividing the loyalty of a principal subordinate.

On the positive side, the conception of the NCTC is rooted in the understanding that in an age of terror, the counterterrorism mission is intelligence-rich; thus, planning needs to be intelligence-driven. It has brought the interagency process in-house, with a permanent set of agency representatives – at about the one-star level – housed at the NCTC. In general, the federal government achieves interagency coordination in two ways: either designating a lead agency or passing the coordinating responsibility to the White House – for instance, to the NSC. If an agency leads, it then constructs its own means of achieving interagency coordination. The CTC at the CIA, for example, recruited liaison officers from throughout the intelligence community. The military's unified CENTCOM has its own interagency intelligence center, recruiting liaison officers from all the agencies from which it might need help. The FBI has joint terrorism task forces (JTTFs) in eighty-four locations to coordinate the activities of other agencies when action may be required.

The December 2004 bill indicated a mix of coordination by the NCTC and by the White House, presumably the NSC but perhaps the Homeland Security Council.[22] The NCTC was to coordinate planning but then turn execution over to lead agencies. The operational coordination presumably would be accomplished by some combination of those lead agencies and the NSC. In general, counterterrorism operations tend to range across diplomatic, law enforcement, military, and intelligence instruments, thereby posing difficult challenges to coordination – particularly to lead-agency coordination.

The first challenge for the director of the NCTC and the DNI was to sort out the turf battle between the NCTC (and the TTIC before) and the CTC. The WMD Commission pointed to this tug-of-war over resources, authorities, and responsibilities – a guerrilla war that has raged since the creation of the TTIC. A division of labor is easy to imagine but has been difficult to reach. The CTC would concentrate on support to operations while the NCTC focused on intelligence analysis and planning, and not all competition between the two need be negative. However, sorting out the roles of the two agencies, a first test of whether the DNI and his team were really in charge, remains inconclusive. Moreover, not only was it a work in progress what "strategic operational planning" would mean in practice, the reach of NCTC planning into the operations of the major agencies, especially the military, also remains uncertain.

Create National Intelligence Centers

With the NCTC as the prototype, creating national intelligence centers under the authority of the DNI and organized around issues was the most sweeping change in the way intelligence does its business proposed by the 9/11 Commission. The centers were to both deploy and use the information, technology, and staff resources of the existing agencies – the CIA, the DIA, the NSA, and others. They were to be, in the 9/11 Commission's vision, the "unified commands" looking to the agencies to acquire the technological systems, train the people, and execute the operations planned by the national intelligence centers. They were to bring together analysts, information collectors, and operations specialists around problems or issues, not collection sources or agencies.

The 2004 bill licensed the creation of centers but had little to say about those other than the NCTC. The idea was much less a centerpiece of the bill than it had been of the 9/11 Commission report, which had suggested that they would be organized around a mix of functional and regional issues – WMD, crime, Russia and Eurasia, and the like. At present, several centers, such as the existing CIA CTC, bring together officers from a number of intelligence agencies. The 9/11 Commission's proposal would have intensified these liaisons by making the national intelligence centers the primary way that the intelligence community does its work. Earlier centers were, and are, still the creatures of the agencies; in the 9/11 Commission's proposal, the agencies were to become their supporters. Ideally, those who use intelligence would be drawn toward the centers and would know where to go for "one-stop shopping" in their areas of interest in this age of terror.[23]

There were and continue to be several lines of concern about an organization by centers, and the first DNIs did not encourage the idea. The first concern is that there is no real infrastructure to support the concept, in technology or personnel. There is little tradition of intelligence officers moving and little incentive for them to do so – despite the beginnings of DNI efforts to require of intelligence officers something like the "joint" appointments that are the prerequisite for senior leadership in the military. The technical shortcomings are obvious at the NCTC, where analysts' computers continued to be accompanied by a half-dozen "pizza boxes" – that is, different agency information sources that had to be integrated by the analysts.

Also on the capacity-building side, the major analytic agencies resist thinking of themselves as force providers; they regard themselves as the doers. Well before 2004, the agencies expressed concern about "center-itis," the rise of numerous specialized or issue-oriented centers.[24] The agencies tended to think of personnel assigned to those centers as lost to the real work, which happened back home at the agency. Changing that view to regard the real work as done by the centers, with the agencies in a supporting role, will entail a sea change in organizational culture. It is interesting that the existing culture that comes closest to reflecting the required change is that of the CIA's directorate of operations, where the real workers are the spymasters abroad and those remaining at headquarters are regarded as in a supporting role.

Second, and more legitimately, the existing agencies argue that the centers as the primary producers of intelligence would be inclined toward focusing on current intelligence and would tend to produce worst-case analyses. Based on the experience of the military's unified commands, those are serious objections – although at this point, the analogy between the centers and the military commands begins to break down. The unified commands tend to have short time horizons and to worry about worst cases, for understandable reasons: if war broke out today, they would have to fight it. In a similar way, the centers would be the first to be blamed if crises developed without warning, and their plans would be the first to be exposed if remedies failed. So, the bias toward current intelligence and the dramatic over-warning that now afflict all of U.S. intelligence could get worse.

In the end, it is a matter of degree and of countervailing pressures. Already, the bias toward today's hot issues is pervasive. With a changed structure, a DNI would need to ensure that there were places, such as the existing NIC or the CIA's Strategic Assessments Group (SAG), that lean against the wind and have at least a little protection from the urgency of the immediate. The fate of the SAG, however, is cautionary. It was disbanded in 2006 in a way that raised questions about both substance and process. In substance, apparently, the criticism of SAG was that it had not *produced* enough, where "production" apparently was equated with production for the PDB – just the short-term commentary the SAG presumably was intended *not* to do. In process, it is not clear that anyone outside the Office of Transnational Issues at the CIA had any voice in the decisions – not even the CIA's deputy director of intelligence, let alone the DNI.

The WMD Commission recommended creating a second center, a National Counterproliferation Center, and it was indeed created. The WMD Commission imagined – and the Bush administration created – the center in a structure very different from the NCTC. In its conception, the center was to be small and focused on overseeing collection and analysis. Planning and operations would be left to wider interagency groupings. There is also a National Counterintelligence Executive (NCIX); it builds on earlier similar organizations and is less a "center" in the Senate bill's sense of the term than a focal point for a specialized intelligence task: counterintelligence.

The WMD Commission also suggested building on the center concept by appointing "mission managers" for priority topics, and the Bush administration adopted that idea as well. Those managers, who work for the DNI, are meant to drive collection and oversee analysis in their areas, and they serve as a clearinghouse for senior policy makers seeking expertise in that area. It is interesting that this conception is akin to the original notion of NIOs in the early 1970s. Influenced by their experience with a special assistant for Vietnam affairs, DCIs James Schlesinger and William Colby fashioned the NIOs as points for one-stop shopping in their respective areas.[25] As suggested in Chapter 3, the challenge that the mission managers will face is the same one that NIOs have faced before them: knowing enough about collection sources and technologies to actually have some effect on collection. By 2008, the DNI had created three such mission managers: for Iran, North Korea, and Cuba–Venezuela.

Make the DCI Separate from the DNI

In the 9/11 Commission's vision, more or less incorporated in the final bill, the DCI was to be primarily responsible for building a better espionage capacity for the nation. The DCI at the time, then the CIA director, Porter Goss, appointed in 2004, indeed made that his priority, almost his exclusive priority. The task includes, in the Commission's words, "transforming the clandestine service by building its human intelligence capabilities; developing a stronger language program, with high standards and sufficient financial incentives; renewing emphasis on recruiting diversity among operations officers so they can blend more easily in foreign cities; ensuring a seamless relationship between human source collection and signals collection at the operational level; and stressing a better balance between unilateral and liaison operations." The Bush administration also made the DCI the national manager of human intelligence, with a deputy charged with the wider responsibility of overseeing human intelligence across the intelligence community.

No DCI had wanted to surrender direct management of the CIA, fearing that the loss of "troops" would mean a loss of power. The 9/11 Commission recognized that risk but argued that clandestine operations are tactical and require close attention. In any case, if the DNI ran the CIA, that official would be an advocate for CIA funding as well as the administrator of overall intelligence funding, which is a conflict of interest. It also noted that the law charges the CIA with *foreign* intelligence, while a critical task for the DNI will be to coordinate intelligence across the foreign–domestic divide.

It is interesting that when the CIA was first created in the 1940s, it was intended to be what its name implied – a central coordinating office. It was not expected to produce much analysis of its own, nor was it expected to conduct clandestine intelligence operations abroad. The State Department's distaste for clandestine operations soon got the CIA involved in operations, and the military's lack of interest or cumbersomeness in developing spy planes and spy satellites got the CIA into the technology business. Soon, it had become not the coordinating agency but rather another agency needing coordination, and so the conflict of interest between the DCI's roles as director of the CIA and overseer of all intelligence emerged. That conflict was muted only because the DCI did not have much authority in the overseer role.

More important, having the DNI also continue to run the CIA would have created an overwhelming workload, even worse than the one faced by the DCI. As the 9/11 Commission stated: "The DCI now has at least three jobs. He is expected to run a particular agency, the CIA. He is expected to manage the loose confederation of agencies that is the intelligence community. He is expected to be the analyst in chief for the government, sifting evidence and directly briefing the President as his principal intelligence adviser."[26] The 9/11 Commission hoped a DNI would be able to exercise the third responsibility while actually managing the second. In fact, DCIs mostly wound up doing the first: running the agency they could command. It was theirs and close at hand; moreover, running operations abroad was both interesting and politically delicate, so constant tactical management is required – just as the 9/11 Commission observed.

The DNI still has two jobs, and balancing the two will be no easy feat. A DNI who tilted the balance between managing and advising too far toward the former would risk losing the credibility to manage. Conversely, tilting it too far toward the latter would risk losing the time to manage – the preference that dogged Negroponte. To be sure, the relationship between the DNI and the DCI will be complicated. One insider likened the early rounds in the process of working out which CIA and intelligence community functions housed at the CIA would stay there and which would go to the DNI to the "partition of India."

Will both the DNI and the DCI meet the president in the morning with the PDB? Who would prepare that brief? The new DNI,

Negroponte, seemed to win the early rounds, with the president indicating that he, not the DCI, would deliver what has been the CIA's "crown jewels," the PDB. Eventually, the relationship between the two might evolve to something like that between the attorney general and the FBI director: in form, boss and subordinate, but for some purposes more like equals. Negroponte's successor, Mike McConnell, reportedly tried to divest himself of the role of delivering the PDB, but the president insisted. Hardly anyone in Washington ever turns down "face time" with the president, but the cost to the DNI's other role is apparent. As one of his senior deputies told me in 2008, "The DNI spends his days waiting outside the Oval Office for the President, trying to manage the community on his Blackberry."

As the DNI attempts to build authority over budgeting and executive hiring decisions and to be the president's principal intelligence office, he or she will need the assistance of a dedicated intelligence staff. The NCTC, along with the other centers, might effectively serve as such a staff. So might the NIC, whose role is underscored by the 2004 bill and subsequent decisions – for instance, to create a Long-Term Analysis Unit at the NIC and later to make NIOs responsible for preparing Office of the Director of National Intelligence (ODNI) principals for major interagency committee meetings, those of the principals and the deputies (PCs and DCs in "governmentese"). The NIC, however, is likely to be stretched by the tension between an enhanced role in current intelligence, as overseer in some form of the PDB and preparer of interagency meetings, and its traditional role as producer of deeper and longer term intelligence, especially the NIEs.

In one area, paramilitary operations, the 9/11 Commission would have had the CIA cede responsibility for directing and executing operations to the military. However, the Commission found the Afghanistan precedent of joint CIA–military teams a good one and suggested that CIA capabilities and people should be integrated into military-directed teams, giving both the CIA and the Special Operations Forces the opportunity to do what each does best. The 2004 bill was silent on this issue, and the CIA and the military decided that both would remain in the paramilitary-operations business.

Like other major recommendations of the 9/11 Commission, this one also had a long and hoary history. The arguments for giving control to the military historically have been those the commission cited:

the requisite capabilities are military, the task has not been a continuous priority for the CIA, and it makes no sense for the nation to build two parallel capacities. On the other side of the argument is concern that the military was never agile or discreet, let alone covert. That concern may have diminished but it has not disappeared, as the Special Operations Forces have developed a wide variety of units and types of operations.

Whatever else is occurring, the Special Operations Forces and the CIA are being thrust together, which seemed an effective partnership, especially in Afghanistan, and the 9/11 Commission applauds it. However, it raises thorny questions of authorization and accountability – questions that are not settled by the Commission's recommendation (and which are discussed in Chapter 8).

Operations by the military would give those carrying them out the status of combatants under international law, at least if they were visibly soldiers. CIA covert actions require a presidential finding, one transferred in secret to the relevant committees of Congress. By contrast, a similar operation conducted by the Special Operations Forces could be set in motion simply by the chain of command from the president as commander in chief. The difference may be less than meets the eye, however, if findings have become so broad in the war on terrorism as to cover almost any CIA operation. If so, however, the problem lies with the breadth of the findings.[27] If they are so broad as to cover almost anything, then the finding process has become a sham. This issue is explored in more detail in Chapter 8.

Do Not Create a Separate Domestic Intelligence Agency

Both Commissions decided and Congress agreed that the arguments for creating a separate domestic-intelligence service in the early years after September 11 were not persuasive and that the FBI should be given time and encouragement to build its own intelligence capacity. The WMD Commission, however, went further than the 9/11 Commission and recommended creating not just a DI within the FBI but also an NSB, incorporating intelligence plus the FBI's CTD and the CD. It feared that even an enhanced DI would lack the ability to task the FBI field offices for information or control the intelligence budget, most of which is spent by the CTD and the CD. In the WMD Commission's phrase, "The Directorate of Intelligence may 'task' the field offices to collect against certain requirements ... [but] its 'taskings' are really 'askings.'"[28] It envisioned an FBI national-security service with about the same relationship to the DNI that NSA and NGA will have.

As a critical step in remaking its mission from law enforcement to intelligence-driven prevention in the fight against terror, the FBI took the WMD Commission's recommendation and created a NSB along the lines suggested. Yet, the question of whether law enforcement and intelligence can – or should – be combined in the same agency will remain on the agenda. Is the FBI likely to remain – and perhaps should remain – primarily a case-based law enforcement organization? It is good at that. Yet, can pursuing individual cases the way the FBI does build a comprehensive intelligence picture, even if the cases are intelligence, not law enforcement? Or, are the two disciplines – law enforcement and intelligence – such different disciplines that they cannot or should not be combined in the same agency? These issues will remain on the agenda, especially if there were another major terrorist attack on the United States. Chapter 5 discusses these issues in more detail.

5

The Agenda Ahead

The main challenge ahead is also the reason for having a DNI in the first place – to better manage the entire set of U.S. intelligence agencies so that the nation gets the most for the $43-plus billion it spends each year on intelligence. For Negroponte to deliver the PDB was a bureaucratic victory, but the nation did not need a DNI to deliver the PDB; for that, the prior DCI was fine. Negroponte's relatively brief tenure as DNI was distinguished mostly by bureaucracy-building, thereby reinforcing the argument of the skeptics that the creation of the DNI would only add one more layer of organizational "clutter." Negroponte conveyed the air of a person who had taken the job out of duty rather than real interest or commitment. He seemed from the start eager to return to his career home, the State Department, and made the move quickly in 2007 when the position of deputy secretary was offered. Indeed, that he was prepared to trade the post of DNI for the number-two job at State was a commentary on the status of the reshaping of intelligence – and not a good one.

Much of the task ahead is implicit in the DNI's mandate to break down the stovepipes, asking how best the United States might get the information it needs. The challenges to existing organizational culture are daunting. The DNI needs to be a major player in programmatic decisions, especially about collection systems, which consume most of intelligence's budgets. The need becomes more pressing as the distinction between "national" and "tactical" systems blurs, meaning that the intelligence agencies and the Pentagon share systems and compete for priority.

The second challenge will be to drive the intelligence community to try to become a collection of adaptive-learning organizations. Again and again, I participate in variants of the same conversation with colleagues and observers, ranging from former CIA officers to the Swiss diplomat who tried in vain to make Switzerland's agencies into a real intelligence community. The conversation begins with the quality of the people. I say to CIA audiences – and mean it – that person for person, the CIA is as good an organization as I have known, public or private, from RAND to the Harvard faculty.[1] When speaking, I am usually too polite to say it, but the private conversations almost always end with the plaintive observation, "Too bad those good people are trapped in such a dysfunctional organization" – and the CIA is far from the worst.

The drive to create learning organizations runs across agencies and tasks, but it has a particular force with respect to intelligence's most precious asset – its people. The rapid growth of intelligence organizations, coupled with an age structure that puts large fractions of existing employees at or near retirement, opens an enormous opportunity for those organizations to reshape themselves. However, it also poses grand challenges not just in mentoring the newcomers but also in adjusting work practices to attract and retain them.

The third challenge is domestic intelligence and how it relates to what has been thought of as "foreign" intelligence. In the 2000s, the body politic was inclined to let the FBI continue with its reshaping, from an almost pure law enforcement organization to one giving pride of place to prevention and intelligence. Bureau leaders committed to a fundamental change in mission and practice. Terrorism is a matter for both intelligence and law enforcement, and now the "wall" that used to separate the two – including the wall that existed within the FBI – has been all but erased. Officials seeking intelligence can share information with colleagues who are investigating a criminal case. This did not seem the right time to tear apart that incipient cooperation by creating a separate intelligence agency outside the FBI. Only time and the future of an age of terror will tell whether this continues to be the right decision.

This chapter outlines the three challenges, those that lie beyond the structural change outlined in Chapter 4: developing centers and mission managers to enable the United States to do its intelligence business around issues or threats, not sources or agencies. Chapter 6 addresses the especially important task of improving intelligence analysis.

The 2004 legislation creating the DNI was a beginning. The first two occupants of the job, John Negroponte and Mike McConnell, came to the task from different histories: the first, someone not from intelligence but versed in it and, perhaps more important, who knew how to make the government work; the second, a former director of the NSA and consummate intelligence insider. The challenge for them was and will be for their successors to use the license of the law to hunt for real authority.

A few years into having a DNI, there was not much evidence of an impact on major programs. McConnell sought to pick up the pace of reform with a 500-day plan.[2] Emphasizing jointness, it mostly aimed to harvest low-hanging fruit. The internal wrangling in 2007–2008 over rewriting Executive Order 12333, the basic document covering intelligence, was vivid evidence of just how elusive that real authority for DNIs continued to be.[3] The revisions mostly reflected the changes made in the 2004 law, especially the creation of the DNI, and updated the order to include NRO and NGA. It increased the authority of the DNI in only two areas and only modestly: giving the DNI new authority over any intelligence information collected that pertains to more than one agency – an attempt to force greater information exchange – and to make acquisition decisions on certain NIPs.

The collapse of the Future Imagery Architecture (FIA) – at a loss perhaps exceeding $4 billion – is indicative of the challenges.[4] It also underscores that DNIs will require a much greater analytic capacity than what they inherited if they are to be compelling inside the executive branch as well as with Congress. It was one of several satellite programs to break down in recent years, leaving the United States with outdated imaging technology. It was especially revealing of the challenge facing DNIs in managing complex contracts when those contracting are multiplying. The idea was a good one, another stage in the successful transition of the so-called national technical systems from puzzle-solving about the Soviet Union to tactical support to military commanders – the transition that is discussed earlier in this book.

The transition meant that by the end of the twentieth century, familiar targets such as Soviet air bases and missile factories were being supplanted by the more varied and elusive threats of the post–Cold War world. At the same time, the armed services, eager for increased tactical intelligence after the 1991 Persian Gulf War, were demanding satellites that could instantly stream battlefield data to warfighters around the globe.

In 1996, a DCI commission, chaired by Robert J. Hermann, who ran the NRO from 1979 to 1981, recommended building a fleet of light, small, relatively inexpensive satellites. Together, they could be at least as effective as the Lockheed-built behemoths then in orbit – at a cost of about $1 billion each and about the size and weight of a Greyhound bus, my RAND colleagues had dubbed them "Battlestar Gallactica."[5] Smaller and more numerous satellites would increase "revisit times" – that is, the number of times a day that satellites pass above target sites – thus keeping better track of moving targets and making deception through camouflage more difficult to sustain. Lighter satellites would require less expensive and less powerful rockets than the Titan IVs then in use, which could cost up to $450 million per launching. The commission also envisioned saving money and time by taking advantage of technologies developed by commercial satellite companies.

It did not turn out that way. Boeing, which had not built such satellites before, won the bidding with an innovative (and cost-conscious) proposal. However, given the overlapping of military and civilian purposes, the requirements multiplied as intelligence and military services competed to influence the satellite design. Boeing's initial design for the optical system that was the heart of one of the two new satellite systems was so elaborate that optical engineers working on the project claimed it could not be built. Engineers constructing a radar-imaging unit that was central to the other satellite could not initially produce the unusually strong radar signal that was needed. In that sense, the FIA was flawed from the start. In Hermann's words, "The FIA contract was technically flawed and unexecutable the day it was signed. Some top official should have thrown his badge on the table and screamed, 'We can't do this system at this price.' No one did."

To be fair, the riskiness of the initial conception was compounded by factors that the intelligence community could not control. As part of the Clinton administration's effort to downsize government, control of big military projects was transferred to contractors on the theory that they could best manage engineering work and control costs. Meanwhile, America's best engineers were being attracted to Google and Apple, not government contracts; therefore, intelligence was losing expertise in systems engineering – the science and art of managing complex engineering projects to weigh risks, gauge feasibility, test components, and ensure that the pieces come together smoothly. Finally, given concern about NRO's free spending in the past, Congress demanded rigid spending guidelines for the satellite project. The FIA thus became a trifecta of risk: a high-concept technology on a fast schedule with a tightly managed budget.

The government continued to hear reassuring words from Boeing while more than one internal review panel was expressing concerns about the feasibility of the project, given its budget cap of $5 billion (and $1 billion per year). As Albert D. ("Bud") Wheelon, who founded the Directorate of Science and Technology at the CIA in 1963 and played a leading role in the early development of spy satellites, said, "Writing winning proposals is different from building winning hardware." By the time the FIA was killed in September 2005 – a year after the first satellite was originally to have been delivered – cost estimates ran as high as $18 billion. Although the FIA was ambitious and innovative, it was so within a stovepipe where the NRO had been a technological leader – building reconnaissance satellites.

BREAKING DOWN THE STOVEPIPES

Yet, the strategic management task requires not just driving trade-offs within the stovepipes but across them as well. At present, U.S. collection produces too much data and too little information, and collection techniques, especially for imagery, are fairly well understood by targets. New technical collection systems, especially for imagery, threaten to overwhelm processing; however, according to the WMD Commission, in the case of Iraq, both IMINT and SIGINT "produced precious little intelligence for the analysts to analyze."[6] Moreover, the official cover-based Cold War espionage practices that occasionally worked against Soviet-bloc diplomats will not work on Al Qaeda operatives. The challenge is to be less passive and quicker in innovation. For signals, that means getting closer to targets; for imagery, it means smaller platforms, more use of stealth, and employing more of the spectrum. For espionage, it means more diversity in spymasters and moving out of official cover. However, it also means being patient.

"The intelligence failure in Iraq did not begin with faulty analysis. It began with a sweeping collection failure" – so said the WMD Commission. Every blue-ribbon panel called for improving America's espionage, or HUMINT. The call is worthy, but expectations have to be reasonable. Beyond HUMINT, much of the U.S. collection architecture, like satellites for imagery and eavesdropping, is fairly well understood by would-be adversaries. Those adversaries routinely camouflage sensitive activities when they know satellites are overhead. Thus, the long-term challenges for U.S. intelligence are to move away from passive surveillance techniques toward more directed collection and to shorten the cycle of innovation in order to be less predictable for would-be targets.

On the espionage side – however one judges the past half-century of U.S. espionage – doing better against tomorrow's more difficult targets, such as terrorists, will not be easy. The required actions – such as making more use of America's ethnic diversity or moving spying out of official cover – take time and money. For instance, the experience with spymasters under nonofficial cover, called NOCs, so far has been mixed at best. Other countries have done better – for example, the Soviet Union during the Cold War and China now – so patience is required. NOCs are expensive in money and time to deploy and sustain and, because they have to actually live their cover, their time for recruiting spies is limited. Thus, they are costly for the information they provide. Lacking the diplomatic immunity of official cover, recruiting spies under nonofficial cover also can be dangerous.

The difficulty of the task is not an argument against trying to do better.[7] It is, however, an argument against expecting too much. Successful espionage requires both patience and a willingness to traffic with unsavory characters. Neither comes easily to the American system. The dilemma runs still deeper: in many respects, effective spying requires attributes that are precisely the opposite of accountability in America's governance. Spying requires giving considerable discretion to case officers in the field. Government, by contrast, tends to the opposite: narrowing discretion downward while it pushes accountability upward.[8]

This means that while the United States can do better at espionage, in the end, it will still be dependent on friends – and even nonfriends – who have access where we do not and perhaps may employ methods that we would not. This means not only tending the rather "clubby" liaison relationships of the Cold War – most of them with fellow English-speaking nations – but also engaging in specific and limited sharing and trading with nations such as Syria or Somalia, where the overlap of common interest is present but limited.

Beyond espionage, intelligence faces the paradox of too much data but too little information. During the Cold War, information on the Soviet Union was in too short supply. Now, however, two things have changed. First, although terrorists are secretive, they (like the rest of us) leave a trail through their travels, purchases, licenses, and so forth. Their cell phones and providers know where they are – until they purchase a new card. Thus, data that are not secret (e.g., telephone numbers and driver's licenses) are also relevant, which imposes on intelligence the need to develop ways to search huge amounts of data – a need more difficult for an intelligence community that for reasons of secrecy and culture has not been at the forefront of the IT revolution.

Second, intelligence's own technical capabilities to produce secret information, such as imagery from spy satellites, have mushroomed. Each new round of collection systems dramatically increases the take, especially in imagery; however, the capacity to process and analyze that take falls farther and farther behind.[9] As one example among many, even before September 11, the NSA could collect the equivalent of the holdings of the Library of Congress in three hours.[10] As a result, the big collectors of signals and imagery intelligence – the NSA and the NGA – will be tempted to solve their processing problem by turning the fire hose of data on intelligence's analysts. After all, that is the way to ensure that the collectors are not the culprits for the next intelligence failure; they passed the data, even if the critical items were lost in torrents. A better balance is needed between investments in the emerging new-generation collection systems and enhanced forms of analytical capability. The latter means a greatly expanded investment in quality personnel and new technologies that assist analysts instead of overwhelming them. Simply stated, terabytes of data collected but unprocessed and unanalyzed are useless to policy makers.

At the same time, all that collection risks producing less information even as it produces more data. The changed nature of the target is part of the reason, just as that change is the major challenge for analysis.[11] As Chapter 2 indicates, the objects of scrutiny broadened. During the Cold War, those objects were big and central; now, they also include the small and peripheral. Then, the focus was the Red Army on the central front in Europe; now, given the harm that small groups or individuals can wreak, they are the objects of scrutiny – and they may be located in places like Afghanistan that are not of much interest for any other reason.

Spy satellites are good at seeing large armored formations but cannot "see" terrorist networks; easily follow small, fast-moving groups; or help us know what is occurring inside chemical plants. Moreover, U.S. adversaries know much about U.S. techniques, often including the orbits of satellites, and therefore they conceal their activities. Some state adversaries, such as North Korea, have invested enormously in underground facilities to protect – as well as to hide – their WMD or related activities.

SIGINT faces even sharper challenges from digitizing, packet-switching, fiber optics, and encryption.[12] Digitizing makes it possible to send huge amounts of information over a single channel, thereby vastly compounding the challenge of sorting out particular communications of interest. Packet-switching means that the routing of a message may be changed in the middle of a communication and that the addressee of a message can be sent in a different packet from the message itself. With the improvement in cable transmission made possible through fiber optics, fewer messages are sent into the open air, where satellites or ground stations can intercept them. The United States must get physically close to the communications channels it seeks to intercept.

On the technical side, U.S. collection must be more targeted and more innovative. The Iraq case suggests that IMINT and SIGINT were driven by the capabilities that existed, not by what was needed. Intelligence was much better at locating large formations than at obtaining the locations of important individuals, much less infiltrating their conversations.[13] The demands of "force protection" – in this case, detecting signs of threats to U.S. and allied pilots flying patrols in the northern and southern "no fly" zones – limited the resources that could be devoted to understanding the WMD problem. Before the creation of the DNI, the Intelligence Community Management Staff had begun to sharpen targeting through its Collection Concepts Development Center. That center drew in knowledgeable outsiders to take a fresh look at collection with respect to a particular target or mission. Those reviews necessarily were driven by questions, not sources, and therefore began to bind collection and analysis together around issues.

Intelligence's impressive technical achievements during the Cold War are now "long in the tooth," and the primacy of satellites remains. The United States needs to broaden its collection means and shorten the cycle of innovation. As in Silicon Valley, innovations may remain secret but not for long; therefore, intelligence will have to adapt faster than its targets if it is to stay ahead. For signals, adapting means finding new ways to get closer to targets; for imagery, it means more use of smaller satellites, or drones, or stealth technology. It also means using new parts of the spectrum, such as hyperspectral imagery, to identify effluents from buildings or factories, as well as a range of technologies in what is called measurement and signatures intelligence (MASINT).

Pushing innovation and making better choices across the collection stovepipes is the chief rationale for having a DNI in the first place. It is the collectors that consume three quarters of the $40 billion intelligence budget. If the DNI does not have the power to collapse the stovepipes, he or she can develop more analytic capacity to make trade-offs across them: "How do ground stations compare with satellites for particular SIGINT missions? Can HUMINT do a mission less expensively?" Many intelligence successes are the result of cooperation across the INTs: HUMINT or open sources may provide tips, which then lead to places to be imaged and communications lines to be monitored. However, to take advantage of such cooperation, analysts and collection managers need to know what the various INTs are doing and can do.

The WMD Commission suggested that the DNI create an "integrated collection enterprise" for the intelligence community to provide for coordination across the entire cycle from planning new systems, to developing strategies for deploying existing systems against priority targets, to processing and exploiting information that is produced. The DNI's centers for counterterrorism and counterproliferation, as well as the issue managers for North Korea, Iran, and Cuba–Venezuela, are steps in the right direction, although so far relatively modest steps. So is the still more recent creation of the DNI's National Intelligence Coordination Center (NIC-C), which is very much a work in progress. The DNI's Integrated Concepts Development Office (ICDO), a descendant of the Collection Concepts Development Center, has a similar charge to push innovation with regard to particular intelligence challenges, especially in collection.

In any event, much of the initiative still rests with the Pentagon, and DNIs have been and will continue to be hard-pressed to move fast to create troops, build authority, and work out arrangements with the secretary and undersecretary of defense. The law provided for the transfer of the NIC to the DNI, along with the NIC's counterpart for the business of the intelligence community, the Community Management Staff (CMS). As it existed in 2004, however, the CMS was incapable of helping DNIs actually manage the community; recognizing that situation, the law provided for 500 new official positions for the DNI, plus 150 to be seconded from other agencies. Previously, the CMS's budget function was largely confined to arguing for programs and to a "bean-counting" review; in conflicts with the Pentagon, it almost always lost. Building analytic clout to fashion an intelligence program and budget that will be compelling to both internal administration decision makers and Congress has taken considerable time. Meanwhile, the DNIs have risked not being major players on precisely the intelligence decisions that were the reason for creating the position of the DNI in the first place.

LEARNING FROM LEARNING ORGANIZATIONS

In the process, the organizations that comprise the intelligence community need to become more adaptive, learning organizations. What can be learned from other organizations that seek to embody high performance and learning?[14] The concepts of a learning organization and organizational learning both arose from organizational theory in the 1970s. Everyday use and the media do not generally differentiate between them and, for convenience, neither does this chapter. The concept of a learning organization is more applied and practical, found in the management consulting industry and promoted by popular writers such as Peter Senge.[15] Its propositions rest on little scientific foundation; therefore, it borrows intellectual capital and concepts from organizational learning, which is an amalgam of principles from organizational development theory, learning theory, complexity and complex adaptive theories, and, more recently, social-network theory.

For immediate purposes, learning organizations practice organizational learning: establish infrastructure, roles, and procedures to capture and exploit knowledge of internal processes and of the causes and consequences of success and failure at the organizational and individual levels. Learning based on cumulative, analyzed knowledge enables the continuity and continuous improvement of internal processes, change in organizational and individual behavior, adaptation to changing environments, and competitive advantage.

The work on knowledge diffusion and management naturally converges with that of organizational learning. The theoretical and experimental work in the area has grown considerably in the past twenty years, but critics note with more than a little irony that the body of research is not coherent and fails to coalesce into a cumulative body of knowledge. For the critics, some articles on both learning organizations and organizational learning tend to produce conceptual complexity without clarity and to reify jargon, resulting in what one paper called the "mystification of the field" – certainly something never seen in intelligence![16]

Nonetheless, the intellectual ancestry of organizational learning includes such respected scholars as Edgar Schein, Chris Argyris, and Kurt Lewin, among other pillars of organizational psychology. Some of the concepts are provocative, providing intuitive value as models of organizational development and effectiveness. Organizations high in learning competence are said to cultivate a culture, internal language, and systems for understanding how internal and external environments interact to affect the organization's mission and success and when they signal a need for internal change. They have a structure and process, including feedback loops that cross both individual and organizational levels, for assessing failure and success and managing and propagating knowledge that affects them. Proponents of organizational learning construe these systems as strategic assets that confer competitive advantage on corporations or other groups.

There also is consensus among practitioners and students about the requisites of high-performance organizations, in the public as well as the private sector.[17] High-performance organizations evince the following:

- a clear, well-articulated mission
- a strategic approach to partnerships
- focus on needs of clients and customers
- strategic management of people

Mission. Because most public-sector organizations lack the convenient bottom line of profit and loss – that is, a clear if limited index of progress or lack of it relative to goals – clarity in mission is critical.[18] The Volcker Commission, formally the National Commission on the Public Service, emphasized the need for missions that are clear and unambiguous.[19] *Government Executive*'s examination of five years of reviews of agencies' performance did so as well.[20] High-performing agencies begin with missions that are clear and clearly supported by their authorizing bodies, especially Congress. For instance, the Social Security Administration (SSA) mission is straightforward – to get checks and information to people who need them.

By contrast, the old INS and the Forest Service ranked poorly in part because of split missions – for the INS, to keep illegal immigrants out of the United States *and* to help legal immigrants become citizens and receive federal benefits; for the Forest Service, to preserve public lands *and* produce resources from them. The Forest Service also suffered from changing minds in Congress about where to strike that balance. Changes have been even more of a problem for the Internal Revenue Service (IRS), which would seem to have as a mission the clear mirror image of the SSA: collect taxes from those who owe them. Yet, in different political seasons, the IRS is alternately criticized for letting tax cheats get away and for harassing innocent citizens.

Perhaps the single greatest "growing pain" of DHS – which brought together 180,000 employees from twenty-two existing agencies – was that the constituent agencies did not and still do not share a single mission – far from it. By one rule of thumb, the constituent agencies in a merger like DHS ought to overlap in mission by at least half.

When the Cold War ended, intelligence looked for new consumers and, at first, found them in domestic agencies such as the Department of Commerce, which wanted staff work as much as intelligence analysis. Then, after the attacks of September 11, its consumers mushroomed – this time including state and local officials and private managers of infrastructure. As a service industry, intelligence found it difficult to turn away customers. As a result, for instance, intelligence's analytic mission has become ever more dominated by question-answering, not deeper analysis. As more than one interviewee stated for a RAND study: "We used to do analysis, but we now do reporting."[21] Plainly, analysis needs to include both reporting and analysis, but deciding where to strike the balance – both within and across agencies – is not easily done.

The question of mission applies with specific force to the FBI, but the CIA's future also raises it. Reshaping the FBI's mission to intelligence-driven prevention still leaves it combining law enforcement and intelligence; it will only shift the priority between the two. Does continuing to try to do both mean risking the confusion of missions that has plagued the Forest Service or the former INS, and has kept them from focusing on becoming high-performance organizations? How to do domestic intelligence in an age of terror, and the implications of choices for the FBI, will remain on the agenda.

The future of the CIA, and especially its Directorate of Intelligence, is an intriguing teaser in this regard because the DNI has absorbed what were core DI functions. Long ago, the NIC and the NIE process passed from being a CIA operation to being a DCI operation, but the upgrading of the NIC with the creation of the DNI has rendered the change more important. After 2004, responsibility for the PDB also passed to the DNI through the NIC, although the DI continued to provide the majority of PDB material. In those circumstances, what is and should be the mission of the DI? For whom should it work? Should its analysis become primarily targeting analysis, with its primary customer being its CIA counterpart, the directorate of operations? Or, should (some of) it move in the other direction, accepting the loss of its current intelligence "crown jewels" and doing more in-depth studies that were its hallmark two decades ago when Robert Gates was its head?

Partnerships

Government agencies, intelligence included, are increasingly more dependent on partners – both domestic and foreign – in carrying out their missions, which came through loud and clear in a RAND survey of both public and private organizations. Both sectors reported the need to build more partnerships; however, public organizations after September 11 found themselves compelled to seek partners in all directions.[22] That is manifestly true of intelligence, which is now dealing not only with new police and intelligence services abroad but also with the eighteen thousand law enforcement units at home – not to mention private citizens. Dealing with domestic law enforcement has raised the difficult problem of sharing information with new partners – all the more difficult for intelligence because virtually none of those new partners have security clearances. The new partnerships also invoke questions of how accountability is to be shared – questions that have been visible in debates over who warns Americans about terrorist threats, when, and on what basis of information.

Customer Needs

This is hardly a new challenge for intelligence, which has always been in the service business, but it is more difficult now because there are so many new customers with new needs – an issue discussed in more detail in Chapter 7. Cold War intelligence served mostly political and military leaders of the U.S. federal government, which was enough of a challenge because intelligence was, for consumers, essentially a free good; thus, there were no easy metrics for judging value. A series of efforts – of which the most recent is the National Intelligence Priorities Framework (NIPF) – sought to interrogate customers about their priorities and then assemble the results in a framework that would provide guidance to intelligence collectors and analysts alike.[23] The new challenge is finding out what, for instance, state and local partners need by way of information and analysis, and then finding ways to get it to them.

For some agencies, such as the Department of State's INR, customers are clear and present. However, for other agencies such as the CIA, working for everyone or the president could mean working for no one in particular, and CIA leaders have sought carefully to establish connections in the policy world. The creation of the DNI has further confused who does what and for whom. For instance, three different agencies seemed to have responsibility for intelligence connections with state and local officials after the 2004 Act: the DHS, which had the congressional mandate; the FBI, which had the troops in the field through its field offices and JTTFs; and the ODNI, which had the stake.

DEALING WITH THE PEOPLE OF INTELLIGENCE

What is true for high-performing organizations is manifestly true of intelligence, as it is for service organizations in general: people are its premier asset. All the agencies must thoughtfully review and possibly redo how they deal with the lives and careers of those assets. For instance, intelligence has been second only to military service as a lifetime career; lateral entry has been rare, particularly given the demands of security clearance, and a large fraction of those who joined have stayed for an entire career. This may well be less true in the future. Many young professionals seek continual challenges. They will want to come in and then move on, perhaps returning later, pursuing what might be called "portfolio careers," which combine experiences in different sectors.[24]

All the intelligence agencies have grown like Topsy since September 11, 2001. For the CIA, the exact numbers are classified, but the directorates of analysis and operations both set the goal of doubling their size. Between FY2001 and FY2006, the FBI budget grew by three quarters, and the national-security portion from under a third to almost a half. The number of agents working counterterrorism and counterintelligence rose from 2,514 in FY2001 to 4,634 at the end of FY2006. Meanwhile, the Bureau more than doubled the number of intelligence analysts, from 1,023 to 2,161. At the other "three-letter" agencies, like NSA or NGA, the situation is similar: if growth has been constrained, it is because of a shortage of qualified applicants. Meanwhile, entry-level training programs for intelligence analysts have sprung up at universities around the country.

The growth is a wonderful opportunity but, as usual with opportunities, also a challenge. The young recruits grew up on Google and are used to reaching out, not sitting back and waiting for information to come to them. They are used to being connected in a hundred directions, not limited by "need to know." To overstate for effect, this new generation is fast, not slow; does parallel processing, not serial processing; gives pride of place to graphics, not text; does random accessing, not step-by-step processing; is connected, not stand-alone; is active, not passive; mixes work and play; is impatient for results; combines fantasy and reality; and definitely sees technology as a friend, not a foe. These ten characteristics can either be a great future asset for intelligence or a considerable liability, depending on how the resources are channeled to solve key intelligence challenges.

The intelligence community will not attract or will soon lose these young people if it does not accommodate to their way of thinking and learning. Now, however, the intelligence community suffers because tools and technologies are rarely, if ever, available in an open-architecture system within the agencies, due to both legacy architecture and the constraints of security. As a result, for instance, young analysts do not have access to these commonly available tools, which means that they will have less capability internally (for their job) while having less familiarity with the innovative ways that others (in their target community) are experimenting and innovating with the same tools. They find, in short, that their workstations at their job are a generation behind their electronic gadgetry at home.

The new entrants are also untrained and, given the aging of the intelligence agencies, they will lack for mentors. This problem could be turned to an advantage if intelligence emulated the best Wall Street firms, which build "gray-green" teams, combining the savvy of veterans with the fearlessness of new recruits. If the future of much intelligence work is more off-site with less direct contact, officers with more sensitive social skills and acuity to compensate for the decrease in social cues and contact among distributed teams will be required. The research on dispersed (i.e., virtual) teams reveals decrements in performance. Virtual teams also raise questions of security – information-security policies and technology as well as counterintelligence-risk monitoring.

All agencies will have to dramatically rethink how they deal with the life and career of their people. The new cohorts can open and enrich intelligence in precisely the ways it needs – but only if intelligence makes major changes in how it recruits, trains, and clears its people. Managing the people of intelligence has been stovepiped by agencies. Thus, there is virtually no common training across agencies and little understanding by officials in one agency of what their counterparts elsewhere do or how they do it.[25]

The creation of the DNI and the DDNI for analysis, along with a DNI-wide human-capital officer and the DNI's five-year strategic human-capital plan, offers the opportunity to think much more strategically across the agencies.[26] For instance, to begin to build more joint learning in analysis, the DDNI began in 2006 a course known as "Analysis 101" for new analysts across the sixteen agencies of the intelligence community. Yet, even this initiative encountered resistance from the various agencies on the grounds that it undermined their separate "branding" and, slightly bizarrely, that it might lead to "groupthink."[27]

If there has been virtually no strategic management of human resources across stovepipes, there also has not been much within them.[28] For example, intelligence organizations, like the government in general, offer relatively generous mid-career training opportunities for analysts as well as others. However, those opportunities are usually ad hoc, not systematic; initiated by individual officers, not planned strategically across the agency or integrated into a developmental program of professional growth; and the numbers of participants are small by comparison to, for example, the analytic cadres.[29]

Psychologists are also clear in that what gets measured and rewarded gets repeated.[30] For instance, the CIA reward structure elevated and still elevates items in the PDB; analysts report it is a career goal and may spend a week writing a single item and negotiating it through the daisy chain of clearance. In thinking about reward systems, as for other issues, the variety in the intelligence community is an ongoing experiment, and its leaders should mine that experiment. What, for instance, are the real reward systems for analysts at the CIA versus INR versus the NSA? What are the effects of those differences? The inquiry is more timely as the intelligence community aspires to become more *joint* and as managers acquire more flexibility in rewarding performance.

As an example from the front end of the personnel cycle, when the NSA and the NGA sought to reshape their missions from "gathering" to "hunting and gathering," they encountered questions about metrics for judging performance as well as skills needed to perform.[31] Traditionally, the two agencies' initial processing and analysis were driven by what they collected; the process was gathering – what might be called "efficient production." An NSA veteran remembers having delivered each morning the take from "her frequencies" – several Soviet communications channels that the NSA was monitoring – and her job was to process that take. Gathering will continue – in populating databases, for example – and it will remain a type of industrial process, albeit often a sophisticated one.

However, the "hunters" may need to be different than the "gatherers" in background, temperament, and training. The hunters will reach out for data, looking across datasets and INTs. They will be engaged in what might be called "innovation operations," and they probably will need, first, to be judged by different metrics than the producers and, ultimately, may be different people than those the agencies traditionally have sought.

The 2004 bill said the right things about training, emphasizing training across disciplines and training that would facilitate rotations of intelligence officers across agencies. The WMD Commission recommended a National Intelligence University to promote jointness in training. However, the bill spoke of language training first and then devoted most of the discussion of training to creating an Intelligence Community Scholarship Program to provide stipends to university students in exchange for commitment to later service in intelligence. The National Intelligence University has been established, but it has been slow in beginning to make a difference; the agencies pushed back, even in language training, if it seemed that the DNI was preparing to evaluate their performance.

In interviews across the analytic agencies, none had much familiarity with the analytic techniques of the others. In all, there tended to be significant emphasis on "skill-level" certification, organizational processes, and writing and communication skills with less emphasis on analytic methods. There is a striking absence of community-wide common course components of emphasis on community-wide perspectives.[32]

That driver is one among several that leads to an emphasis on *credentials* in training, perhaps at the expense of techniques more directly related to immediate analytic work. The CIA University, for instance, confers bachelors and masters degrees, which the Joint Military Intelligence College (JMIC) offers well. Of course, there is nothing wrong with degrees and other credentials. However, operators express concern that the schools are too distant from the needs of operators to be as helpful as they might be. From the perspective of the trainers, the concern was keeping up with the pace of needs – usually defined as knowledge about a specific new area or country – in circumstances in which the most knowledgeable possible "teachers" were precisely those experts in highest immediate demand. The CIA's Sherman Kent School for Intelligence Analysis (part of the CIA University), for instance, offers eighty courses on specialty disciplines.

Initiatives in tradecraft are also isolated. The Kent School, for instance, tries to keep up with best practice in the private sectors by sustaining four small teams: one team handles outreach; another focuses on product evaluation; a third looks at methods, including tools; and a fourth team treats integration, which means trying to keep the School's offerings matched to the needs of the CIA's DI. With the rush of immediate need, there are few opportunities or mechanisms for jointly looking at tradecraft, for understanding how other agencies do "analysis" and what might be learned from them, or for developing centers of training excellence that develop comparative advantage instead of duplicating what has been done elsewhere.

Regular joint training experiments and field tests in tradecraft – in both analysis and operations – would make sense, first, because there is a basis in methods that is shared across different tasks of intelligence analysis. Now – while there is debate about how deeply the U.S. military should engage in espionage – would-be military spymasters train at CIA schools. Second, that training could begin to foster more sense of joint tradecraft, more community awareness on the part of intelligence officers of what their counterparts in other agencies do or could do. The process could contribute to advancing joint efforts more generally across the intelligence community.

In the early 1990s I had the opportunity to create the Intelligence Fellows Program. The idea was to give several score of the intelligence community's future leaders, those who had just been selected for Senior Intelligence Service (SIS) – the equivalent of Senior Executive Service in the rest of the government – an opportunity for two weeks away from the job to come to know each other and their work, reflect on their own work, and confront cases and other materials that would broaden their perspective as they began to not only manage but also lead their agencies. Fortunately, the program has continued and there is a counterpart more focused on management. The National Intelligence University needs more such flagship programs.

The vision for intelligence training should emulate the military – joint and integral to careers. In interviews, officials engaged in analysis endorsed the idea of some initial joint training of analysts – like Analysis 101 – but also said another joint training experience at perhaps five years into a career would be at least as valuable because by then, officials in one agency are more likely to actually need to work with other agencies. At present, intelligence is far from that vision: training is discretionary and individual, not required and strategic. Training is far from the expectation on the way up; indeed, too often the best intelligence officers are deterred from training by the imperative to not "leave the flagpole." Intelligence agencies do not have the slack in their officer ranks that would permit officers to routinely depart for several months or even a year.

Recent legislation has freed the DHS and Department of Defense from many civil-service constraints. Now, more than half of the civilian federal government employees do not work under traditional civil-service rules. While intelligence agencies are not generally bound by those rules, in practice, they have until recently followed them. However, managers across the agencies have more latitude in managing and rewarding performance.[33]

To be sure, in shepherding that most precious of assets, people, the opportunity is a double-edged sword. The experiment is on, but the stakes are high and the jury is out. The intelligence community has just as much opportunity to succeed as to drive down performance and drive up attrition, absenteeism, security violations, and other symptoms of a bad personnel-management system. So far, the experience has been that discretion to reward performance often goes unused; superiors hold back from taking the responsibility that goes with using the discretion they have, more frequently if performance metrics are ill defined. The last position intelligence should take is to fall back to the easier metrics, such as numbers of agent recruitments for CIA operators or PDB items for analysts.

Obtaining access to the best people also means rethinking what is done in-house and what can be reached outside government. Air Force intelligence, for instance, faces this challenge in trading depth for breadth. Given the demands of the current business, there simply is no time to "train up" an analyst on a new current "hot-button" issue with any serious depth. Existing programs for reaching outside only scratch the surface of what will be needed. For instance, the NIC is addressing the outsourced-expert issue through its NIC Associates Program, which preestablishes ties to subject-matter experts in critical areas throughout the world and facilitates their use to address key intelligence challenges. The program expanded in recent years, numbering approximately 160 experts in 2008.

A similar program – the Science and Technology Experts Program (STEP) – has been underway for several years, although with the same concerns about size and scope of the program relative to demand. As currently configured, the STEP provides the NIC and other agencies with access to a few dozen organizations with subject-matter experts in key areas of science and technology. This resource may be tapped for specific advice on intelligence problems. However, the resource is primarily amenable to limited-scope efforts of short duration. Program activities are manifestly consultative or advisory in nature and are difficult to translate into improved core capabilities for the intelligence community.

Intelligence needs to open new ways for lateral entry; in this regard, the NIC experience is indicative. In many areas, such as top-flight economists, the government is and will continue to be hard-pressed to compete with the private sector. The government will have difficulty attracting and retaining such talent for a career. However, the NIC has recruited that talent for several-year stints: top-flight professionals, many of whom have no more worlds to conquer where they are, are motivated by a combination of patriotism and a desire to see how the government works.

INTELLIGENCE AT HOME . . . AND ABROAD?

In the wake of September 11, there were calls for creating a domestic-intelligence service. U.S. Senator Bob Graham (D-FL) was representative of those calls: "I think [it is time] to look seriously at an alternative [to the FBI approach], which is to do as...many other nations have done, and that is to put their domestic intelligence in a non–law enforcement agency."[34] Indeed, the joint congressional investigation into the September 11 attacks recommended that the Bush administration "consider promptly...whether the FBI should continue to perform the domestic intelligence functions of the United States Government or whether legislation is necessary to remedy this problem, including the possibility of creating a new agency to perform those functions."[35]

Looking back at September 11, the villains were precisely those legacies outlined in Chapter 3 – the "opposition" in mission and operating style separating intelligence and law enforcement and, especially, the FBI as captive to a law enforcement approach to the world. As the 9/11 Commission stated, the Bureau focused its resources on "after-the-fact investigations of major terrorist attacks in order to develop criminal cases."[36] Agents were "trained to build cases [and] developed information in support of their own cases, not as part of a broader more strategic [intelligence] effort."

By this argument, the FBI was cleft on the stick of diverging missions. It was and was likely to remain – and perhaps should remain – what it was good at: primarily case-based law enforcement.[37] Yet, pursuing cases the way the FBI did, even intelligence cases, simply seemed contrary to building a comprehensive intelligence picture. If the FBI identified a suspected terrorist in connection with a Hamas investigation, for example, the suspect would be labeled a Hamas terrorist with relevant information kept in a separate "Hamas" file that would be easily accessible to and routinely used only by "Hamas"-focused FBI investigators and analysts. The UBLU would be unlikely to know about the FBI's interest in that individual. In the case of Moussaoui, when agents from the local field office began in August 2001 to investigate his flying lessons at a Norman, Oklahoma, flight school, they did so in ignorance that the same field office had been interested in the same flight school two years earlier because a man thought to be bin Laden's pilot had trained there.

The FBI and its director, Robert Mueller – who had been on the job only one week before the September 11 attacks – were keenly aware of the pressure to cede domestic intelligence to a new agency. Mueller moved quickly to reorient the Bureau toward prevention and intelligence, sending his reorganization plan to Congress in November 2001. He moved to centralize the management of the Bureau's counterterrorism program by terminating the office-of-origin system for terrorism cases. Instead, headquarters personnel oversaw all terrorism cases, regardless of where they originated. Arthur Cummings, SAC for counterterrorism at the Washington field office, explained the rationale for centralization: "There is no such thing as a local terrorism problem. Something might happen locally, but within two seconds, you discover national and international connections."[38] SACs had been the barons but were now required to cede power to the center.

As the FBI grew in budget and size, it also increased the number of JTTFs – bringing together FBI agents, state and local law enforcement officials, and representatives from other federal agencies to investigate terrorism cases – from 34 to 101 throughout the country. Yet, the JTTFs remained primarily in the business of *investigation*, especially because FBI Director Mueller promised after September 11 that no tip would go unpursued. To a considerable extent, the JTTFs sought to deconflict investigations by assigning them to a particular federal, state, or local agency and then ensuring that they did not cross in harmful ways.

In May 2003, Mueller created a more independent Office of Intelligence, hiring Maureen Baginski from the NSA and naming her EAD of Intelligence, reporting directly to the deputy director. Her mandate was to create state-of-the-art processes and standards for intelligence-gathering throughout the Bureau; find and prioritize gaps in intelligence; and evaluate field-office performance in closing those gaps. Field Intelligence Groups (FIGs) in each field office would analyze and disseminate intelligence, and they would serve as a central point of contact for intelligence among field offices working on related cases as well as between them and headquarters. In some field offices, however, the role of FIGs remained ambiguous and ill defined – in part, reflecting the powerful legacy of agents and law enforcement. The WMD Commission worried that intelligence still lacked clout: "The Directorate of Intelligence may 'task' the field offices to collect against certain requirements...[but] its 'taskings' are really 'askings.'"[39] In early 2005, only 38 of the Bureau's 1,720 intelligence analysts worked within the DI itself.

The next stage of reorganization, in 2005, put the expanded Office of Intelligence back together with Counterintelligence and Counterterrorism in the NSB, as the Bureau quickly embraced the recommendation of the WMD Commission. In effect, the FBI created a service within a service but without the formal personnel track to match. Later, the Bureau created an intelligence career track (one of five) for special agents as part of its more general effort to upgrade the status of intelligence within the organization.[40]

There is no gainsaying the difficulty of the FBI's transformation. For intelligence-gathering, for example, it means to look "at threats in the U.S. and determine how to address gaps in our understandings of those threats" – the words of Philip Mudd, who moved from the CIA to become the first deputy at the NSB. Following cases, those typically opened in reaction to some incident or tip, might lead to an arrest but might also leave dangerous gaps in the FBI's intelligence about terrorist threats. Instead, agents should work with analysts to "map their domains," assess the potential threats in a region, and then build an intelligence-gathering strategy to mitigate those threats. Joseph Ford, the FBI's de facto chief operating officer, described the shift:

> With this new approach, we want agents to ask if the issue that just popped into their in-box [as a conventional case] is more important than filling a critical intelligence gap. It's all about forcing them to make these tough but important choices about how to spend your time and resources.[41]

Changing the Bureau's approach would not be easy. In Mudd's words, "There are thirty-one thousand employees in this organization and we're undergoing a sea-change. It's going to take a while for what is a high-end national security program to sink down to every officer."[42] By interview accounts, in many field offices, the FIGs and their intelligence analysts are becoming valued members of FBI squads – and not just in counterterrorism. By the same accounts, they continue to be torn because what their immediate field colleagues need most is operational support, while headquarters is eager to have them develop broader intelligence and threat analyses.

For the time being, the nation's political leaders were persuaded to give the FBI a chance to reshape the Bureau's mission. The WMD Commission had considered but then rejected the idea in favor of the service-within-a-service structure, regarding the hybrid nature of the

Figure 5.1. Core functions of domestic intelligence.

FBI as a strength. Mueller and his colleagues, at least at the top, were committed to a fundamental change in mission and practice. Terrorism is a matter for both intelligence and law enforcement, and now the wall that used to separate the two – including the wall that existed within the FBI – has been all but erased. Officials seeking intelligence can share information with colleagues who are investigating a criminal case. To both commissions, and to the body politic, the mid-2000s, less than a decade into the age of terror, did not seem the right time to tear apart that incipient cooperation by creating a separate intelligence agency outside the FBI.

THINKING ABOUT A SEPARATE DOMESTIC-INTELLIGENCE SERVICE[43]

However, the issue of creating a separate domestic-intelligence service will not go away, and it will come powerfully to the agenda if there is another serious terrorist attack on the United States. To some extent, the issue serves as a focal point for a cluster of issues about domestic intelligence, many of which are not significantly affected by the form of an organization. Consider Figure 5.1, which illustrates the core functions of domestic intelligence.

Function by function, it is noteworthy that collection depends only in part on organization. *How much* is collected depends more on how much money is spent and how large the collectors are than on which form of organization does the collecting. By the same token, *how* collection is accomplished depends more on which guidelines are in effect and which capabilities are provided than on the specific organizations involved. *What* is collected could well be affected by the choice of organization because, as the Mudd quote suggested, a pure intelligence service might give more attention to filling out the map of the domain and less to following specific leads than would a hybrid intelligence–LEA; indeed, that would be the main point of creating a separate agency.

Such a service presumably would not have arrest or other "action" authority; thus, that function is irrelevant. With regard to information storage, organizational form does not seem to matter much because the question would be whether a new agency became the focal point for databases and other information storage or simply one more agency storing information – which is more a question of policy than organization. The same is true in moving information – "Would a new agency become a focal point for what is called information-sharing or just one more sharer?" – except in one critical detail.

That particular detail is moving information back and forth across the intelligence–law enforcement "seam." That seam exists no matter what the organization because at some point, a decision has to be made about whether a specific suspected terrorist group may be close enough to attack so that information-gathering should cease and law enforcement tactics should roll up the group. To make that decision, intelligence and law enforcement officials have to be in close contact long before – whether they work in the same or separate organizations. After September 11, given the FBI drive to reshape itself and erasure of the wall, the United States decided, implicitly at least, that having intelligence and law enforcement in the same agency had advantages in working across that seam.

It is in *analysis* where the choice of organizational form would appear to matter most because that is where the gap between intelligence and law enforcement is the widest. In a law enforcement organization, the purpose of information is prosecution; what is not relevant to a possible case is not relevant. In such circumstances, those who provide and process information – that is, analysts – are rewarded for information that leads to prosecution and conviction.

By contrast, for intelligence, the purpose is to provide a mosaic of understanding of the threat – "mapping the domain" in Mudd's language; thus, a piece of information that was irrelevant to a particular prosecution, if stored away, may provide the invaluable piece to the mosaic months or even years hence. To that end, analysts should be rewarded for valuable contributions to that mapping – plainly, a less tangible metric than for information that leads to a conviction. Not only would a domestic-intelligence service conduct and reward analysis differently than a law enforcement organization, it probably also would recruit a somewhat different set of professionals. It would seek a wider set of skills including, for instance, historians, anthropologists, and country or regional specialists.

It is interesting that virtually all of the United States' closest friends abroad have domestic-intelligence services separate from national law enforcement.[44] National context matters enormously, especially in comparisons with the United States, which is more than three times larger than any of the six countries in this survey – Britain, Canada, France, Germany, Australia, and Switzerland – and with a more diverse federal system. That said, the other countries suggest, first, several potential advantages of having a dedicated domestic-intelligence service, as follows:

- Services with no functional law enforcement powers of arrest or detention can devote the totality of their resources to preemptive information-gathering, analysis, and dissemination. By comparison, the FBI's "case-based" culture and tendency to select leaders from law enforcement run the risk that its intelligence function will take a secondary role to its policing responsibilities.[45]
- With no immediate requirement for prosecutions, the services can concentrate on long-term surveillance of terrorist suspects, trying to foster what might be called a "culture of prevention" with respect to political extremism.[46] For instance, threat assessments have been a major stock-in-trade of most of the services, and several are the drivers of interagency threat-assessment processes in a way that the FBI is not.
- The lack of police power may make it easier to develop community liaisons, as especially the Australian and Canadian services have done. These activities not only give the services a more public face, they also can be a "force multiplier" in enhancing the potential scope of national surveillance efforts and in affording a direct conduit for assessing the residual threat emanating from homegrown extremism. These overt contacts add to what is provided by informants in foreign-minority communities.
- They may be able to draw on a wider, more diverse recruitment pool. More specifically, they are perhaps more able to attract individuals who would not normally be interested in entering a law enforcement profession, such as linguists, historians, social scientists, psychologists, economists, and country and regional experts.

- The division between intelligence and law enforcement, perhaps somewhat paradoxically, has compelled the creation of domestic coordinating mechanisms across that seam, which, in turn, has spurred the institution of wider, integrated antiterrorism plans. Rather than blurring the wall, the continued separation requires agencies that work on both sides of the wall to understand in detail the requirements and working habits of the other side.

To be sure, it is difficult to judge how much of this is the effect of having separate police and intelligence agencies and how much of it stems from smaller size and from history. British arrangements look impressive: "Britain Counterterrorism, Inc." Yet, while the core may be a domestic-intelligence service without police power, Britain is only a fifth of the population of the United States, and its internal cooperation stems from a nearly forty-year history of dealing with terrorists in Northern Ireland, England, and abroad.

Perhaps the most relevant experience is that of America's immediate neighbor, Canada. Like the FBI, the Royal Canadian Mounted Police (RCMP) combined policing and intelligence. In parallel with the FBI's COINTELPRO, it was revealed that the RCMP Security Service (RCMP-SS) harassed the separatist Parti Québécois: stealing mail; breaking into offices; illegally opening mail; burning a barn in Quebec where the Black Panther Party and Front de Libération du Québec were rumored to be planning a rendezvous; forging documents; and conducting illegal electronic surveillance.

In response, a Royal Commission, the McDonald Commission, investigated and recommended the creation of a separate intelligence service.[47] The Canadian Security and Intelligence Service (CSIS) began operations in 1984. In effect, the United States and Canada had come to the same pass, both realizing that their domestic-security arms had imposed their own view of what the nation's security implied, but then they divided over action to take. For the United States, the solution was the famous wall; for Canada, it was a separate service. The primary argument for creating the CSIS was legal: to have clear legislation and detailed oversight. However, a secondary argument was concerned with effectiveness: absent major terrorism or a spy scandal, the RCMP-SS would lose in the internal competition for resources to the Mounties' main law enforcement mission. It was likely to suffer a boom and bust cycle as terrorism and spying rose and fell on the public's agenda of concern.

The principal negative from the experiences of other countries is that for all the various initiatives, integrating intelligence and law enforcement in the fight against terrorism remains a parlous enterprise. Of course, having a separate service is no panacea for inter-agency conflict: Britain's MI-5 domestic-intelligence service and the Metropolitan Police Special Branch argued for years over which would take the lead in intelligence operations on the British mainland against Irish Republican terrorism. Operationally, how to collect information for evidentiary purposes while simultaneously protecting the identity of covert sources and surveillance/monitoring methods remains a problem. Tactical intelligence for immediate law enforcement purposes is different than strategic intelligence about threats. The difference is reflected in the inherent tension between continuing to gather intelligence on suspicious activity, on the one hand, and rolling up that activity through law enforcement (or another disruption) on the other.

In that sense, the FBI hybrid model may be attractive in quickly moving information across the seam, from information-gathering to actionable law enforcement, because its transformation still renders it a case-based culture but seeks to view those cases as collection platforms as well as law enforcement units. There may be benefit to having one agency deal with particular cases, using "case" broadly – from "grain to bread," as the Swedish service puts it.

Developments in the arrangement of America's foreign partners suggest that benefit. Britain has launched regional task forces, seeking to better integrate MI-5 and the police, and France's *Direction de la Surveillance du Territoire* (DST), or Territorial Surveillance Directorate, is set to integrate *Renseignements Generaux*, or General Intelligence, which is a police intelligence unit akin to the Special Branch of Britain's Metropolitan Police. Of course, the creation of a domestic-intelligence agency, whatever its merits, cannot in and of itself address the larger problem of working across the intelligence–law enforcement seam, in deciding on action as well as in continuing to share information.

By the same token, whether systems for oversight and accountability are easier or more effective with a separate domestic-intelligence service is difficult to disentangle from history, culture, and size. The experiences of other countries, along with the COINTELPRO history, suggest that domestic intelligence might be better and safer for democracy if it were separate, not the tail of a law enforcement dog, which was the Canadian argument for the CSIS.

Conversely, the lack of any effective parliamentary oversight over France's DST could be seen as a separate service's successful argument for more autonomy. However, again, that lack of oversight probably has more to do with the specifics of the French case than with anything inherent in fashioning a separate domestic-intelligence service. The Cold War history of Communist Party members in governing majorities raised the fear that any parliamentary oversight would leak sensitive information to Moscow.

Moreover, the context of all the countries is not only less federal than that of the United States, it also tends to be one in which citizens are generally less skeptical of their governments and more inclined to defer to its powers. To be sure, the point should not be overstated – yet, Australia, which often seems closer to the United States than Continental Europe, speaks to it. In Australia, for instance, the enabling act empowers the head of the domestic intelligence service to decide the strategic direction of the agency and to determine what does and does not constitute a legitimate target for surveillance. Since 2003, so called Questioning Warrants have accorded intelligence officers a limited right to detain, interrogate, and hold terrorist suspects without charging them with a specific offense. Taken together, these provisions, in practice, produced an intelligence service that is not only self-tasking but also quasi-executive in nature.

Neither is a separate service any guarantee against abuse: witness both COINTELPRO and the RCMP-SS. Purely domestic-intelligence services have been abused for political purposes. In several countries, including Britain and France, the services have been accused of spying for political purposes, particularly on figures of the political left. In the case of France, domestic and foreign intelligence was mixed and used by leading politicians to bolster their political arguments. At a minimum, the other countries' experiences highlight the need for appropriate firewalls, more so now that the principal wall that separated intelligence and law enforcement has been dismantled in the United States. To be sure, firewalls can hamper operations by making it more difficult to work across the seam from foreign or domestic intelligence to law enforcement, but the experiences abroad at least reinforce the old lesson that the United States learned about the risks of bypassing mainstream intelligence structures and normal oversight bodies.

In the end, perhaps the most powerful downside of creating a separate domestic intelligence service in the United States would be the transition costs. Purely practically, it would have all the growing pains of any new agency – pains on vivid view at DHS – and additionally would need to duplicate the range of offices and infrastructure that the FBI now has.[48] Critically, the existing FBI JTTF infrastructure, both physical and human, for reaching out to state and local authorities either would or would not move to a new agency. If it did not, the new agency would have to create it afresh; if it did, the FBI would have to re-create it for law enforcement purposes.

The history of government reorganization in the United States is eloquent about the fact that the results are political compromises, those that may reflect what no party intended. In the words of one seminal study: "American public bureaucracy is not designed to be effective. The bureaucracy arises out of politics, and its design reflects the interests, strategies, and compromises of those who exercise political power."[49] There would be a host of questions about where it would be located: Justice, DHS, or somewhere else? Or should it be a service within a service, like the FBI's NSB but with distinct career tracks for counterterrorism and intelligence and even more autonomy that is being created for the NSB – a kind of MI-5 within the FBI?

Critically, to return to the functions cycle outlined previously, how big would it be and with what authorities? How could it be constructed to make it more likely to become the hub of information and information-sharing – and not just one more agency trying to get in on the act? How high and wide would its bureaucracy be, with what latitude for selecting and training professionals? How many political appointees would it have? As always in life, the devil would be in the details, and those details themselves would be political compromises.

When RAND assembled a panel of distinguished experts and former practitioners to assess the nation's existing arrangements for domestic intelligence, the assessments were low, none more than 3 on a 1-to-5 scale for any dimension of those arrangements.[50] Perhaps paradoxically, if the experts did not positively assess current arrangements, neither were they enthusiastic about possible alternatives. None of the alternatives offered was assessed more than slightly above 3, again on a 5-point scale. The highest score was given to the idea of an autonomous service within an existing agency (a more autonomous version of the FBI's existing NSB) – largely because the experts reckoned the transition costs for it to be lower than the other alternatives.

The paradox suggests that the experts were pessimistic about the ability of the U.S. government to do much better, were more sanguine about the threat than some political commentary would have it, or both in some combination. A kind of "We're not doing well but are doing better and, besides, the near-term threat has been hyped" explanation was hinted at by the experts' response when asked how much the risk of terrorism has been reduced since September 11. Notwithstanding their negative assessments of current capabilities, they still thought the risk had diminished by a third.

THE NEXT FRONTIER IN THE AGE OF TERROR

What foreign countries do can hardly settle the issue of what the United States should do. In the end, analytically, the choice principally turns on one main cost, one main benefit, and one that could be either – none of which can be reduced to a numerical estimate. It is reasonable to believe, given the task and experience of other government agencies, that the transition cost of creating a separate domestic-intelligence service would be high. The principal benefit would be the *quality* of intelligence collected and analyzed by a separate dedicated agency. The "either/or" would be whether working across the intelligence–law enforcement seam was reckoned better or worse with a separate agency. To justify the costs, the benefit would have to be judged as considerable, and the either/or a wash or a benefit.

If foreign experience cannot settle the *what* for the United States, they are suggestive of *how* the United States might build a domestic-intelligence service if it decides to do so. The experiences of other countries also can provide useful ideas about how relationships among federal, state, and local LEAs can be strengthened. In Canada, for example, the CSIS established a network of regional-liaison officers, who help facilitate the flow of information between local and provincial police agencies and the federal authorities. The German service, the Federal Office for the Protection of the Constitution (*Bundesamt für Verfassungsschutz* [BfV]) has regional offices in each *Land* (i.e., state) responsible for domestic intelligence and internal security, which operate with considerable independence but are linked to and report back to the federal BfV in Cologne. The BfV's single database is also suggestive in that it provides a repository for all information and intelligence from the various state offices as well as BfV headquarters, and it does so in a way that is both secure and accessible to appropriate officials at the local level.

Ultimately, however, the logic of intelligence for an age of terror would drive discussion to a place well beyond where it has gone so far because that logic destroys not only the wall between intelligence and law enforcement but also the wall between foreign and domestic. By the logic, the United States should create a new agency that has both law enforcement and intelligence functions at home and abroad but perhaps whose jurisdiction is limited to dealing with international terrorist groups targeting Americans.[51] Such an agency would focus on Al Qaeda, its kin, and descendants wherever they are, aiming to prevent terrorist acts and prosecute terrorists. The new agency would be the clearinghouse for information on the small number of terrorist groups.

To be sure, making it easier to work across several seams also would create new seams – a reminder that there is no ideal organization. Such an agency would have to cooperate in intelligence abroad with the CIA, and at home with the FBI and others in both intelligence and law enforcement. It would have to find ways to reach out – either directly or through the FBI or the DHS – to state and local authorities. Presumably, it would have to run the gauntlet of different approval procedures for both intelligence and law enforcement, both at home and abroad. The FBI, however, already manages different procedures for intelligence and law enforcement, and the new agency's relationships with the CIA, the FBI, and others would not be much different than, for instance, relationships the FBI already has with the Secret Service, the Drug Enforcement Administration (DEA), and the Bureau of Alcohol, Firearms, Tobacco, and Explosives.

Other nations' intelligence services have blurred the domestic–foreign line. For instance, Canada and Australia, which have services that were predominantly domestic in orientation, found that transnational threats such as terrorism required equally transnational responses. As a result, both services found they needed to increase their activities abroad, and the CSIS has been given authorities for foreign intelligence. In response to the Sikh extremism of the 1980s, for instance, the CSIS began to give pride of place not to counterintelligence but rather to counterterrorism. It recruited informants in the Sikh community in Canada, but then followed them as they moved abroad. It came to resemble, in fact, what the Netherlands has formally – a single service, the General Intelligence and Security services, with both a domestic and a foreign branch. It is both a security and an intelligence service; in its latter capacity, it operates abroad.[52]

For the foreseeable future, however, thinking of integrating foreign and domestic intelligence will remain a challenge too great for the United States. Creating a domestic-intelligence service, however, will remain on the agenda. It is worth thinking about and discussing now because if such a service were created in the aftermath of a major terrorist attack on the United States, all bets would be off in the political panic of the moment. The details that can make a significant difference could be lost, and the country could be left with domestic-intelligence arrangements that were both more intrusive *and* less effective.

6

The Special Challenge of Analysis

If the season of analysis as the object of blue-ribbon panel post-mortems was unusual, so was the scathing language used by both the WMD Commission and the Senate Select Committee in describing analysis in the run-up to the Iraq war. One critical part of the agenda for reshaping intelligence is analysis, and the need is dramatic. Current and future threats to the United States such as terrorism are global and adaptive, blurring distinctions among crime, terrorism, and war. Analysts of the future will need to think more like homicide detectives, trying to see patterns amid incomplete information. Most important, given the asymmetric nature of the threat, future analysis becomes net assessment, where understanding "blue" – what the United States is doing – is as critical as understanding "red," U.S. foes. However, this runs directly against the powerful norm in U.S. foreign intelligence: "Thou shalt not assess America or Americans."

In these circumstances, there are no easy solutions to improving analysis; legislation or reorganization or exhortation cannot produce more creativity. The shortcomings run deep into organizational culture; for instance, most intelligence analysis in the U.S. government has made little use of either machines or formal methods. Thus, there is no substitute for a rich variety of pilot projects and experiments, many of which involve dramatic departures from current practice. For instance, psychologists tell us that harried people are not likely to be creative; creativity requires having some reflective "down" time. However, intelligence analysts are now frantic all the time; therefore, creating special units enjoined from immediate production but encouraged to think makes sense, but it cuts against the organizational grain.

Improving analysis requires putting consumers at the center of the process. Ultimately, analysis is neither information nor elegant papers reflecting deep judgment. Rather, it is improved understanding by people who have to make a decision. Intelligence, and especially analysis, will not be truly reshaped until it changes how it thinks about its *products*. When I ran the NIC, I realized that NIEs were not our real product; rather, our real product was NIOs – not paper but rather people – experts – in a position to attend meetings and offer judgment. A starting point for the reshaping would be recognizing that "analysis" is plural, covering many consumers with many different needs for intelligence.

Recent failures are the point of departure for this chapter, but its aim is to garner for intelligence analysis the lessons of high-performance and learning organizations. The chapter begins with an assessment of recent postmortems and then turns to the dramatic changes over time in the target of intelligence and how those changes shape the task of analysis. It then looks at attributes theoretically associated with high-performance and learning organizations and their implications for analysis. Finally, it turns to implications from the perspective not of analysts but rather of *consumers*: What do they need and want from intelligence analysis?

THE SEASON OF POSTMORTEMS

The first five years of the 2000s comprised the season for postmortems of failed intelligence *analyses*, while in most other seasons in the past half-century, it was intelligence *operations*, especially covert action, that typically were the focus of post-failure assessments. Several of this season's postmortems were detailed and thoughtful.[1] Some of the recommendations, discussed in more detail herein, were embodied in the 2004 intelligence reform legislation, and others have been adopted by the DNI and the various agencies.[2]

Most of that is all good. Nevertheless, as the legal saying has it, "hard cases make bad law."[3] The social-science equivalent is that single cases – or a linked series of failures in the 9/11 case – make idiosyncratic lessons; it is too tempting to conclude that if analysts did X and failed, then they should do *non-X* (or *anti-X*) in order to succeed. All of these postmortems tend to carry the presumption that intelligence analysis is a singular enterprise. Yet, it is not; it comprises a variety of purposes and relationships to consumers and, therefore, data and methods. Intelligence analysis is plural, and so must best practices be plural.

As emphasized in Chapter 5, organizations must learn if they are to compete. If organizations fail to learn, they risk not staying current with a changing world, all the more so when adversaries are continually trying to frustrate the efforts of U.S. intelligence. How should they learn and – more to the point – how can they become a learning organization? The military services, especially the Army, have formal lesson-learning organizations – in the Army's case, the Center for Army Lessons Learned (CALL). The intelligence community has been through no shortage of postmortems: from 9/11 to WMD in Iraq, to the overthrow of the Shah of Iran, to India's nuclear tests.[4]

Yet, it is far from clear that learning lessons by examining celebrated cases is the best path. The examinations tend to be rare and in the full glare of publicity – and of political stakes. They often focus on finding guilty villains to blame as much as improving practice. Even if they do not focus on "Who shot – or who missed – John?," they still are methodologically flawed. They focus on a handful of incidents, each with its own peculiarities – but whose lessons are then generalized to inevitably different circumstances. They tend to assume that if analysts did *X* and failed, then doing do *non-X* (or *anti-X*) would have produced success and would do so in future circumstances akin to those examined. By this point, the inquiry is on thin epistemological ice indeed.

The examinations also focus on *failures*, which have several consequences. Most obvious, they raise the defenses of those intelligence organizations that feel their copybooks are being graded by the exercise. It is perhaps little surprise, for example, that the first efforts by the DNI to create a joint lessons-learned center ran into resistance from virtually all the analytic agencies. Focusing on failures also downplays what might be learned from successes or even middling outcomes. The preoccupation with major error may also produce a pendulum swing. One reason among several that U.S. intelligence overestimated Iraq's WMD program in 2002 was that it had underestimated them in 1990 – and had been taken to task for doing so.

Perhaps most important, the assessments are seldom explicit about what constitutes intelligence failure.[5] Not every failure is an intelligence failure; in principle, there could be intelligence successes and policy failures. A dramatic example is the NIE on Yugoslavia in the autumn of 1990, which predicted Yugoslavia's tragedy with a prescience that is awe-inspiring.[6] It concluded that Yugoslavia's breakup was inevitable. The breakup would be violent and the conflict might expand to spill into adjacent regions. Yet, the estimate had no impact on policy whatsoever. None. Senior policy makers did not believe it, or were distracted by the impending collapse of the Soviet Union, or did not believe they could do anything about it.

To the extent that policy officers saw and digested the estimate, intelligence could not be said to have failed. To qualify as an intelligence failure, flawed intelligence analysis has to be seen and acted on by policy, leading to a failure. There has to be a decent case that better intelligence would have induced policy officials to take another course, one that was likely to have led to a more successful policy. By that definition, intelligence on Iraqi WMD in 2002 certainly was flawed, but it may not qualify as an intelligence failure to the extent that a better estimate, within the bounds of what was possible, probably would not have changed the policy outcome.

In these circumstances, most of the quick lessons from the recent postmortems are apt. However, they tend to be relatively superficial, reached by wise people who usually are amateurs in the esoterica of the trade. For their part, the experts are likely to be seen as biased, even responsible for the failures at hand, and thus excluded. The lessons of these postmortems are in the nature of reminders that analysts might post on their computers, not so much lessons as good guidance that is too easily forgotten. After the fall of the Shah, both intelligence and policy reflected the major lesson from the case: do not assume that the Shah understands his politics any better than U.S. intelligence does. Both intelligence and policy applied that conclusion to the next similar case: the fall of Ferdinand Marcos in the Philippines. In that event, the *lesson* produced a success.

By the same token, intelligence took on board the headline from India's nuclear test postmortem: all politics may be local but no less important for it; therefore, take seriously what politicians actually say they will do. That lesson may not have been applied forcefully enough to Osama bin Laden, but intelligence analysts were not likely in any case to repeat the mirror-imaging of the Indian case when it was child's play for Americans to assume that India would not test: Why suffer international opprobrium, even sanctions, when India could have its cake and eat it too, being regarded as "nuclear" without testing again to force the hand of the international community? Bin Laden presented a different challenge; he was too different even to be seen in the mirror.

The headlines from the Iraq WMD case were also reminders mostly about good tradecraft, even good social science: validate sources as much as possible and do contrarian analysis (e.g., "What is the best case that Saddam has *no* WMD?"). The report on the biggest of all recent failures, September 11, is wonderful history with a strong lesson about the importance of sharing and integrating information across U.S. intelligence organizations, not sequestering or cosseting it. Yet, even that postmortem cannot escape a certain historical determinism to which case histories are vulnerable: everyone knows how the story ended and, knowing that, the pointers along the way are painfully obvious. It is easy to underestimate the noise in the data or even, in the case of September 11, the good reasons why the CIA and the FBI did not share information freely or why the FBI did not go knocking on flight-school doors in the summer of 2001.

Moreover, however valuable these reminders are, they fall short of best practice in learning lessons for intelligence. Warfare, in which lessons-learned activities are becoming commonplace, tends to be an episodic activity. By contrast, intelligence – especially in an era of nonstate as opposed to state-centric threats – is more continuous. At any one time, intelligence provides estimates of what exists (e.g., "How many nuclear weapons does North Korea have?"), what will be (e.g., "Is India planning to test a nuclear weapon?"), and what might be (e.g., "How would Iran react to the overthrow of Iraq's government?"). Intelligence exists to give policy makers reasoned assessments about parameters whose truth value is not otherwise obvious. Much of Cold War intelligence was about what exists: puzzle-solving, looking for additional pieces to fill out a mosaic of understanding whose broad shape was a given. By contrast, intelligence and policy are now engaged in a joint and continuing process of trying to understand the terrorist target in the absence of convenient frames of reference.

At any point in time, the intelligence agencies are assessing an array of enumerable possibilities, each of which can be assigned a likelihood. An NIE is a consolidated likelihood estimate of selected parameters. Such estimates are not (or, at least, should not be) static. To be valuable, each must be open to adjustment in the face of new information or reconsideration. Recall my CIA friend and colleague: "We're all Bayesians now." The November 2007 NIE on Iran is discussed in more detail in Chapter 7. Whatever its shortcomings in asking the right question, the NIE's tradecraft was careful, and it clearly announced that intelligence's judgment had been altered in light of new information.

Sometimes, the new information fixes the estimate firmly (e.g., India tests a nuclear weapon). More commonly, each event can influence the confidence with which an estimate is held. The analyst's art, and one in which the ability to learn lessons is valuable, is in collecting the right facts, developing or choosing the right rule for integrating those facts, and generating the right conclusions from the combination of facts and rules.

This art can be considered a process, and the goal of a lessons-learned capability is to improve the process continually. Toyota, the automobile company famous for its success in implementing quality control in manufacturing, calls the process of continuous improvement *kaizen*, which is critical to its success.[7] How does such a process work? It is Bayesian in the sense outlined in Chapter 2.

Consider, for instance, an estimate of the likelihood that Iraq had a serious nuclear weapons program. New evidence was then found of Iraqi commerce in aluminum tubes. This evidence had to be interpreted and, once interpreted, it should have affected the judgment of whether Iraq had a serious nuclear weapons program. Conversely, if another week went by in which inspectors again failed to find a serious nuclear weapons program in Iraq, that event should have reduced the belief that such a program existed (by how much is another question). Perhaps needless to add, success at finding the information that would make the greatest potential difference in those estimates is a critical measure of success for intelligence, but only because it feeds the estimates.

There are many formal, mathematical approaches to making inferences.[8] However, they are not panaceas and tend to be more useful in more complex problems involving great uncertainty and multiple variables (e.g., estimates, forecasts, and warnings) rather than those involving interpretive reporting of events underway. Human judgment is and will remain the core of the analyst's art. Yet, there certainly is analytic value in at least being explicit about the inputs to an assessment and how they were treated. At a minimum, explicitness permits the validity of such assessments to be scrutinized before third parties. Intelligence analysts should compare their estimates over time; for example, "How do last month's events alter my estimate about the likelihood of any particular outcome in North Korea?"

Having noted such deliberations, it is easier to discover why the processes succeeded or went awry. If they went awry, where? Was it the failure to collect evidence and, if so, what kind? Was it the misleading template that was used to process the evidence and, if so, in what way? Which unexamined assumptions were made in generating the estimate?[9] Was it the failure to integrate properly the evidence into the estimate and, if so, what kind of failure?

The process might start by making explicit the following issues:

- What is believed to be true and with what probability or degree of certainty?
- What is believed to be not true (i.e., things that are unlikely to happen; e.g., many intelligence failures arise because possibilities such as the fall of the Soviet Union are simply not given enough credence to be evaluated systematically)?
- Among the many indicators tracked, what is deemed to be more or less important to support or disconfirm a judgment? Many intelligence failures arise not from failure to predict events per se but rather the failure to realize the significance – the predictive value – of antecedents or triggers.
- If a particular estimate is true, which indicators would be observable and supportive, and which disconfirming indicators should not be observable (or have evidence that is not credible)?
- What are the conditional, if–then assumptions by which evidence is interpreted to support or disconfirm estimates? For example, if rulers are known to commit atrocities, then their national standing will decline. Furthermore, which facts or established principles (e.g., evidence from this situation, the history of other situations, or

validated psychological theories of attitude and behavior change) should cause analysts to doubt the validity of these assumptions?

• Which rules of thumb are used to assess how much a correct estimate matters in the sense that such a judgment (1) would change policies, programs, or operations if there were better intelligence and (2) such changes would have made a difference to national security or comparably significant outcomes?

Explicitness can serve two purposes. It can display the continuous nature of the intelligence process, making plain that the process sustains an array of estimates, not unlike currency markets, which are ever-changing around the clock. The more operational reason for explicitness is to make it easier to review the process by which assessments are generated. In that sense, explicitness is like the flight data recorder in an aircraft or the log file on a computer process. Explicitness – if adequately captured as part of the development of an estimate – can be useful even if feedback on many estimates comes long after the fact, if at all.

FROM TRADITIONAL TO TRANSNATIONAL TARGETS

The starting point for thinking about reshaping analysis is the observation that while the manner in which the United States analyzed state-centric targets may have been appropriate during the Cold War, those methods are not appropriate now when transnational threats are at least as important as state-centric threats (see Chapter 2). Table 6.1 highlights the differences and suggests how best practices need to be reshaped, driven by the focus of analysis, and then encompass organization and workflow, sources and methods, and analysts' characteristics.[10]

Traditional intelligence as practiced during the Cold War focused on nation-states; nonstate or "transnational" actors were secondary. Now, the priority is reversed, as discussed in Chapter 2, and the principal targets are nonstates, like Al Qaeda. States are of interest as facilitators of terrorism either willingly or because they lose control of their territory. Chapter 2 also describes the differences between state and nonstate actors as targets of intelligence. There is much less shared story about nonstates, which come in many sizes and shapes;

Table 6.1. *Analysis: Past, Present, and Future*

	1970s and 1980s	1990s and 2000s	Possible Future
Focus of Analysis	Continuing large well-defined issues and adversaries, primarily states	Emergence of complex, rapidly shifting issues and adversaries, especially transnational actors	Complex, rapidly shifting issues and adversaries and large well-defined issues and adversaries
	Space for longer term thinking	Bias toward current intelligence	Both immediate question-answering and deeper analysis
	Large centrally organized and managed	Large centrally organized and managed	Tailored to rapidly adapt to shifting foci
	Hierarchical	Still hierarchical, although problem-oriented "centers" added	Flat, problem-centric networks
Organization and Workflow	Institutional and operational memory mostly in analysts' minds	Institutional and operational memory mostly in analysts' minds	Technology helps to notice what analysts are watching and asking
	Time pressure persistent but low intensity (mostly)	Time pressure drives toward premature closure	Technology's advantage in memory affords easy tracking of data, hypotheses, and debate – in effect, expanding time
Sources and Methods	Dominated by secret sources	Broader range of sources, but secrets still primary	Draws on a wide variety of sources, open and secret
	Analysts are separated from collectors	Analysts are also their own collectors	Analysts are their own collectors
	Analysts mostly passive recipients of information	Limited searching of available data	More aggressive searching and reaching for data, both classified and unclassified

	1970s and 1980s	1990s and 2000s	Possible Future
	Analysis focuses on previous patterns	Same, although growing interest in new methods and tools for shaping, remembering, and examining hypotheses	Formative pattern-recognition and data-mining capabilities searches for out of the ordinary
	Analysts operate on basis of own experience and biases	Limited use of formal method and technology	Not discrete methods but rather a continuous process of integrated and integrative activity that combines everything in a process that engages everyone communally
	Many analysts are deep specialists	Many, perhaps most, analysts are generalists	Mix of generalists and deep specialists, both technical and political
Analysts' Characteristics[11]	Analysts mostly work alone or in small groups	Analysts mostly work alone or in small groups	Analysts work in larger virtual networks
	Analysts, not machines or method, control key analytic choices	Analysts, not machines or method, control key analytic choices	Analysts, not machines or method, control key analytic choices

their forms combine network and hierarchy. Understanding them is less bounded; more outcomes are possible. Because many state targets, such as the Soviet Union and Iraq, were secretive, intelligence's secret sources were critical. Terrorist groups are hardly open; therefore, secrets still matter. However, signals about bad people or bad weapons are also there to be ferreted out of the vast "noise" of customs declarations or motor-vehicle records, not to mention Web chat rooms. The Soviet Union was not only hierarchical but also ponderous; discontinuities in its behavior were rare. Al Qaeda has been shown to be patient; however, discontinuities in the terrorist threat – new groups or new weapons or new modes of attack – are all too possible. Finally, and perhaps most important, while Soviet behavior on many issues (for starters) could be assumed to be relatively independent of what the United States did – recall Brown's quote about Soviet nuclear programs – the interaction of what we do and how terrorists respond is more consequential. After all, terrorism is the tactic of the weak; thus, terrorists cannot be understood in isolation from what we are doing to counter them. Even the capabilities of the terrorists turn on us. The 9/11 hijackers did not come to their tactic as a preference; rather, they chose it because they had found seams in our defenses.

Intelligence analysis was not only stovepiped by agency, it also was organized hierarchically. Fritz Ermarth, a former chair of the NIC, once mused: "Why, at the turn of the millennium, is intelligence analysis still organized like the Roman legions?" Intelligence, analysis in particular, needs to be in flat and highly networked organizations. In that sense, the main 9/11 Commission recommendation other than the creation of the DNI – to organize the analytic part of the intelligence community around *issues* in "centers," perhaps more virtual than real, with the NCTC as the model – is the right direction. However, it carries the risk of increasing the urgency of the immediate.

In understanding terrorism, in contrast to the states of the Cold War, the need for collaboration is greater, not just across sources or specialties in federal intelligence agencies but also with foreign partners and with state and local officials. Intelligence's customers also were limited during the Cold War, mostly politico–military officials of the federal government. Now, intelligence is called on to serve a wider range of consumers – from foreign partners of the United States, which may have access to places and people we do not, to private citizens who own the national infrastructure that terrorists may target – and intelligence is often linked to action on a continuing basis.

During the decade-long lull between the Cold War and the war on terrorism, intelligence's budgets declined and its deep expertise on the Soviet Union dispersed. To be sure, public rhetoric often exaggerates the decline. Both political parties sought a "peace dividend" after the Cold War, but most of that dividend came from defense. For its part, intelligence, whose budgets had risen faster than defense in the 1970s and 1980s, declined more slowly in the 1990s. The counterterrorism mission took only a small hit; indeed, its budget began to grow rapidly after the first World Trade Center attack in 1993.[12]

At the same time as budgets tapered down, intelligence needed new customers and new missions. It found new customers, especially in economic agencies like the Department of Commerce. Those new customers were interested mostly in immediate support, more like staff work than longer term analysis. With more customers and fewer resources, the intelligence agencies were hard-pressed to keep up with the flood of short-term questions they were asked. Because intelligence is in the service business, turning away new customers or sloughing off old ones is painful; what got squeezed was the capacity to accomplish deeper analysis.

The lament of insiders was quoted in Chapter 5: "We now do reporting, we used to do analysis." The dominance of question-answering is pervasive, even where it would not be expected. The intelligence agencies of the military services, for instance, report that they spend as much as half their time answering specific, usually short-run, questions, not doing their traditional job of assessing the military capacities of potential U.S. foes. The "crown-jewel analysis," the PDB, is jokingly referred to as "CNN plus secrets." It *is* very current, often a new piece of secret information, although analysts do add commentary to put that information in context. Answering questions from a wide variety of customers may be done best with generalist analysts; however, longer term understanding requires deep specialists.

In fact, intelligence needs to do both; it needs to answer immediate questions and open space for longer term thinking. Both will require dramatic changes in the way intelligence does its business. Instead of relying heavily on secret sources, intelligence has to reach out to a wide variety of sources. In a world of secret sources, analysts could be separated from intelligence collectors; in the world of the Web, analysts are also their own collectors. In that world of secrets, analysts were mostly passive users of the information that was delivered to their computer screens; now, they need to actively search and question data, something that comes naturally to the younger generation that has grown up on Google.

The challenges to analytic practice from changing targets – less boundedness and more uncertainty, no shared story, more contingency on our actions, and too much information of widely varying reliability[13] – can be sharpened by dividing analytic issues into the following three types, which are outlined in Chapter 2:

- *Puzzles.* These are questions that could be answered with certainty if only with access to information that, in principle, is available. Dave Snowden, in his business-related writing about the philosophy of information, calls them *known problems*, for which there is a unique relationship between causes and effects.[14] The challenge is to correctly categorize the problem, obtain the necessary data to solve it, and apply accepted formulas. Military-targeting issues are puzzles; so are many issues about capabilities. Much of Cold War intelligence was puzzle-solving: looking for additional pieces to fill out a mosaic of understanding whose broad shape was a given.

- *Mysteries.* No evidence can definitively settle these mysteries because they typically are about people, not things. They are contingent. Snowden labels these *knowable problems*, which involve contingent relationships between a limited set of causes and effects. In this realm, analytic techniques can be used to predict outcomes, at least probabilistically. Russia's inflation rate for this year is a mystery; so is whether North Korea will dismantle and abandon its nuclear program. While Soviet capabilities were primarily a puzzle, those of terrorist groups are a mystery because they depend until the last moment on the actions and vulnerabilities of their foes.

- *Complexities.* These are *mysteries-plus*, involving a wide array of causes and effects that can interact in a variety of contingent ways. Large numbers of relatively small actors respond to a shifting set of situational factors. Moreover, because interactions reflect unique circumstances, they do not necessarily repeat in any established pattern and are thus not amenable to predictive analysis in the same way as mysteries. To be sure, the distinction between transnational and traditional intelligence problems should not be overstated: there are some state-to-state problems, such as battlefield situations or crisis diplomacy, in which situationally driven interactions among a large number of players can also produce a wide variety of outcomes.

The analytic products and some of the processes that produce them differ across these types of problems. For puzzles, the product is *the* answer: North Korea has X nuclear weapons; Soviet missiles have Y warheads. To be sure, the answer may not be definitive; it may remain a best estimate. If that is so, however, it is not because of inherent uncertainty. Rather, it is so because information that is available in principle is unavailable in fact.

As Table 6.1 suggests, in solving puzzles, analysts could work alone or in small groups, perhaps specializing in one puzzle piece, such as understanding Soviet submarine propellers. Relatively traditional, hierarchical organizations could then assemble the various puzzle pieces. As Table 6.1 indicates, U.S. intelligence analysts during the Cold War did not make much use of formal tools or methods except in technical areas.[15] Those analysts operated on the basis of their experience or that of their immediate work unit. Previous assessments or patterns were the point of departure, with analysts looking for information that would confirm those patterns – a tendency abetted by time pressure, which drove analysts toward early closure on open issues.

The needs of the future are not lost on U.S. intelligence agencies. Yet, the press of the present is so intense and the legacy of the past so powerful that innovations so far have been piecemeal, if also promising. Moving toward an organization by center will permit wider virtual networks to be put in place. However, those centers will need to be accompanied by a wide range of experiments and innovations in analysis. The groups inside intelligence that are thinking beyond the immediate – the NIC, for instance, or the CIA's SAG – need to be reinforced.

For mysteries, the product is a best forecast, perhaps in the form of a probability with key factors identified, as well as how they bear on the estimate. For instance, analysts do not and cannot know what Russia's inflation rate will be this year. However, from Russia's experience as well as that of other countries, analysts know which factors will be important in determining that rate and, at least roughly, how they will combine to produce it. So, the answer can be conveyed by laying out those determinants along with quantitative or qualitative assessments of where they stand and how they are moving, which can lead to a best forecast, along with some bounds of uncertainty. To sharpen both the forecast and the bounds, sensitivity analyses (e.g., using scenarios or a variety of quantitative methods) could test the effects of different levels of determinants on outcomes.

The first challenge in dealing with complexities is what, if anything, intelligence can say about them, other than to identify them as complexities. The goal is to convey a sense of emerging patterns with an eye to reinforcing or disrupting, respectively, positive or adverse patterns. Communicating that sense may be difficult in a discrete paper or stream of electrons. Rather, it may be done best with the active participation of policy officials – for instance, using computer power to *fly through* a wide range of variables and scenarios, looking for patterns.[16] Such processes run into two familiar obstacles: (1) the canonical separation of intelligence from policy; and (2) the fact that policy officials, in particular, are always hard-pressed for time. Because the product is a sharpened sense, the problem is not one simply of communication; the sense needs to develop out of shared analytic work. Thus, there is a premium on ways to facilitate that interaction. This chapter returns to that issue in its conclusion.

CHARACTERISTICS OF LEARNING ORGANIZATIONS

The experience of learning organizations also emphasizes six themes in addition to those discussed in Chapter 5 – tacit knowledge; free access to information; redundancy as part of organizational design, not waste; simultaneity, not sequence; systems for learning from experience; and continuous innovation.[17] All of these themes are relevant to intelligence analysis, at least of some types, and most are foreshadowed in Table 6.1.

Tacit Knowledge

Tacit knowledge is deeply embedded, often not conscious, difficult-to-articulate knowledge and intuition.[18] It is what a person knows about one's own life, work, and subject matter that may not be in awareness but is essential to one's success and therefore to the organization's performance. It is derived from direct experience; unrelated to formal learning; nonverbal; outside awareness; and essential to everyday life, leadership, and organizational success. It may become more critical as intelligence seeks to anticipate complex threats under both time pressure and uncertainty. In such circumstances, newly observed qualities of an object or body of data that are unconsciously related to past experience or accumulated patterns – apperceived – may trigger an idea. The idea must become stated and then fully articulated as a working hypothesis to be subjected to explicit analysis.

However, the ironies about tacit knowledge are three. The practical value of tacit knowledge is in leveraging it for the good of the organization by communicating it to others. Yet, because it is both preverbal and outside people's conscious awareness (like intuition), it is not susceptible to communication or analysis. Theorists debate whether tacit knowledge can ever be made explicit, codified, and shared.[19] However, much theory and applied research – as well as billable consultants' time – has been devoted to that purpose.

The literature on judgment and decision making, especially the research of Phillip Tetlock, a political psychologist, is cautionary.[20] His work pointed out that hunches, intuition, scenario-planning, and other explanations offered on the basis of reputation (not evidence) stimulate confirmation bias (i.e., seeking confirmatory data or self-justifying elaborations). Furthermore, he demonstrated in political predictions an inverse correlation between the analyst's confidence in the judgment and the eventual accuracy of it. Although tacit knowledge should be brought into the light, it also warrants a process of careful vetting and analysts' discipline in bringing it into explicit form and subjecting it to inquiry. Tetlock developed a training scheme for calibrating political judgments, which might be adaptable to making tacit knowledge explicit.

His effort follows in a long tradition of techniques for trying to be rigorous about eliciting and displaying subjective judgments – a tradition that goes back to RAND's creation of the "Delphi" technique a half-century ago.[21] Policon, FACTIONS, SENTURION, and other similar methods in the "expected utility" family of techniques have been used in intelligence, sometimes with powerful results.[22] Early in the Clinton administration, for instance, the CIA did a FACTIONS analysis of what it might take, in policy terms, to persuade Serbian leader Slobodan Milosevic to scale back his objectives in Bosnia. The midpoint judgment of that analysis – military strikes on industrial targets in Serbia proper – was striking to me, at a time when the administration was still promoting consensual peacekeeping under UN Article 6 and was years away from the Dayton Peace Accords and the muscular Intervention Force (IFOR). However, because they are time- and resource-consuming, these more formal methods have been regarded by analysts as occasional luxuries, not a regular feature of analysis.

Moreover, consumers can easily react to their results, and more so to unprocessed tacit knowledge, as mere bets rather than as refined analyses. They can ask, "How do you know that?" – or demand, "Prove it." Clever defense lawyers discredit ballistics experts by asking them how they reached their judgment. By the same token, chess masters can be reduced to middle-weight status by having to explain their strategy. For both, the knowledge is tacit, born of comparing the current pattern, almost unconsciously, with a thousand previous circumstances in ways that they themselves would be hard-pressed to describe. To be sure, the skepticism is warranted; it is both natural and responsible analytic supervision and policy making to grasp the foundations of the analysis on which critical policies are staked. Cognitively, the task is to use all of the various *ways of knowing* in a synergistic manner to enrich the story for the customer. Tacit knowledge would be folded in using this approach.

The experience of one experiment, the so-called terrorism futures market, is an intriguing case in point. Developed by the Defense Advanced Research Projects Agency (DARPA), it was officially the Futures Markets Applied to Prediction (FutureMAP), a Web-based market in which investors would buy futures on the likelihoods of specific events or conditions occurring in the Middle East. When it came to light two days before it was to begin enrolling investors, it was overwhelmed in political outrage – left, right, and center. As then–Senate Minority Leader Tom Daschle (D-SD) said on the Senate floor: "...I can't believe that anybody would seriously propose that we trade in death..."[23] The next week, however, analysts across the political spectrum rallied to the idea as a way of using the market to gain information. Financial analysts bet their own money before they are willing to make specific recommendations to clients. In this case, too, with uncertainty large and information in short supply, using a futures market to get experts to bet their hunches made good sense.

To ensure adequate and appropriate processing of expert judgments arising as gut feelings or hunches and to deliver defensible products, much of analytic tradecraft as it developed in the last generation presumed a normative, rational process, in which the vagaries of human cognition – such as mindsets, biases, and shortcuts – were to be eliminated.[24] In that sense, traditional analytic tradecraft (overstating to make the point) tried to turn people into machines rather than dividing the labor into what people and what machines do best. The premise here is that tacit knowledge is badly undervalued and warrants recognition, even pursuit.

Thus, reshaping best practice to incorporate tacit knowledge will require dramatically rethinking the analytic process, at least for issues that require deep understanding, in which the *expert* is more important than the *expertise*, as reflected in a piece of written analysis. By definition (if it exists), tacit knowledge, like judgment, is the domain of the expert deeply steeped in the subject matter. Thus, organizations would benefit from devising a means by which senior analysts coax their preconscious tacit knowledge into awareness and expression, to produce finished intelligence as well as to enhance the competence of junior analysts.

Tapping into tacit knowledge also will require further muting distinctions, especially between collector and analyst. During the Cold War, that distinction may have made sense, but it does so no longer. NSA translators, collectors who had listened to conversations of foreign leaders at all times of the night and day, were valuable sources of advice about those talkative subjects. They could offer analytic judgments and rich syntheses of volumes of collection over long periods to anyone who thought to ask, but they were almost never consulted for those judgments. They were not analysts. In contrast, today analysts act as collectors. They debrief, search and browse, and go to public forums to observe their principals or targets. The best collectors surfing the Web are analysts, who know what they are looking for and can distinguish wheat from chaff. The line between collector and analyst is already blurred in practice.

Similarly, closer connections between the CIA's analysts and its spymasters are good for both: analysts can help spymasters avoid passing along explicit knowledge in spy reports that is true but not new, and analysts can benefit from the practical knowledge of their operations colleagues on the streets of foreign lands (which is why analysts often highly value the personal "think pieces" that station chiefs sometimes forward).[25]

Access to Information

Opening access to information is one of the most difficult challenges intelligence organizations face – and it is a major subject of Chapter 7. In the wake of September 11, it was driven by the need to reach out to state and local authorities and was labeled *information-sharing*. In fact, the challenge is about how intelligence does its business because innovations in intelligence *analysis* run directly into existing security procedures, which are designed to limit information to those with a need to know it, not share it. Yet, new analytic insights are likely to arise precisely from those who come to information with a fresh perspective, who may have *no* need to know. On these matters, more discussion will come later.

Desirable Redundancy

Private companies value redundancy, even competition, among units as a way to avoid the perils of groupthink.[26] Intelligence's analytic community has considerable redundancy – Congress is forever chiding it over the waste – but little management of that redundancy. Most of the redundancy results from separate agencies tailoring similar analytic products to the needs of disparate consumers – for instance, State Department analysts write for their policy counterparts, while DIA officers tailor their products to the needs of senior Pentagon officials. Because analysts are relatively inexpensive by comparison to collection, that tailoring makes sense. Beyond that, multiple perspectives can be valuable; however, because redundancy is not managed systematically across the community, it is not part of a deliberate scheme for achieving quality or accuracy – which is indicative of another challenge for the DNI.

Redundancy becomes unhelpful in two circumstances (expanded on in Chapter 7) but could be helpful under one condition. If multiple views seem pure cacophony, policy officials will rightly say the process is not producing useful intelligence at all. If there are several views – and if customers have little basis for judging their relative quality – then policy makers will "cherry-pick," naturally opting for the interpretation that is most congenial given their current agenda, bias, or policy favorite. Without common quality standards and a system that ensures comparable rigor, multiple analytic teams can come to different conclusions with different degrees of validity and objectivity. Ideally, quality – the most rigorous, objective, and cogent product – should dominate, but cherry-picking allows policy makers to choose the one that serves political purpose without regard necessarily for quality.

Competing analysis – a traditional, directed approach mandated in Executive Order 12333 and encompassed in what is now called *alternative analysis* – is a type of redundancy with a long tradition.[27] An underlying assumption in competitive analysis is that a common standard applies to all comers; the system applies equally an articulated quality-assurance process and criteria to sources, data, and tradecraft. However, experience – revealed in disseminated products and public discussion of how they were crafted, as well as in postmortems from both internal and external reviews – has shown that the common standard is applied inconsistently at best, if it exists at all.

Simultaneity

As Table 6.1 suggests, when the primary task of intelligence was the puzzle of Soviet capabilities, a linear, serial process made sense. For instance, one analyst or team might seek to understand Soviet submarine propellers and then see their work integrated with other pieces to judge the capabilities of the submarine overall. Now, however, the less bounded nature of the target means that analysts on many issues need to work in teams, sometimes extremely diverse, with the various components of the team's work brought together not each in turn but rather in parallel and continuously. This is part of the reasoning behind analytic centers, which combine multiple disciplines under a common management. They are based on the model of matrix project teams that arose in the defense industry to deal with complex, multifaceted design, engineering, and manufacturing. Not only is the product cycle for intelligence faster now, but for some issues the product itself also is changing, which is discussed later in regard to sensemaking.

Systems for Learning

Lesson-learning is a parlous art in government, not just intelligence, as suggested previously in this chapter. Postmortems in the intelligence business are usually conducted in the full glare of publicity and therefore tend more toward assessing blame than learning how to do better. When run internally, they are often matters for the IG (perceived or actual matters of wrongdoing) or management accountability – in any case, the postmortems are conducted under the banners of accountability and blame. This contrasts with the military's long-time practice of conducting after-action reviews (AARs) following operations as a matter of course. The cultural expectation in military units that examining what went right and wrong after significant operations renders this reflection routine, providing an opportunity to do so out of the limelight. The WMD Commission recommended a special lesson-learning unit, which the DNI moved to establish for the intelligence community. This could lead to a new view of lessons learned, as outlined previously – not a series of cases or postmortems either of failures or successes but rather a process of continuous improvement and a codified set of lessons indeed learned.

APPLYING BEST PRACTICES TO ANALYSIS

Suppose the application of best practices in analysis started not with analysts but rather with consumers. What do consumers want and need? It would be possible to identify scores of different consumer needs, but a compromise between reality and manageability might produce eight or ten. Moving down the list corresponds – but only roughly – to the shift from puzzles, to mysteries, to complexities.

Table 6.2 summarizes these types of needs, issues, and likely demands from and on policy officials.

The last five columns of Table 6.2 suggest analytic best practice for each: Does it require analysis or is it primarily reporting? Is it driven by collection or by problem? Does it require specialists or generalist analysts? Can it be accomplished by individual analysts or small teams without much formal methodology, or does it require larger teams and more by way of machine and method? Must it be done inside or can it be outsourced? To be sure, the more fragmented the process

Table 6.2. *Intelligence Needs, Types of Issues and Demands from and on Policy Officials, and Best Practices*

Intelligence Need	Type of Issue	Likely Demand from Policy	Demands on Policy Time	Reporting vs. Analysis	Collection vs. Problem-Driven	Generalist vs. Specialist	Staffing, Use of Technology or Methods	Insiders or Outsiders
Easily validated tactical information	Puzzle	High	Low	Reporting	Collection- or source-driven	Generalist, collection expertise	Teams of special kinds	Insiders
Warning with predeveloped indicators	Mystery turned into puzzle	High	Medium	Reporting, with context	Collection- or source-driven	Generalist	Singles, small teams, limited technology and methods	Insiders
Warning with more subjective indicators	Mystery	Medium	Medium	Analysis	Problem-driven, collection key	Specialist	Singles, small teams, limited technology and methods	Insiders, if classified
Tactical nonmilitary support	Puzzle, sometime mystery	Medium to High	Medium	Reporting or analysis	Collection, and problem- or issue-driven	Generalist or Specialist	Singles, small teams, limited technology and methods	Insiders

(*continued*)

Table 6.2. (*continued*)

Intelligence Need	Type of Issue	Likely Demand from Policy	Demands on Policy Time	Reporting vs. Analysis	Collection vs. Problem-Driven	Generalist vs. Specialist	Staffing, Use of Technology or Methods	Insiders or Outsiders
Recognizing patterns	Puzzle, sometime mystery	Medium to High	Medium	Analysis	Problem- or issue-driven	Generalist	Teams, heavy reliance on technology	Insiders
Categorizing emerging issues	Mystery	Medium to small time window	Medium	Analysis	Problem- or issue-driven	Specialist	Singles, small teams, limited technology and methods	Insiders, if classified
Assessing implications of policy choices	Mystery	High if agree, low otherwise	High	Analysis	Problem- or issue-driven	Specialist	Singles, small teams, limited technology and methods	Insiders, if secrets and policy require
Framing the future	Mystery	Low	Medium	Analysis	Problem- or issue-driven	Specialist	Teams	Insiders plus outsiders
Sensemaking about the future	Complexity	Unknown	High	Analysis	Problem- or issue-driven	Specialist and generalist	Teams	Insiders plus outsiders
Expert views of deep mysteries and complexities	Mystery or complexity	Low	Medium	Analysis	Problem- or issue-driven	Specialist	Singles, small teams, limited technology and methods	Insiders or outsiders

of analysis, the less likely is an integrative, continuous process and common quality standards. This is not necessarily an argument against outsourcing, but it does stress the importance of the fusion function.

Consider each of the following categories of consumer needs:

- *Easily validated tactical information.* This information consists of the solutions to tactical puzzles, solutions that will immediately be proven right or wrong, such as the locations of an enemy facility or tank column. Many but not all of the solutions require little or no processing; the processing protocols can be developed in advance. An example is generating targets for weapons, what the Pentagon calls designated mean points of impact (DMPIs, pronounced "dimpies"). Such targeting intelligence in wartime will be driven by collection, although the specific collection should also be driven by the needs of targeting. The work is more reporting than analysis, but it is reporting of a specific type. The human needs fall closer to the generalist end of the generalist–deep-specialist spectrum, although considerable understanding of the collection systems is required. They will be teams and require technologies, again of a specialized type. Theirs is work for insiders, although contractors could assist with technology.

- *Warning, generally of military moves or threats, that is not easily validated but does rely on predeveloped indicators.* When the number of those flashing indicator lights increases, the warning level escalates. Analysis is necessary first in developing the indicators and then in providing context for the change in blinking lights. This is also collection-driven. Although it is primarily reporting, it does require analysts to provide context for the change in blinking lights (indicators). It requires primarily generalist analysts, who can work alone or in small groups, without much method more than the collection and warning system; it too is a job for insiders.

- *Warning, perhaps more of a political and economic character, for which the indicators are less precise.* Examples include coups or changes of government or failed states, the indicators of which are less clear than troops out of garrison, but there is a shape to the warning problem and some history of where to look for indicators. The propensity toward a certain outcome can be identified, but specific triggers that will produce that outcome are more difficult to foresee. This type of warning is more driven by issue or problem than collection, although collection may provide particular insights. The task is more analysis than reporting, and there is a higher premium on substantive expertise. Individual experts can work without formal methods, although there is value in bringing nonexperts into the team. Fairly sophisticated methods, such as FACTIONS, may advance the messier and more political challenges. Indeed, one intelligence project of the 1960s, Project Camelot, aimed to build a general social-systems model to predict significant political events, such as coups in Latin America. Alas, it ended by poisoning relations with those social scientists when CIA funding was revealed. Still, for this need, insiders have an advantage over outsiders only to the extent that secret sources provide special purchase on the issue.

- *Immediate tactical support to nonmilitary consumers.* This is mostly puzzle-solving, perhaps through stealing the other side's negotiating plan or discovering critical information about secretive foreign leaders with whom U.S. policy makers are about to meet. It might range from primarily reporting, in the case of negotiating plans, to more analysis, in the instance of the leadership and psychological analyses that are a popular stock-in-trade of the CIA's DI. This is reporting, perhaps with some commentary, although it shades into analysis with, for example, leadership profiles. It can be both collection-driven, in the case of particular secret-source insights, and more issue-driven, in the case of impending visits by foreigners or ongoing negotiations, for example. It is done by generalists, shading into country specialists in the case of leadership. It can be done by individual analysts or small teams without much recourse to technology or method. It is the province of insiders, given that usually the government would not like it known that it has the source or is conducting the analysis.

- *Recognizing patterns.* This is mostly puzzle-solving. It ranges from assembling the enemy's order of battle from a variety of sources, to rapidly iterating to field commanders information of tactical value, to assembling information – and perhaps using machines to see or resurrect patterns – to confirm patterns or detect anomalies, such as the infamous flying lessons taken by the 9/11 hijackers. It is driven by problems, although sources will matter. It mostly requires generalists, and some of it can be done by individual analysts, but it will be aided by technology and often by teams of diverse backgrounds and approaches. Given classification, it is probably mostly a task for insiders.

• *Identifying or categorizing emerging issues.* This is a different type of warning, more mystery-shaping than puzzle-solving. Is a near-visible issue or a change in a particular political constellation a big deal or a small one? Is it an apple or an orange? The challenge here is that policy makers may be interested in this open-ended information only briefly and at a stage in which intelligence does not have much to report. This mystery-shaping analysis is also driven by issues and problems. It can be done by individual analysts, without much methodology; however, those analysts need to be specialists. Intelligence insiders have an advantage, again, only to the extent that secret sources provide purchase on the issues (which is not likely, given that not much collection attention will have been given to the issue yet).

• *Assessing the implications of policy choices.* Intelligence is not asked to do this enough and seldom knows enough about the alternatives at play to do so on its own. Moreover, this is mystery-framing because the choices have not yet been made. Because few policy makers, at this point in the process, are disinterested choosers, many would seek this intelligence only if they were confident that it would support a preferred choice, which is similar to the previous category. The main difference is that insiders have an additional advantage to the extent that they may know more than outsiders about the immediate agenda for government decision. Whether teams and methods are necessary will depend on the nature of the issue.

• *Framing the future.* This might be thought of as a variant of the previous category, but one that involves scenarios, what-ifs, red-teaming, and other forms of alternative analysis.[28] Again, the policy market for it is likely to be thin but may be present if the issue is difficult enough and not settled solely by ideological preconceptions. What to do about North Korea's nuclear program is an example: there are no good answers and reality confounds preconceptions (e.g., "Don't negotiate with tyrants"). The difference between this and the previous category is that secrets will matter much less here; therefore, outsiders are not handicapped and may even be advantaged to the extent they have fresh or different views. Also, teams and methods will be imperative.

- *Sensemaking about the future.* This is similar to the previous category but for complexities rather than mysteries. The methodology for sensemaking – creating a unified, explanatory, consensual understanding about the world that leads to principled, consistent action – requires forms of analysis and interactions with consumers that are not yet developed, well known, or widely used. It is explicit about what is implicit in most of the other analytic needs and, because it requires common understanding, it probably requires more interactive intelligence process than products. After all, the real need is not good analysis on a piece of paper (too often in intelligence, these paper goods are treated as ends in themselves); rather, the need is for improved understanding by officials who will decide or act. It is more difficult to draw the implications for this task because it is not yet fully developed or implemented; it remains largely a theoretical construct. Teams, methods, and both generalist and specialist analysts will play essential roles. Because a common understanding of the world is at the core of sensemaking, being close to and interacting with consumers will be imperative; thus, insiders have the advantage on that score.
- *Expert views of deep mysteries and complexities.* These are questions without answers: "Where is China headed?" "Do events in Latin America herald a broad backlash against globalization?" Here, the challenge for intelligence is proving it has value, for even prescient insights may not appear to help policy makers with the press of immediate decisions. This is more traditional deep understanding, driven by issues and accomplished by experts, functional or regional. They may be helped by formal methods, but usually the separate views of individual experts are more useful than team conclusions, which might homogenize or suppress the individual insights that add value. Insiders have no advantage; it all depends on the expertise.

In developing best practices based on these guidelines, experiments or pilot projects can be extremely useful. For instance, virtually all of the 2000 postmortems called for more creativity in analysis – a steep hill to climb. Yet, psychologists are eloquent about busy, harried people being less likely to be creative.[29] Rather, creativity arises from reflection, from down time. An experiment might create a cell for understanding, for example, Al Qaeda and its strategy. That cell might be enjoined from current production but instead empowered to reflect, to attend conferences, to walk in the park, to consult outsiders, to brainstorm – passing insights only when it had them. A well-designed experiment could be used to quantitatively measure any improvement in problem-solving performance as compared to a standard analysis cell. Unfortunately, to describe such an experiment is to display why it is more likely to win a congressional "waste in government" award than actually to occur.

Experiments with different forms of teaming would also be a natural. Some research and experiments are beginning to be undertaken – for instance, by the CIA's DI. For all the concern about groupthink, teams perform many tasks better than individuals working alone. Sometimes, the sheer complexity of the problem demands more heads than one to account for the range of expertise needed. For example, the terrorist target seems to require teams of people who can think about religion, region, strategy, business, leadership, and – as mentioned previously – our own assets and vulnerabilities. What kind of teams would be optimal? Experiments might form different kinds of teams – those that mixed ages, professional specialties, and – given advances in cognitive testing – different mental capabilities and styles. Again, the various agency practices would constitute natural environments for experiments. The experiments could also help answer the questions of what kinds of teams, for what kinds of tasks, and under what circumstances.

The aim of the experiments and pilot projects would be to take analysis beyond alternative analysis. While traditional intelligence analysis generates forecasts or explanations based on logical processing of available evidence, alternative analysis seeks to help analysts and policy makers stretch their thinking through structured techniques that challenge ongoing assumptions and broaden the range of possible outcomes considered. The 2004 Act made a gesture of support toward analysis by requiring alternative analysis (defined somewhat oddly as *red-teaming*, but practice could include many more varieties of methods) and mandating the DNI to appoint a watchdog for integrity and objectivity in the analytic process.[30]

Alternative analysis serves as a hedge against the natural tendencies of analysts – like all human beings – to perceive information selectively through the lens of preconceptions; to see the world as an extension of themselves (i.e., mirror imaging and ethnocentrism); to search too narrowly for facts that would confirm rather than discredit existing hypotheses – the bias that Rob Johnston's study found so pervasive in the analytic culture; and to be unduly influenced by premature consensus within analytic groups close at hand.[31] In theory, use of alternative analysis techniques can help to reduce the likelihood of failure. The text box on page 164 illustrates a range of alternative analysis techniques.

Yet, in the end, the division between traditional or conventional analysis and alternative analysis is itself the heart of the problem of uneven application. There is no alternative analysis, only analysis. Within that realm are nested a variety of techniques, which can be prescribed as better or avoided as worse under specifiable conditions (e.g., types of problems or questions, cycle time for production, types and parameters of data, sophistication and needs of consumers). There can be guidelines for how they are used. Because organizations tend to get what they measure, management systems would have to give less attention to counting things (e.g., papers produced per analyst per unit and numbers of tools used per unit of time) and more attention to assessing the *quality* of analysis or incremental value added, which would relate to applying a variety of analytic techniques as a type of triangulation on certain problems. This would move away from box-checking to meeting criteria for good analysis, within which a number of options would be available.

Moreover, the demands of future analysis will raise critical issues about the mix and levels of cognitive capabilities that may make future analysts different than today's. Conceivably, some of the analysts will require more cognitive flexibility and complexity to match the higher speed and density of data flow, complexity of available analytical tools, and speed with which analysts will able to generate and test hypotheses with tools; higher visual/spatial reasoning to make use of new visual analytics (e.g., today's tools include Starlight and IN-SPIRE); and faster cognitive speed to leverage the speed and bandwidth of technology without suffering attention overload. Socially, not everyone functions equally well with the temporal-spatial distance and autonomy likely afforded virtual teams and telecommuters. Some people need more human contact or imposed structure. All these issues have implications for analyst-selection standards; procedures; and policies, training, and workplace design and ergonomics.

There is no shortage of tool-building happening – for example, at the CIA's In-Q-Tel and Advanced Technology Programs; the intelligence community's Advanced Research and Development Activity and Intelligence Information Innovation Center; and the Pentagon's DARPA. The initiatives are focused not only on mining large datasets but also on remembering discarded hypotheses and seeing new patterns, as well as providing analysts with better ways of working together. As yet, however, the initiatives are scattered and often driven by technology. With no clearinghouse for matching what analysts want and what technology can provide, there is the risk that innovations will remain just sophisticated terabytes of technology, not real advances in analytic method.

Therefore, a DNI should move to create a focal point for tool-building and innovation in using the tools. If, for instance, all analysts had more or less similar workstations, it would facilitate moving them around the intelligence community, including to newly created centers. A focal point for learning lessons would make sense for all the reasons discussed previously.[32] The DNI's effort to create a lessons-learned unit first foundered on precisely the common image of postmortems – that the unit would grade the copybooks of the analytic agencies. For the CIA, its Center for the Study of Intelligence, which published the Johnston book cited previously, would seem to be such a focal point, and it was charged with taking that role when General Michael Hayden became DCI. So far, the Center, which publishes a sold journal, *Studies in Intelligence*, has been mostly a producer of internal CIA histories. The Center's bias is that of historians and covert operators, both of whom are preoccupied more with the particularities of cases than with possible lessons for the future.

ENGAGING CONSUMERS

In engaging consumers, especially at the sensemaking end of the list of needs, analysis should be perceived as a continuous, integrative process. The deliverable would be process, not product, including a recursive dialogue between analyst and consumer in which tools engage the consumer to create and test hypotheses (to "what if?")

directly with the data as part of the process. In much of the current practice of analysis, most of the time is spent on writing, editing, and coordinating, not on thinking or sensemaking. Thinking of analysis as a process, not a product, and construing the engagement with sources and consumers as integral might help rebalance the investment of time and commensurately improve the analysis.

Selected Alternative Analysis Techniques

Contrarian

• *Devil's Advocacy* analysis in which an analyst is assigned to use available evidence to develop an argument contrary to the prevailing analytic line.
• *A Team/B Team* analysis in which naturally arising differences among analysts are brought to the fore (rather than suppressed as in groupthink) by dividing them into teams tasked with producing conflicting interpretations of evidence.
• *Red Team* analysis in which analysts try to think or act like an adversary in order to test prevailing assumptions about Red's intentions or behavior.

Contingent

• *What-If?* analysis in which an analyst varies a key assumption and speculates how this might lead to different behavior by an actor. In a variant:
• *Low Probability/High Impact* analysis, the same operation is conducted but with the aim of testing an unlikely but plausible outcome with dramatic consequences (e.g., "What if poor but aggressive Ruritania obtains *the bomb*?").
• *Alternative Scenarios* (called *scenario planning* in the business community) involve a more complex effort to conceive two or more plausible alternative outcomes by identifying and then exploring the interaction of underlying drivers of behavior and situational triggers and enablers. The outcomes are transformed into stories – hence, the term *scenarios* – to allow policy makers to more deeply understand the path to, nature of, and implications of the alternative outcomes.

An important step in this direction has already been mentioned: *sensemaking*, as developed particularly by the noted organization theorist Karl Weick. It is a process through which organizations, not individuals, comprehend the complex environment with which they contend.[33] Sensemaking is a continuous, iterative, largely intuitive effort to paint a picture of what is going on in the environment of a target. It is accomplished by comparing new events to past patterns or, in the case of anomalies, by developing stories to account for them. Sensemaking, in fact, is conducted every day in current intelligence, which is a continuous, largely informal effort to update the storyline on an issue. It also underlies the key warning concept of recognition or discovery of patterns of behavior.

A compelling example at the tactical end of analysis is called *multi-INT*. The key is rapid iteration of information from more than one sensor. In one sense, multi-INT is not conceptually different from what intelligence calls *fusion* or even *all-source analysis*. However, in Afghanistan and Iraq, it has involved analysts from the NSA (handling SIGINT) and the NGA (handling IMINT) in networks to permit rapid responses in support of operational decisions made under intense time pressure.

In principle, however, multi-INT could be accomplished within a single INT or even a single organization. In the incident during the summer of 2001, for instance, the Phoenix FBI agents who were interested in Zacarias Moussauoi's flying school did not know that their colleagues had been interested in the same school two years earlier on suspicion that Osama bin Laden's pilot had trained there. The FBI did not know what it knew. It tripped on an "unknown known," to extend Rumsfeld's terms. In this case, what was required was not rapidly laying information from several INTs on top of each other but, rather, ways of assuring that what was known did not become unknown – that previous interests in particular behaviors did not vanish if they had not been pursued to fruition before.

More generally, the aim of sensemaking would not be to examine rigorously alternative assumptions or outcomes but rather to prompt analysts to be continually alert to different types of patterns. To borrow another concept used by organizational decision-making experts, it would aim to promote mindfulness within the analytic intelligence organization.[34] According to organizational literature by proponents,

mindfulness – an intellectual orientation favoring continuous evaluation of expectations and assumptions – is found in many organizations
that successfully deal with high levels of complexity and uncertainty,
such as aircraft carriers and nuclear power plants.

Such organizations accomplish effective sensemaking of their environments, as indicated by exceptionally low rates of accidents (a
minor equivalent of an intelligence failure). According to Weick's theory and some associated research, high levels of mindfulness are associated with, among other things, a preoccupation with past and potential failure and a learning culture in which it is safe and even valued
for members of the organization to admit error and raise doubts.

In shaping those processes, the watchwords are as follows[35]:

- *Social*: People do not discover sense, they create it, usually in conversations. Those conversations are critical.
- *Identity*: The first identities that surface in an inexplicable event,
  identities such as "victim" and "fighter," lock people in to overly
  limited options. Moving beyond first identities is imperative.
- *Retrospect*: Faced with the inexplicable, people often act their way
  out of their puzzlement by talking and looking at what they have
  said in order to discover what they may be thinking. The need is to
  make it possible for people to talk their way from the superficial,
  through the complex, to the profound.
- *Cues*: People deal with the inexplicable by paying attention to a
  few cues that enable them to construct a larger story. They look
  for cues that confirm their analysis, and, in doing so, they ignore a
  great deal. Expanding the range and variety of cues is important.
- *Ongoing*: Sensemaking is dynamic and requires continuous updating and reaccomplishment. Groups cannot languish in thinking,
  "Now we have it figured out."
- *Plausibility*: What is unsettling when people face the inexplicable is
  that they tend to treat any explanation as better than nothing. That
  is healthy, but the first plausible account cannot be the last possible
  story.
- *Enactment*: Most of all, in inexplicable times, people must keep
  moving. Recovery lies not in thinking and then doing but rather
  in thinking *while* doing and in thinking *by* doing. People need to
  keep moving and paying attention.

The watchwords are fairly abstract, but they suggest the goals in both designing organizations and especially fashioning processes within and across them. Suppose, for instance, the FBI and the CIA officers who met in New York in June 2001 had engaged in a sensemaking conversation instead of mutually holding back information they were not sure they could pass to one another. They might have led to the joint discovery of where two of the September 11 terrorists had been and, in fact, were. Broadened, it might have introduced flight schools as a jolt, which might then have triggered another round of conversation in an effort to make sense of that inexplicable piece.

Mindfulness is critical not only in the sense of being open-minded but also in the sense of being aware of just how uncertain the complexity of reality can be and how possible it is that the group will be surprised. Sustaining mindfulness among time-pressed consumers would be even more difficult than getting them to read alternative-analysis papers on occasion. Again, a portfolio of research and experiment would make sense; several have already been mentioned. *RapiSims* is one way to let consumers work through the various implications of different intelligence conclusions and to do all of it at their desk.[36] Robust decision making, similar in spirit, uses the power of computers to let analysts (and decision makers) alter variables, looking for assessments (or policies) that are robust across a wide range, perhaps hundreds, of scenarios.

If being too close to consumers breeds bias but being too far away leads to irrelevance, why not test this proposition with experiments, giving analysts different degrees of proximity to policy and the policy agenda? Indeed, this might not be conducted through experiment but rather through mining the experiences of the many intelligence analysts who have served rotations in policy positions. In the end, analytic practice will not be reshaped until the *product* of analysis is reconceived – not as words or bytes in a finished document but as better understanding in the mind of policy makers.

7

Many Customers, Too Many Secrets

The specific concern in the infamous debate over the Iraqi "WMD that weren't" was *politicization* – the risk that intelligence would be under pressure, usually more implicit than explicit, to produce assessments that suited the preferences of national administrations. Yet, too often in my experience, politicization was avoided at the cost of irrelevance – those interesting but not useful analyses that answered questions no one was asking. Analysts in the intelligence "tribe" could avoid politicization from their counterparts in the policy tribe by remaining aloof from them.

Thinking about the future of analysis requires considering from whence the pressures toward politicization will arise and perhaps rethinking the ways to protect against it without condemning analysis to irrelevance. In that future, the principal danger may be more subtle than overt politicization. It may be the temptation – seen in what has become the almost regular declassifying of NIEs – of administrations and their leaders to use intelligence to justify their policies, which puts intelligence in an unwanted and exposed public position.

The federal agencies call reaching out to the vastly expanded tribe of consumers – those 700,000 law enforcement officers in eighteen thousand government jurisdictions, plus the private-sector managers of "public" infrastructure – *information-sharing*. That is precisely what it is not. First, the language implies that agencies own their information, sharing it only as they see fit; in that sense, the language only reinforces the existing stovepipes. Second, the language of sharing implies that if information could only move more freely, presto!, all would be well.[1] Third, it implies that the challenge of sharing intelligence with state and local authorities, down to the cop on the beat, is technical – enough information pipes to move information freely. It is not. Technology can help, but the challenge is one of policy, not hardware.

Fourth, and perhaps worst, the language implies that the sharing goes in one direction, with the federal agencies as providers and the other as grateful recipients, and that what gets shared downward is information. Yet, the new consumers are producers as well; the flow needs to be both information and analysis, and it needs to move in both directions. In fact, the heart of the issue is how intelligence does its business. Existing business practices, with each intelligence agency controlling the information it produces, make it difficult enough to share across U.S. intelligence, let alone get information to state and local authorities.

The core of the policy problem begins with intelligence – with existing security procedures that are designed to limit information to those with a "need to know," not share it. Yet, fresh analytic insights, for example, are likely to arise precisely from those who come to the information with a fresh perspective, who have *no* need to know. The fundamental challenge is reshaping how the U.S. government thinks of information as well as how information should be produced, used, and controlled.

INTELLIGENCE AND POLICY TRIBES

The mushrooming of consumers compounds the challenge of communication between intelligence and its consumers, which was difficult enough at the federal level before September 11. Table 7.1 illustrates some of the contrasts between the federal tribes of intelligence and policy.

Washington policy officials live and die in policy contests at home, which is where their stakes lie and their attentions follow. By contrast, the main intelligence agencies, from the CIA to the INR to the DIA, were all oriented toward foreign countries; that preoccupation derived from mission but also, in many cases, was reinforced by law. The agencies were enjoined from operating at home: recall the distinctions of the Cold War intelligence legacy. Thus, intelligence officials often understood Moscow better than Washington, Botswana

Table 7.1. *Contrasting Intelligence and Policy "Tribes"*

Intelligence "Tribe"	Policy "Tribe"
Focus on "over there," foreign countries	Focus on "here," policy process in Washington
By personality, reflective, want to understand	By personality, active, want to signify
Strive to suppress own views, biases, ideology	Act on strong views, biases, ideologies, at least some of the time
Time horizon is relatively long	Time horizon is short; assistant secretaries' average tenure about a year
Analytic products improve with time	Want the help yesterday
Understand the complexity of the world, perhaps overstate it	Want (and wont) to simplify
Know that sharp answers or predictions will be wrong, so spell out scenarios and probabilities	Ideally, want "the" answer
Tend to take the world as a given; it is there to be understood	Take the world as malleable; it is there to be shaped
Thus, tend to be skeptical of how much U.S. action can affect the world	Thus, tend to overstate what the United States (and they) can accomplish
Work in an almost entirely written culture	Work in a culture that is significantly oral

better than main-street America. That has changed over time, and the change has been sharper since September 11, but intelligence officers often are still uncomfortable thinking, let alone writing, too much about what is happening at home. At the NIC, I would gently suggest to my colleagues that while understanding foreign places was intelligence's stock-in-trade and should remain so, the effort of spending a few minutes thinking about – perhaps even inquiring into – the policy officials they were trying to help would be richly repaid.

Intelligence analysts are reflective by nature; they want to understand. That has not changed much because of September 11 because those who are drawn into intelligence analysis – even analysis of domestic intelligence – have alternatives. As one analyst told me years ago, "If I had wanted to sell shoes, I would have gone into that line of work." Thus, expecting many analysts to be entrepreneurial, to reach out with their stories, is expecting too much. Policy officials, by contrast, tend to be active; they want to do, not just think. They came to Washington to signify; they want to make a difference.

The contrasts between the tribes run to time horizon and operating style as well. If policy officers are to signify, they have to do so quickly; the average tenure of an assistant secretary is not much more than a year. Moreover, most of those officials – Congress is a provocative exception – are driven by their in-boxes, which are now electronic, not physical. They may have some idea of what they want to accomplish in the next few months but they usually have little idea of what they will be working on next Tuesday. Thus, when they want something, they want it yesterday. For intelligence, the result is the classic process of "hurry up and wait"; instant deadlines arise instantly and then disappear just as quickly if policy is distracted by another immediate crisis.

From the perspective of intelligence, those congressional consumers – members and staffers alike – are interestingly but dangerously different. Although members are harried by the incessant round of committee meetings and traveling to their home districts, they – and even more so their staffers – are less driven by those electrons in their in-boxes, which is especially the case when Congress is not in session. Congressional consumers are thus interesting to intelligence because, for them, more information is not always a bother as it almost always is for executive branch officials. They are on the alert for ways to make a difference, and information can be useful. Yet, for precisely that reason, they are dangerous for intelligence. They are hardly disinterested consumers; rather, they want to *use* information. In America's divided government, they often use it against intelligence's ostensible masters in the administration in power.

Not only is the perspective of intelligence analysts longer in time than executive branch officials, their intelligence products also benefit from additional time. More time almost always permits collecting new information or refining the analysis, as well as coordinating with other agencies to seek agreement or sharpen differences. Part of the failing in the October 2002 estimate on Iraqi WMD was simple shoddiness. Doing an estimate in several months does not seem challenging from the outside, but it is from the inside when representatives from a dozen or more agencies argue about every shade of nuance in every line.

Intelligence officers are in a service industry; they work for the government, not administrations or individuals. Thus, they try hard not only to avoid partisanship but also to keep their ideologies or biases out of their work. To be fair, because they are human, they do not always succeed, but still they find it surprising when policy officials assume that anything they receive from anywhere, including intelligence, is an argument for or against a policy position. Those policy officials live in a world of advocacy, not analysis. In classes I teach for intelligence professionals, I tell outside presenters that, of course, they cannot check their policy views at the door, like guns in Old West saloons. However, the intelligence participants will be discomforted by explicit discussions of particular policy issues, such as whether the Iraq war was wise or foolish. For them, intelligence is an input, not an argument.

Preoccupied with the world "over there," intelligence seeks to understand and display the complexity of that foreign reality. In the process, it is more likely to exaggerate that complexity than to understate it. There is always one more factor to consider. By contrast, policy officials, impelled to act, are prone to simplify both cause and effect. They would like *the* answer, preferably the answer for which they are looking. They usually are smart enough to know that they seldom can have *the* answer, let alone the one they seek, but their life would be easier if they could.

Finally, and perhaps most important, the impact of the terrorism and other transnational issues is slow to change the orientation of intelligence toward the world, which is to take it as a given. Intelligence officers regard their task as understanding that reality. For many of them as experts, not only is that reality overdetermined – the product of a long list of factors – it is also likely to be resistant to change. Given this orientation, not only is intelligence hard-pressed to imagine discontinuities, it also is skeptical of opportunities for U.S. action to make much difference. If intelligence is likely to understate how much U.S. action can affect the world, policy officials are likely to exaggerate it. Where intelligence sees fixity, policy sees malleability.

Transnational targets such as terrorism of necessity are changing that orientation of intelligence – a change emphasized in this book. Intelligence is becoming net assessment, where even the capabilities of terrorist groups cannot be understood apart from knowing about U.S. defenses and vulnerabilities. However, the change is doubly difficult for intelligence. First, it runs against that basic orientation that the world is a given, to be understood. Second, it raises the discomfort of blurring the line between "over there" and "here" for professionals, most of whom thought their analyses and their jobs stopped at the water's edge coming from abroad. It means that spending time thinking about what is happening with "us" is imperative, not just a luxury that might enable analysts to better target their products.

The tribal markings of intelligence and policy are not indelible, although many are deeply rooted in personalities and the career choices they drive. People move back and forth across the tribal boundaries, and they take some knowledge of tribal customs with them. NIOs who were career intelligence professionals did better as NIOs, in my experience, if they had served a stint in a policy job because, as a result, they had a richer understanding of the pace, orientation, and needs of the people they were trying to help as NIOs. Yet, the extent of the difference between the tribes is still striking. I wondered not that intelligence and policy sometimes miscommunicated but rather that they ever communicated at all.

PARSING POLITICIZATION: THE WMD THAT WEREN'T

It is in this context that politicization arises. The starting point is to parse what *politicization* can mean. John Gannon, a former deputy director for intelligence at the CIA and former chair of the NIC, defines it as "the willful distortion of analysis to satisfy the demands of intelligence bosses or policy makers."[2] I would broaden that definition to "commitments to perspectives or conclusions, in the process of intelligence analysis or interaction with policy, that suppress other evidence or views or blind people to them." Seen that way, politicization can have at least five different, if overlapping, meanings, and several forms can be at work at once, as follows:

- *Direct pressure* from senior policy officials to come to particular intelligence conclusions, usually those that accord with those officials' policies or policy preferences.

- *"Cherry-picking"* (and sometimes growing cherries), in which senior officials, usually policy officials, choose their favorites from a range of assessments.
- *Question-asking*, in which – as in other areas of inquiry – the nature of the question takes the analysis a good way if not to the answer then at least to the frame in which the answer will lie. A related version of this form occurs when policy asks a reasonable question but continues to ask it repeatedly, which deforms analysis by depriving it of time and effort to work on other questions – even if it does not directly politicize it.
- A *"house line"* on a particular subject, which shifts the focus of the bias from policy to intelligence. Here, a particular analytic office has a defined view of an issue, and analysts or analyses that suggest heresy are suppressed or ignored.
- A *shared mindset*, perhaps one running across intelligence *and* policy. This is perhaps the limiting case; if it is politicization, it is more self-imposed than policy maker–imposed.

Table 7.2 lists these forms of politicization and suggests ways to mitigate them.

The saga of WMD before the Iraq war demonstrated elements of all five forms of politicization, although the limiting case – mindset – was by far both the most important and the most difficult. From reports of the WMD Commission and the Senate Select Committee on Intelligence, the first form – *direct pressure* by policy officials – was absent.[3] It is crude – hence, rare – and analysts would hardly yield or admit to it in any case.[4] It is also fair to report, however, that some intelligence analysts believed they were under pressure to produce the "right" answer – that Saddam Hussein had WMD. As in all human interactions, the effect is subjective. Policy officials are not likely to order intelligence to heel. Rather, they often have strong policy preferences, which intelligence knows, so the question becomes at what point the growing force of the policy preference amounts to undue pressure on intelligence.

In the WMD case, the form of *the question* did matter because it became, simply, "Does Saddam have WMD?" It was as though the logic train from a single chemical canister to war was visible for all to see: witness Secretary of Defense Rumsfeld's statement that the

Table 7.2. *Defining Politicization*

Type	Description	Ways to Mitigate
Direct pressure from policy	Policy officials intervene directly to affect analytic conclusion	Rare but can be subtle – logic is to insulate intelligence
"House" view	Analytic office has developed strong view over time, heresy discouraged	Changed nature of target helps, along with need for wide variety of methods and alternative analyses. NIE-like process can also help across agencies
"Cherry-picking"	Policy officials see a range of assessments and choose their favorite	Better vetting of sources, NIE-like process to confront views
Question-asking	How the question is framed, by intelligence or policy, affects the answer	Logic is *closer* relations between intelligence and policy to define question, along with contrarian question-asking by intelligence
Shared "mindset"	Intelligence and policy share strong presumptions	Very difficult – requires new evidence or alternative arguments

absence of evidence was not necessarily evidence of absence. Intelligence analysis broadened the question, but issues of how much threat, to whom, and over what time frame got lost in the "Does he?" debate. Moreover, intelligence was asked repeatedly about links between Iraq and Al Qaeda. On the whole, it stuck to its analytic guns – the link was tenuous at best – but the repeated questions served to both elevate the debate over the issue and contribute to intelligence's relative lack of attention to other questions.[5] Repeated asking of the question seemed to imply that there *must* be something new to the answer. Question-asking had a political effect on intelligence. The *house* views inside intelligence also played a role. In this case, the fact that intelligence had underestimated Saddam's WMD programs a decade earlier certainly contributed to a readiness to err – if at all – in the other direction this time around.

The other two forms of politicization, however, were critical in the WMD case. *Cherry-picking* is awkward to deal with because having more than one set of analytic eyes on particular evidence and logic usually seems wise, as suggested in Chapter 6. Analysts are inexpensive in comparison to collection; therefore, multiple if not competing perspectives are often valuable. Indeed, what looks to some – congressional overseers, for example – like duplication of analysis can be regarded by others as useful tailoring of analysis to the needs of different consumers, as it usually has been in my experience.

The presence of multiple perspectives, however, can turn negative if multiple views seem pure cacophony. Then, policy officials will rightly say the process is not producing any useful intelligence. The other negative is permitting cherry-picking, especially by senior policy officials. If there are several views among intelligence analysts and all seem to have about the same status, then why not choose the one I like best? Not all views are equal, however, and in the WMD case, the question being asked in some parts of the government – implicitly if not explicitly – was still narrower than "Does he?" It was, "What's the best case that he does?"

Worse, the cherries were not just picked but also grown – by a special unit in the policy office of the Secretary of Defense and labeled the Office of Special Plans. Some of the evidence supporting those cherries was rotten, provided by Ahmed Chalabi and the Iraqi National Congress, which had long been discredited in the eyes of the mainline intelligence agencies.[6] Therefore, it was not a case of multiple sets of eyes looking at the same facts in different ways. The evidence was also different or judged differently. There is no evidence that the Pentagon operation had a direct effect on the October 2002 NIE, but its perspective became part of broader "intelligence" in the run-up to war, supporting political arguments that the mainline intelligence agencies did not.

In the end, however, the WMD story was one of a deeply flawed mindset, one that ran widely across intelligence and policy and also included European intelligence services whose governments were opposed to war. If most people believe one view, arguing for another is difficult. It is not just the analysts' fault; rather, it is compounded by having policy makers who share – even advocate for – flawed analysis. There is little pressure to rethink the issue, and the few dissenters in intelligence are lost in the wilderness.

This form may be more groupthink than *politicization* in the most common uses of the term. Yet, the process occurs not in a vacuum but rather in the presence of powerful arguments, those rooted in political agendas or political convenience or both. For the German invasion of France in 1940, the mindset was "They couldn't attack through the Ardennes."[7] For Pearl Harbor, as for September 11, it was "They wouldn't dare, and anyhow they couldn't." For the 1973 Yom Kippur war, it was "Egypt wouldn't start a war it would lose."[8] For the 1998 Indian nuclear test, it was "They'd be stupid to test, despite their campaign rhetoric."[9] Lest the shortcoming be thought confined to government intelligence, IBM in the 1980s failed to appreciate the implications of personal computers because it assumed the long-term dominance of mainframe technology – a type of politicization stemming from convenience amid the dominance of IBM in mainframes.[10]

Challenging mindset takes something new – new evidence or evidence of some new argument – which is precisely what was *not* available in the WMD case. In that sense, the Iraq failure was as much a collection failure as an analytic failure, which was implicit in the WMD Commission conclusion cited previously. As the Senate postmortem stated, "Due to competing, collection priorities globally and regionally: Operations Northern and Southern Watch, and the emphasis on current, rather than strategic or national, intelligence, there was no focused, collaborative collection effort on the Iraqi WMD target."[11]

For Dennis Gormley, "Intelligence failure is virtually assured when a predisposed analytic mindset is combined with predictable overhead collection systems."[12] Imagery was predictable, and both it and SIGINT were devoted to protecting U.S. and allied pilots patrolling the "no fly" zones. Indeed, by some accounts, the concentration on the no fly zones became a bone of contention between Secretary Rumsfeld and the two agency directors, Michael Hayden of the NSA and James Clapper of the NGA.[13] With no U.S. official presence in Iraq, traditional espionage, or HUMINT, was limited and catch-can, which made British sources valuable and sources from the Iraqi National Congress tempting to those with too little experience – or too much agenda.

In those circumstances, analysts inside and outside government fell back on what *had* been true. To be sure, in a Bayesian sense, each day the UN inspectors did not find evidence of WMD should have shifted the odds a little in the direction of Iraq not having them.[14] (On that score, the Rumsfeld quote about evidence of absence is wrong.)

However, it did not. Virtually everyone believed that some evidence would be found – including intelligence and policy, insiders and outsiders, and Americans (like me) who thought the war a strategic mistake from the start.

In speaking to the WMD Commission, I used the "perfect storm" metaphor to describe the Iraq WMD case. Its report picked up the metaphor but said the Iraq case was not that perfect storm. What the Commission meant was that features of it appeared in other cases as well; because two of their five cases remain classified, it is not possible to know for sure, but it is likely that the Commission was right. What the Iraq case illustrated was a conjunction of pathologies; mindset was the most important. Because there was so little new collection, nothing challenged that mindset or the inferences from past behavior on which it rested. Saddam himself tried to convince us that he had what he did not have, or perhaps he did not know he did not – in any case, it was the oddest of disinformation campaigns.[15]

Given the storm, and especially the strength of the mindset, it is not clear that there was a way to do better. Surely, the infamous October 2002 NIE left much to be desired; in particular, it was overly technical, without much "Iraq" or political context in it.[16] The Senate Select Committee on Intelligence's conclusion, quoted previously, was on the mark: "Most of the major key judgments ... either overstated, or were not supported by, the underlying intelligence reporting. A series of failures, particularly in analytic tradecraft, led to the mischaracterization of the intelligence."[17] At least, the NIC should have commissioned a devil's-advocate piece, perhaps ending as a box in the estimate, seeking to make the best case that Saddam did *not* have ongoing WMD programs. Not that the effort would have made the least difference to the debate or the war outcome because it would not have. However, it would have offered greater integrity to the process and, therefore, some protection to the NIC and intelligence in doing their job.

Something that looked like the opposite of politicization occurred with the November 2007 NIE, *Iran's Nuclear Intentions and Capabilities*.[18] The first sentence of that estimate was dramatic: "We judge with high confidence that in fall 2003, Tehran halted its nuclear weapons program." The NIE seemed to surprise the Bush administration, and it was read by virtually everyone as undercutting the administration's effort to step up international sanctions against Iran. To those who knew less about intelligence analysts, it seemed like the intelligence community was looking ahead to the next administration – or even taking its revenge on the Bush administration.

By all accounts, the NIE was carefully prepared; after the October 2002 fiasco, sources were scrubbed especially hard. It acknowledged, refreshingly, that the intelligence community had changed its mind: "[Iran] is less determined to develop nuclear weapons than we have been judging since 2005." The reason was rethinking in light of new information, especially Iranian nuclear officials who were overheard complaining about suspension of the military program and 2005 photographs of the Natanz enrichment plan, which suggested that it was not designed for the high level of enrichment required for nuclear weapons.[19]

Yet, what the intelligence community had done was provide a good answer to the less important question. The focus of administration policy and the sanctions debate was Iran's so-called civilian-enrichment program, which could take the country to the brink of nuclear weapons, more than the specific nuclear weapons program. The NIE indicated – but only in a footnote – that it was focused on the latter, not the former, and it asserted "moderate-to-high confidence that Tehran at a minimum is keeping open the option to develop nuclear weapons." Only in the fourth key judgment did it pick up the civilian program specifically: "Iran's civilian uranium enrichment program is continuing. We also assess with high confidence that since fall 2003, Iran has been conducting research and development projects with commercial and conventional military applications – some of which would also be of limited use for nuclear weapons."

ADDRESSING POLITICIZATION: TYPES OF INTELLIGENCE

None of the forms of politicization is easily addressed; however, some types of intelligence seem more prone to politicization than others. Recall the categories of consumer needs for intelligence described in Chapter 6. For instance, much of intelligence, especially on the battlefield, is puzzle-solving and is explicitly tactical. The location of the enemy tank column either will or will not be where intelligence says it is; intelligence will be either right or wrong, and in most cases the difference will be quickly apparent. (That is not to say the tactical puzzles will not sometimes be controversial. During the first war in Iraq in the 1990s, for instance, the commander, General Norman Schwarzkopf, was critical of CIA bomb-damage assessments. He had more confidence – misplaced, it turned out – in the assessments of the pilots who flew the missions.[20])

At the other end of a continuum of intelligence types or needs might be deep experts' views of mysteries – however, they are just that, expert views. Because they are views on mysteries, matters that by definition are improvable, they are not likely to be central enough to policy makers' decisions to be subject to intense political pressure. Imagine if some prescient analyst had told the Reagan administration in the early 1980s that policy should not be worrying about the "evil empire" but rather the impending collapse of the Soviet Union! "Sensemaking" about complexities – issues that are "mysteries-plus" in the sense that they do not arise with a history and with some pre-existing shape – will be a rapid and iterative exercise, a search for some sense in a sea of ever-changing complexity. Therefore, sensemaking also does not seem to be a likely candidate for politicization.

Rather, it is the needs in the middle of the continuum that seem more problematic. After all, the argument about Iraqi WMD concerned a puzzle, not a mystery – yet, it was a puzzle the solution to which the administration had hitched its argument for war. I came away from my own experience managing NIEs with more sympathy for the trial by fire that Robert Gates suffered during his confirmation hearings to be DCI in 1991. He was accused, in general, of imposing a hard line on assessments of the Soviet Union and, in particular, of setting in motion a paper that sought to make the strongest possible case that the Soviet Union had been involved in the attempted assassination of Pope John Paul II.[21] Gates was hardly a "shrinking violet," and his views of the Soviet Union were quite different from my own, but his critics seemed to me to have construed hard review of their analytic products as pursuing a policy line – that is, politicization.

For the purposes of this discussion, however, the fault lines in Soviet analysis that exercised the Gates confirmation hearings were not divisions over puzzles, but neither were they over mysteries. They were puzzle-like in that they concerned what was, not what might be. They went to the nature of the Soviet Union: how creative it was and what was driving its actions in what was then called the Third World. Similarly, when in 1976 as DCI, George H. W. Bush commissioned outsiders, a "Team B," to assess Soviet strategic objectives, missile accuracy, and air defense in light of official CIA views, Team A, the first set of issues became a major political controversy.[22] That too was not an argument over a puzzle, but it *was* an argument over what existed – Soviet objectives – not what might be.

The issues that are more subject to politicization, not surprisingly, are those that have or seem to have obvious policy implications. Stated differently, they seem or can be made to seem to turn policy issues into intelligence issues. For much of recent history, the temptation was most visible for Congress. Especially in eras of divided government, Congress was tempted, for instance, to make sanctions against a particular malefactor nation contingent on intelligence's conclusions that it had or had not committed some act.[23] To be sure, this process put intelligence in the most awkward of positions, having been given the gun and told to point it at the head of its ostensible masters in the executive branch of government.

Yet, the narrowing of the question at issue in the run-up to the Iraq war represented the administration's success at turning a policy question – "Should the United States attack Iraq?" – into an intelligence question: "Does he or doesn't he?" In this instance, as administration officials admitted later, they believed there were several reasons to invade Iraq, but WMD seemed the best bumper sticker on which to hang the defense of their preferred policy. It was particularly so with regard to one important constituency: Democrats in Congress. For all the recent failures, intelligence retains some mystique; at least, it is difficult for politicians to defend views that are at odds with intelligence. For the October 2002 NIE to argue that "he does" did not settle the question for Democrats but did make it easier for those who were on the fence to side with a then-popular president.

This increased temptation to use intelligence in support of policy seems to argue for insulating intelligence from policy, for repainting the bright white line that many of us have sought to blur. Therefore, if policy and intelligence can find new ways of interacting, the line between them also will blur and, logically, the risks of politicization will rise. In that sense, the changes in both the politics of foreign policy and the nature of the intelligence target would seem to argue for new ways to protect intelligence from politicization.

In a fascinating conversation in 2006, George Shultz, secretary of state in the Reagan administration, reflected on different DCIs with whom he had worked and on the different relationships between intelligence and policy they embodied.[24] The contrast was marked between what he called the "Helms approach" and the "Casey approach." Richard Helms, DCI in the Nixon administration, embodied the sharp separation of intelligence officers from policy. When he briefed senior policy meetings, he left the meeting after his briefing. His remit was only intelligence. By contrast, William Casey, DCI in the Reagan administration, actively sought Cabinet status and behaved as a Cabinet officer, mixing intelligence briefing and policy advocacy.

On balance, Shultz, a person of the old school, favored the Helms approach, but he recognized the cost. The approach risked irrelevance, those fine answers to unasked questions that so troubled me while in government. For Shultz, the way to square the circle was to have policy officials, including those at the top of government, actively engaged in question-asking and probing. Only then would they be well served by intelligence. Stated in terms of this chapter, for Vice President Dick Cheney to journey to Langley to work through CIA analyses of Iraqi WMD programs before the Iraq war would be a good move, in Shultz's terms, if intelligence hewed to the Helms approach. Shultz did not say it, but Cheney's active engagement with intelligence might risk politicization if intelligence did not feel protected through independence.

Only time will tell whether the changed world of transnational targets and the need it imposes for intelligence and policy to work more closely, in fact, will lead to more risk of politicization. For now, the pressing need apparently is to find new ways of interacting – sensemaking, for instance. Yet, the age of terror and other transnational targets will still throw out puzzles or puzzle-like issues on which policies will seem or can be made to seem to turn: for example, the debate over contacts between Saddam Hussein's government and Al Qaeda. In the future as in the past, policy makers will seek analyses to suit their policy preference, operators will seek intelligence to validate their actions, and agencies will look for assessments to justify their budgets. For all the hits intelligence and analysis have taken, the temptations of leaders to either try to turn policy issues into intelligence questions or use intelligence to make the case for their preferred policies seem likely to grow.

Intelligence is becoming less special or unusual and a more common feature of American policy making. Like it or not, it is also becoming more transparent, if not more open. That gradual change has been driven not only by investigative reporting but also by the change in targets: if the fight against terrorism gives pride of place to intelligence, it also has multiplied the numbers of those who would make claims on intelligence – from foreign cooperators to state and local authorities. In the process, the nature of the business is changing, if perhaps too slowly.

If the changed target has changed the intelligence problem, it has also reconfigured the policy problem. The Soviet threat could be *deterred* but the threat posed by terrorists cannot, at least not in anywhere near the same degree. The terrorist threat has to be *prevented*, which requires policies that seek to work to back up the chain from adversaries' actions to their intentions before they act. If terrorist foes act, policy has failed. Thus, prevention puts a premium on intelligence. The irony is not only that the farther up that chain, the more "iffy" intelligence usually will be, it is also that administrations will want to use intelligence to justify actions taken in the name of prevention, in advance of pressing, obvious need.

These circumstances require a second look at ideas and institutions to insulate intelligence from political pressure. The long decline of the congressional intelligence committees and, especially, their slide into sharp partisanship do not seem likely to be reversed before the bitter divisions of their parent bodies are muted. Neither does the 9/11 Commission's recommendation of a single point of oversight for the two houses seem to have a realistic chance of being implemented. Recentralizing oversight in a single committee in *each* house might be more thinkable and it could make the process of oversight less political by reducing the number of players. I return to these issues in Chapter 9.

Despite its drawbacks, limiting the DNI to a set term, like that of the FBI director, should be rethought. The argument against a fixed term was that of relevance: if the DCI, now the DNI, were to be the president's principal intelligence advisor, he or she should be someone who has a good relationship with the president – a person chosen, not imposed. Now, however, if the circumstances have shifted toward the need for more political insulation, a fixed term for the DNI may not be a bad idea. DNIs would still carefully tend their relationships with the White House, but they would have somewhat more room to tell truth to power in extreme circumstances.

Finally, for all its faults, the risks of politicization over those puzzles or puzzle-like issues underscore the need for a careful process to produce NIEs or something similar. I came away from my time running the NIE process skeptical of both process and product. It was slow and – despite all our efforts to the contrary – both disconnected from the policy process and likely to produce a hedged and lamely worded result. My skepticism was about whether the process could produce enough relevance.

Again, however, the changed circumstances shift the argument. As the flawed October 2002 NIE testified, something like the NIE process is no safeguard against the perils of mindset. However, the process provides some insulation against "house" views by forcing the houses to argue and against cherry-picking by producing one comprehensive intelligence answer. Innovations in process and tradecraft also could provide some insulation. Having the collection specialists in the room should help analysts – and customers – to better judge sources. More "what if?" and other techniques of alternative analysis should broaden the hypotheses that get considered, as would widening the process to consider more information and expertise from outside intelligence and even outside government.

My experience with NIEs also left me admiring the British practice of including officials from policy agencies in their Joint Intelligence Committee process – at all levels from the drafting through the meetings of the Committee itself. Then, my reason for admiration was relevance: perhaps, with policy officers participating, the results of the process might provide an answer to a question someone was actually asking. Now, including policy officials from the start might produce a useful argument about exactly what the question at issue for policy – and, thus, for intelligence – really is.

Table 7.3. *New Intelligence Customers and Their Needs*

New Set of Customers	Needs for Intelligence
Tactical military commanders	Target locations, "DMPIs"
"Domestic" federal agencies	"Help," staff work, question-answering
NGOs	Both customers and sources, especially for tactical issues in contingency operations
Much wider set of federal agencies	Both strategic analysis and tactical information in the campaign against terror
State and local authorities	Both strategic analysis and tactical information in the campaign against terror but, ideally, tailored to their jurisdiction
Police on beat	Tips about what to be on the alert for as they do their usual rounds
Private-sector managers of "public" infrastructure	Both strategic analysis and tactical information in the campaign against terror but, ideally, tailored to their particular sector and location
Private citizens	Information about threat and what to do

NEW CUSTOMERS, NEW NEEDS

All the foregoing reflections on interactions between the intelligence and policy tribes concerned officials who were all Washingtonians, and all were engaged in national-security matters defined narrowly as political and military matters sometimes tinged with economics. Yet, after the end of the Cold War, intelligence's customers expanded and, after September 11, the numbers exploded. Table 7.3 displays the new customers and characterizes their needs.

The first three new sets of consumers predated September 11. The first and, so far, easily the most important is military commanders in the field. Their arrival as customers coincided with the end of the Cold War but was not a product of it. As Chapters 4 and 5 emphasize, the change is dramatic. Technical intelligence-collection systems, most of them satellite-based, were for most of the Cold War too slow in retrieval times to be of use to battlefield commanders. Remarkable advances in bandwidth and other communications technology resolved that problem, permitting targeting information – the

DMPIs – derived from SIGINT and IMINT to be transmitted to air-
plane cockpits within minutes or seconds, not hours. Intelligence from
systems that were originally designed to help understand the Soviet
Union can now be used to produce those DMPIs.

The second new set of customers was a direct result of the Cold
War's end. As it ended, intelligence was on the alert for new customers; it first found them in "domestic" federal agencies, such as
Commerce, whose global reach was expanding with globalization of
the economy. With tight budgets and expanding activities, they were
looking for help wherever they could find it; intelligence, with its service mission, was a natural fit. Those new customers mostly were interested in immediate support, more like staff work than longer term
analysis. With more customers and fewer resources themselves, the
intelligence agencies became hard-pressed to keep up with the flood
of short-term questions they were asked; because intelligence is in
the service business, turning away new customers or sloughing off old
ones is painful. As previous chapters discussed, what got squeezed was
intelligence's capacity to conduct deeper analysis.

After the end of the Cold War, peacekeeping and other contingency operations mushroomed, often in countries that had not been of
high priority for intelligence. In many countries, any foreign presence
on the ground was stray academics but also, in particular, NGOs –
especially those in the business of humanitarian relief, such as the
International Red Cross, CARE, and Médecins san Frontières. They
were often skeptical of government and more so of intelligence; however, they also eventually welcomed the idea that someone cared
about their issues. They knew about local circumstances; therefore,
like the new "customers" that arose after September 11, they were as
much sources as they were consumers.

The other sets of new customers are a direct result of September 11.
Because the war against terrorism of necessity is one of prevention –
a point emphasized throughout this book – it is an intelligence fight.
Intelligence is imperative if terrorists, who cannot be deterred in the
Cold War manner, are to be *prevented* from acting. That means, first,
that a whole new set of federal agencies – from the Border Patrol
to the Centers for Disease Control – is now engaged in the war on
terrorism and thus requires intelligence if the agencies are to be part
of prevention.

Their needs differ across agencies but generally are both strategic and tactical. The Border Patrol and the Transportation Security Administration (TSA), for instance, want both strategic understanding of likely terrorist infiltration routes and more immediate tactical support, such as warning of impending movements or signs of suspicious behavior. Some of the new customers will have considerable intelligence capacity of their own by creating new organizations (e.g., the Intelligence and Analysis organization at the DHS), by enhancing existing intelligence organizations (e.g., the DEA), or by more explicitly conceiving of their work as intelligence-driven (e.g., the Border Patrol).

A second set of new customers consists of those eighteen thousand state and local authorities. Their needs, both strategic and tactical, are similar to the new federal agencies, but they are helped most if both analysis and information are specific to their jurisdiction. If the Washington policy tribe wants intelligence *now,* state and local authorities want it *here.* As discussed later, all except the largest police departments – New York, Los Angeles, and a few others, with New York in a special category – are too small and stretched by ordinary police work to either build much capacity for analysis or conduct special, purposive intelligence-gathering in the fight against terrorism. This means that cops on the beat can be the war's "eyes and ears," but only if they get tips on what to look for as they go about their usual policing.

Most "public" infrastructure, such as information, finance, and transportation, is now in private hands, and those private-sector infrastructure managers comprise another important new set of customers. Their needs are also both strategic and tactical and, for them, specific to both sector and location. The federal alert in 2004 that singled out a threat to financial institutions in the New York and Washington areas addressed that combination of needs. The sectors differ sharply in how organized or prepared they were before September 11, as well as in how ready they are to work with the government. Railroads, for instance, had a number of security measures in place before 2001, although primarily to guard against theft; given their close relationship with the government, they moved quickly to take additional measures.[25] By contrast, the information sector, most of whose managers had spent their career seeking to free their industry of government regulation, shied away from anything that smacked of "security" and, hence, government intervention. The last thing they wanted to hear was, "We're from the government and we're here to help you."

Finally, private citizens are important new customers. They are concerned about terrorism, perhaps well beyond the cold facts – a point emphasized in Chapter 2. Former State Department counter-terrorism chief, L. Paul Bremer, said that "terrorism goes from zero to sixty faster than any other issues in American politics." By the polls cited in Chapter 2, it does not drop back to twenty very fast even in the absence of fresh attacks on the United States. It was in that context that my "RAND answer" – that is, nothing – to the question of what people should do to protect themselves and their families was so unsatisfying. People want information, but the challenge for governments is to warn without terrifying. Terrorism is about terror, and so much of what the U.S. government did in the wake of September 11 accomplished the terrorists' terrorizing for them. On that score, I came up with a bumper sticker for which I still lack the vehicle: "Take the terror out of terrorism." Building the vehicle is the challenge of getting intelligence to private citizens in the war on terrorism.

WHAT'S CALLED "INFORMATION-SHARING" BUT ISN'T

At the federal level, the simple fact of September 11 was a powerful impetus to moving information within and across agencies and to working together.[26] New institutional creations, such as the NCTC and the DNI, have helped but there is a long way to go. Before the attacks, the different cultures compounded the effect of the wall between intelligence and law enforcement. For instance, FBI agents have Top Secret clearances, but few are cleared into the SCI, which is the "woof and warp" of intelligence. Therefore, when faced by unfamiliar FBI counterparts in meetings, CIA officers might be genuinely uncertain about how much they could say, and vice versa for FBI agents, who feared that inadvertent disclosures might jeopardize prosecutions. The safest course was to say nothing. If the conversation turned to domestic matters, then the CIA officials would also be uncertain about how much they should *hear*.

If moving information across federal agencies is the first frontier, the second and third are even more difficult because they are sharing with ourselves, *across* levels of government and *across* the public–private distinction. Despite a number of initiatives, the conclusions of the Markle Foundation task force about the DHS several years ago apply to the government as a whole: "DHS has yet to articulate a vision of how it will link federal, state, and local agencies in a communications and sharing network, or what its role will be with respect to the TTIC and other federal agencies."[27] There is no gainsaying the difficulty of the task; the DHS and the FBI share the responsibility. Not only is infrastructure for moving information lacking but also much of the relevant information is classified. To state and local officials, however, the classification problems often look like a smokescreen that conceals an attitude on the part of federal officials that the war against terrorism is a federal fiefdom.

Although "information-sharing" has become a mantra in the fight against terrorism, existing procedures – with each intelligence agency controlling the information it produces – make it difficult to share across U.S. intelligence, much less get information to state and local authorities. More generally, innovations in intelligence *analysis* run directly into existing security procedures, which are designed to limit information to those with a "need to know," not share it. Yet, new analytic insights are likely to arise precisely from those who come to information with a fresh perspective, who have *no* need to know. The fundamental challenge is reshaping how the U.S. government thinks of information and how that information should be used and controlled. Both the 9/11 Commission and the WMD Commission deserve credit for at least raising the challenge. In addressing it, the language of information-sharing is both tepid and misleading.[28]

Current rhetoric about the "transformation" of the intelligence community celebrates exploiting information derived from the full spectrum of secret and open courses. Such terms as *multi-INT* and *fusion analysis* are the catch phrases; the favorite is *connecting the dots*. Yet, every innovation requires more sharing and therefore runs directly into existing security policies. As a result, paradoxically, some of the most interesting multi-INT experiments we discovered in the course of RAND research have not been virtual; rather, they have depended on place. That is, as long as they were small and experimental, they could obtain license to operate "within the security fence," sharing information in ways that the originating agencies probably would not have permitted on a larger scale. In one example, an analyst literally faces a number of computer screens, "fusing" information by rolling his chair from one screen to the next – what we called "wheeled fusion."[29] At the NCTC, analysts' computers have stacks of "pizza boxes" – that is, hard drives for different information sources than cannot be fused directly. There is a clear need for more candor between the administration and Congress over costs of the current information-security system.

From the outside, the security issues look daunting, but insiders seldom mention them. They are so used to them that they hardly notice – a sad indicator of how difficult change will be. In one sense, the problem of security is less pressing now, at least in principle. During the Cold War, intelligence was dependent on a small number of collectors; therefore, any single-point exposure was deeply damaging. Arguably, that situation is less frequent now with many and varied targets and much more information. Even if that is true, however, it still means that intelligence must recognize (as Silicon Valley has) that innovations that confer advantage are fleeting. If advantage is to be maintained, it will require a short cycle in producing new innovations.

The 9/11 Commission recognized that the issues are less technical-than policy-related in nature. It recommended creating a government-wide "trusted information network" to share information horizontally, using the model suggested by a recent task force organized by the Markle Foundation (cited previously). For the WMD Commission, the December 2004 bill's provisions on that score, however, raised as many questions as they answered. The bill created a program manager to build such a network for the war on terrorism. Yet, that manager was to be located outside the intelligence community and report to the president – a recognition that the information-sharing problem runs well beyond intelligence. In the end, the program manager for the ISE effectively works for the DNI, which is more straightforward even if it limits the manager's mandate.

The ISE mission statement is a terse description of the problem: "Today's ISE consists of multiple sharing environments designed to serve five communities: intelligence, law enforcement, defense, homeland security, and foreign affairs. Historically, each community developed its own policies, rules, standards, architectures, and systems to channel information to meet mission requirements. Prior to 9/11, the need for coordinated and trusted interagency partnerships was not universally recognized and thus gaps and seams existed in the sharing of information across all levels of government.... We envision a future ISE that represents a trusted partnership among all levels of government in the United States, the private sector, and our foreign partners...."[30]

Yet, the ultimate difficulty is not mandate but rather policy. Framed as information-sharing, the solution is one that the nation "cannot get there from here." Rather, the challenge is what might be called *coproduction* – that is, jointly producing information across the federal structure.[31] It requires reshaping security to effectively confront the threats ahead – which requires perhaps the ultimate change in culture. It will not come soon.

In the meantime, a number of smaller proposals can at least ameliorate immediate problems. For instance, intelligence analysts, like other professionals, want to play at the top of their game; therefore, their reports inevitably begin with the most classified – and, thus, least shareable – information. The 9/11 Commission suggested the opposite; that is, starting any report by separating information from sources and writing first at the level that can be most easily shared. (Some agencies, such as the NSA, write different versions but typically start with the most classified, then adjust downward.) If intelligence consumers wanted more, they could query the system under whatever rules were in place, leaving an audit trail of requests. Many – perhaps most – potential consumers would not even know what to ask for now.

Already, many agencies have reached out for translators into pools of people they would not have tapped before: immigrants who have spent much of their adult life abroad. Certainly, it is possible to imagine different types of clearances for different types of jobs. In 2008, the DNI, Mike McConnell, spoke of obtaining clearances within a month for even first- and second-generation Americans. They would then be followed carefully with constant surveillance – "lifecycle monitoring."[32] He also set in motion a review of classification policy.[33]

The military is creative during coalition operations in using "tear line" intelligence so that information can be separated from indications about the source and transferred to non-American coalition partners. There is no reason that the FBI and the DHS cannot be comparably creative in getting information to uncleared partners. Now, the FBI JTTFs are the principal means that the federal government has for working with state and local authorities. Yet, those are built around FBI communications and require state and local participants to be cleared at the Top Secret level.

On the collection side, the terrorist threat to the homeland is impelling agencies – specifically, the FBI and the DHS – to think of their officers as "embedded collectors." Before September 11, FBI agents collected a lot of information but concentrated on the portion that was immediately relevant to the specific case being investigated. As embedded collectors, they would recognize that the information they collect has value beyond the case, to others, if not immediately to them. In addition to the FBI, the DHS has eighteen thousand agents in Customs and Border Protection (CBP), fifteen thousand employees in Citizenship and Immigration Services, and forty-eight thousand screeners in TSA – all potential intelligence collectors – not to mention six hundred thousand state and local law enforcement officers.

DHS only recently acquired the mandate to collect intelligence and the word *collection* remains something of a taboo, but the capacity exists. To be sure, embedded collectors raise a host of civil-liberties issues. More practically, those collectors need to know what to look for and how to pass on what they observe. Gilman Louie, president of In-Q-Tel, the CIA's high-tech venture-capital company, likens the need to having a "soda straw" reaching down to the cop on the beat. Now, however, there is no infrastructure for the straw, let alone guidance and policy to govern what should be pushed or pulled through that straw in either direction.

STATE AND LOCAL RESPONSES TO TERRORISM

The challenge of sharing with ourselves is common to the United States and its major global partners, but the U.S. federal structure poses special obstacles. It means that there are those eighteen thousand authorities at the state and local level to coordinate, of widely varying size, capacity, and vulnerability. As a starting point, it is worth observing that while most discussion of information-sharing in the fight against terrorism after September 11 concentrated on the federal government, state and local law enforcement agencies (LEAs) are the nation's eyes and ears in that fight.[34] So, it seemed useful to some of us at RAND to look at intelligence from the bottom up rather

Table 7.4. *Reported Terrorist Groups Located Within Jurisdiction*

Type of Group	Percentage of All State Law Enforcement Organizations	Percentage of All Local Law Enforcement Organizations
Right-wing	85	17
Race/ethnicity/hate-related	82	19
Religious groups utilize violence	38	3
Single issue/special interests	74	24
Millennial/doomsday cults	8	3
Other	15	7

than from the top down.[35] How widespread is counterterrorism-intelligence activity among state and local LEAs? What are those state and local authorities doing differently now, after September 11, to collect and process information? Ultimately, what might an "ideal" division of labor among the various levels of government look like?

LEAs' involvement in intelligence activities designed to counter terrorist actions ranges from investigation, including electronic surveillance, of possible criminal acts (typically those authorized by Title III) to collecting information in the normal course of policing activities but that is not related to any specific criminal case.[36] Traditionally, that information would have been handed over "the wall" to the FBI for its continued investigation and assessment. Other relevant state and local LEA intelligence activity now occurs in more direct partnership with or supervised by federal authorities. The preeminent authority is the FBI-led JTTFs, which now exist in all fifty-six FBI field offices in the United States and in many other cities as well.[37] The number of JTTFs increased from 36 in 2001 to 101 in 2006.

Of the eighteen thousand LEAs across the United States, only about a thousand have a hundred or more full-time sworn officers. It is not surprising that for many of those LEAs, especially the smaller ones, terrorism is not a major issue. As Table 7.4 indicates, substantial majorities of state LEAs indicated knowledge of terrorist groups within their state, but only a fifth of local LEAs indicated knowledge of such groups operating in their jurisdiction. Most local LEAs (i.e.,

Table 7.5. *Participation in Terrorism-Related Task Forces*

Liaise with or Member of Some Task Force?	Percentage of All State Law Enforcement Organizations	Percentage of All Local Law Enforcement Organizations
Yes	90	42
Of those that do, with which task force(s)?	**Percentage of State Law Enforcement Organizations that Liaised with or Were a Member**	**Percentage of Local Law Enforcement Organizations that Liaised with or Were a Member**
FBI's JTTFs	89	36
State Attorney General's ATTF	77	44
State Homeland Security Office Task Force	77	23
City/county task forces	20	42
Other task force(s)	17	10

88 percent) indicated that no incidents attributed to a terrorist group had occurred within their jurisdiction during the previous five years.

Similarly, state entities had greater experience with incident management and response, incident investigations, and hoaxes. About 16 percent of local LEAs had a specialized terrorism unit, while three of four states reported such a unit. Local LEA terrorism units typically have a more limited mission (i.e., primarily information-sharing); state LEA terrorism units are more likely to take on more expansive roles (e.g., training).

Most LEAs at both the state and local level conducted terrorism-threat assessments. Local LEAs were more likely to have conducted an assessment only after September 11; about half of the states had conducted their assessment prior to September 11. It is not surprising that there was a correlation between the size of the LEA and threat-assessment activity: the larger the local LEA, the more likely it was to have conducted an assessment. As Table 7.5 indicates, only about one of three local LEAs collaborated with an FBI JTTF. Again, the larger the local LEA, the more likely it is that it participated in a JTTF. For local authorities, participating in JTTFs

Table 7.6. *Intelligence and Information-Related Support Needs*

To Improve Response Capabilities	Percentage of All State Law Enforcement Organizations	Percentage of All Local Law Enforcement Organizations
More/better intelligence information on threats and terrorist activity in region	64	42
More manpower dedicated to response planning and/or to counterterrorism activities	87	35

	Of Those Organizations That Indicated a Need for Some Type of Support	
To Improve Assessment Capabilities	Percentage of State Law Enforcement Organizations	Percentage of Local Law Enforcement Organizations
To inform assessment activities, better intelligence on terrorist threat/capability from federal government	47	17

typically means sharing information and receiving training. In contrast, nearly all state LEAs collaborated with JTTFs for the same reasons, as well as for more expansive reasons, such as assisting with investigations.

Most states and close to a majority of local LEAs reported needing more and better terrorism-threat information, and most states and a third of local authorities registered requirements for more manpower (Table 7.6). The need for better terrorism-threat information was confirmed in a 2003 survey, which found that both state and local organizations were looking to the DHS for intelligence information and information about the terrorist threat within their jurisdiction. Of local LEAs, 62 percent wanted more such information.[38]

Despite a desire for more detailed intelligence information, few local LEAs were in a position to receive it. Only 7 percent of local agencies indicated having applied for security clearances for their personnel after September 11; of those that had applied, only half indicated that all of their personnel had received the clearances. Indeed, state offices of emergency management and state public health departments were more likely than LEAs to have sought security clearances for their personnel after the September 11 attacks. Portland, Oregon, withdrew its police from the FBI JTTF, ostensibly over the refusal of the FBI to grant the mayor a security clearance – an issue that is a problem for the JTTFs.[39] It is understandable that many elected officials and senior local police officers chafe at having to be "cleared" by the FBI.

Detailed interviews with eight local LEAs confirmed the survey finding that local police generally have not created separate units for counterterrorism intelligence. Counterterrorism-intelligence–gathering and analysis tend to occur as part of a larger criminal intelligence unit. Neither has the terrorist threat led to large-scale changes in the organizational structure of most local police departments. In general, local police have increased their commitment of human resources to counterterrorism efforts, which usually comes at the expense of other policing areas.

Those departments have little capacity to analyze the information they collect or receive; although federal grants have been available, most of those were used – especially initially – for equipment and consequence management, not analysis and training. The September 11 attacks led to a sharp increase in the amount of counterterrorism information that is shared within and among local police and their federal counterparts. Paradoxically, however, the sheer number of cooperating agencies sometimes inhibits progress in responding to the terrorist threat. Several states quit the Multistate Antiterrorism Information Exchange (MATRIX) out of concerns that included privacy and the social impact of interstate data-sharing.[40] They did so even though MATRIX did not have intelligence-gathering functions but rather focused on enabling information-sharing across state lines.

The survey and case studies portray a varied set of state and especially local responses to the threat of terrorism. For many of the localities surveyed, perhaps most, terrorism is a threat that may come but has not yet. The findings tend to belie the notion that counterterrorism intelligence is a pervasive function among LEAs. Instead, the survey findings, which reflect heightened awareness associated with the Oklahoma City and September 11 attacks, suggest that the "eyes and ears" capability is concentrated among the larger departments. These are the LEAs that are investing in training, response plans, coordination, and other preparedness measures, which, in turn, suggests that the process of shaping and directing state and local LEA involvement in intelligence activities may be a narrower and more focused challenge than is often implied by the eyes and ears metaphor.

Overall, however, state and local intelligence-gathering has increased, at least as measured by wiretaps for law enforcement purposes. As Table 7.5 indicates, state and local intercept orders doubled between 2000 and 2006, and communications per order nearly tripled. Federal orders nearly doubled by 2005, then declined, and communications per order grew somewhat. Table 7.7 reports the numbers of intercept orders for law enforcement purposes approved by federal and state and local judges, along with the average number of communications intercepted per order. The sixth column in Table 7.7 reports the number of federal intercept orders granted under the FISA, for national-security purposes. It is not surprising that those numbers increased sharply after September 11 and doubled between 2000 and 2006.

There has been considerable attention given to privacy and civil-liberties considerations at the federal level, especially after the Patriot Act, which widened authority not just for the FISA but also for investigation and surveillance by other means. By contrast, there has been much less attention given to what is happening or what might be authorized at the state and local level and virtually no research on law and practice at those levels.[41]

The numbers in Table 7.7 should be reviewed with caution. First, the state and local numbers probably understate the facts, for several reasons. In 2001, for instance, forty-six states had laws permitting interceptions, but only twenty-five states reported using that authority. If the states under-report to the federal government, then localities also may under-report to the states. Second, the purpose of the interceptions is not evident because terrorism is a problem for both intelligence and law enforcement. Thus, while by definition the FISA wiretaps were for intelligence, as opposed to law enforcement, they might have generated leads or other information relevant to criminal prosecution. More to the point, although many states are in the process of broadening their authority to intercept communications, in most cases and in most places the purpose is law

Table 7.7. Federal and State and Local Wiretap Orders, 2000–2006

Year	Total Federal Orders	Average Number of Communications per Order	Total State and Local Orders	Average Number of Communications per Order	Total Federal FISA Orders
2000	479	NA	711	NA	1,005
2001	486	2,367	1,005	1,180	932
2002	497	2,354	861	1,335	1,228
2003	578	2,931	864	3,052	1,724
2004	730	3,266	980	3,017	1,758
2005	625	3,555	1,148	2,835	2,074
2006	461	2,862	1,378	2,685	2,181

Sources: Administrative Office of the U.S. Courts, *Wiretap Reports,* available at http://www.uscourts.gov/library/wiretap.html; for FISA, see http://www.fas.org/irp/agency/doj/fisa/index.html#rept. The 2003 report on FISA surveillance from the Justice Department to the Administrative Office of the U.S. Courts is available also at http://www.fas.org/irp/agency/doj/fisa/2003rept.pdf.

enforcement. If the wiretaps generate information that is useful in the war on terrorism but *not* germane to any ongoing criminal investigation, that information will be a by-product.

From interviews with local police departments – Las Vegas, for example – it seems likely that if the local authorities undertook terrorism-related surveillance for intelligence purposes, they almost always did so with federal officials through the JTTFs. If so, then the request for surveillance would go through FISA channels and any subsequent oversight would be through federal courts. The role of state courts in overseeing police investigations usually is in the form of Fourth Amendment litigation arising from a criminal prosecution. It has been – and probably will continue to be – rare to see state courts ruling on the constitutionality of post–September 11 legislation like the Patriot Act.

After September 11, many states began to discuss more permissive reforms of their wiretap legislation.[42] Those measures typically expanded which crimes would justify wiretaps; who could grant authority; who could implement wiretaps; and authorization to conduct "roving" wiretaps across broader geographic areas, as well as the devices subject to interception.

The last measure – expanding authority to new devices – merely brings state laws into line with the prevailing federal statute, the Electronic Communications Privacy Act (ECPA) of 1986, which updated the standards for newer technologies, such as cell phones and e-mail.[43] Thus, the issues raised are mostly those of whether local officials will get the training needed to operate such wiretaps. Similarly, roving wiretaps that permit surveillance of any communications device the target may use, instead of specifying a particular telephone or the like, are mostly a modernization of legislation. Roving wiretaps were permitted under ECPA but not under the FISA until the Patriot Act brought the two into harmony. States are moving to modernize their statutes in the same way. This implies, however, that just as federal judges can issue orders for the entire nation, some states are permitting judges to issue orders that extend beyond the jurisdictional bounds of the court. Florida, Virginia, and Maryland have such provisions.[44] Although these provisions recognize the fact that terrorism respects few boundaries, they raise the prospects of "judge-shopping" and of decreased supervision of interceptions performed beyond the originating court's jurisdiction.

A DIVISION OF LABOR

To what does all this flux in procedures amount? One way to evaluate the "So what?" question is to ask what are the comparative advantages of the different levels of government and of the private sector in dividing the task and then to evaluate what is happening against that ideal. The evaluation, in turn, suggests steps that might be taken to move closer to that ideal.

Given the FISA, federal authorities would naturally take the lead in intelligence-gathering that is not connected to criminal investigation. The local authorities have neither money nor capacity for that type of pure intelligence. The intelligence-gathering also would be guided by federal regulations and overseen primarily by federal courts. Ideally, the state and local authorities would conduct two types of information- or intelligence-gathering: (1) investigation, including electronic surveillance, of possible criminal acts; and (2) collection that is incidental to the normal activities of LEA officers. The latter becomes the eyes and ears of the cops on the beat, and the goal is domain awareness – what is going on in the jurisdiction, what is the state of possible targets, and so on. Here, the shortfalls of current practice against an ideal are two, the first more doctrinal and the other more practical.

The doctrinal problem is that both types of state and local intelligence-gathering involve enormous discretion – not an unfamiliar issue in policing. However, terrorism compounds the problem because the task is inherently preventing crimes, not enforcing the law after the fact. As states emulate the federal government in relaxing their eavesdropping regulations, the line between intelligence and law enforcement blurs for them as well. Yet, the range of state reporting – not to mention state regulation – of eavesdropping is enormous. The problem of guidelines travels all the way down the chain of command: in discussions with police departments, most guidelines for the counterterrorism mission at the local level are ad hoc and derive from the local chain of command.

The more practical shortfall is that local LEAs get neither much guidance about what to look for nor enough intelligence that is sufficiently specific to shape local operations. There is increasing recognition that the problem is apparently only one of hardware – that is, the "pipes" actually to move information. To be sure, the piping remains a considerable problem, especially for many local departments; yet, policy and guidelines are the still more formidable obstacles. As both the surveys and cases suggested, the principal information-sharing mechanism, the JTTFs, is constrained because it requires obtaining security clearances for the state and local participants at the level of their FBI counterparts. The FBI focuses on cases and investigation; one of its key functions is "deconflicting" investigations – that is, parceling out cases to JTTF member agencies for their investigations and then ensuring that the investigations do not work at cross purposes to one another.

The newer fusion centers, a DHS initiative, are meant to be complementary. If JTTFs work on cases once identified, the fusion centers are meant to assemble *strategic intelligence* at the regional level. They also seek to bring together federal officials with state and local officials, including – in principle – reaching out to the private sector. The responsibility of the centers is to fuse foreign intelligence with domestic information in order to facilitate improved policy decision making on issues of counterterrorism, crime, and emergency response.[45] How exactly to accomplish that remains a challenge.

In practice, the fusion centers are experiencing adjustment difficulties, including poor or absent communication among centers. Not all fusion centers have statewide intelligence systems. They also do not all have access to law enforcement data or private-sector information. The problem of interoperability of systems that was widely criticized directly after September 11 still exists. Because of the huge number of systems and the resulting duplication, reviewing incoming information is extremely time-consuming.

Moreover, as outward signs of the terrorist threat wane, many of the centers are changing their focus from a pure counterterrorism mission to an "all-hazards" approach as priorities change at the local and regional levels. That change reflects the simple fact displayed in the survey: for most localities, terrorism is not a major problem. That shift to an all-hazards approach may not be so negative as the "domestication" of the terrorist threat means that it increasingly resembles organized crime.

In parallel, the federal government has encouraged the formation of industry Information Sharing and Analysis Centers (ISACs). Such groups had long existed in some sectors, such as communications and transportation; now, in principle, they are meant to span seventeen critical infrastructure and key resource sectors. The ISACs, along with Sector Coordinating Councils (SCCs), are meant to serve as central points of information-sharing within each of the sectors and also to act as the liaison to the federal government. Their main functions are to funnel threat information to facilities and to receive and collect information from facilities. For instance, the chemical-sector ISAC has supported DNS information-sharing efforts since the department's inception and includes more than six hundred individuals representing more than 430 different chemical companies.[46]

At this point, it is far from clear how or how much classified intelligence information will be shared with private-sector companies and individuals. The 2004 warnings about threats against U.S. financial institutions were still fairly general – although they did apply to particular regions – and specific companies were notified that they might be targets. The IT ISAC stresses – if not the classified nature of benefits to members – at least the nonpublic opportunities to share details of incidents or possible incidents among peers from other companies.[47]

Coproduction is far from a real two-way street and reaching out to the private sector, the third frontier, is particularly troublesome. In the words of one recent assessment, "The flow of information from the private sector to fusion centers is largely sporadic, event driven, and manually facilitated."[48] Like cops on the beat, private managers of infrastructure know their domain better than anyone else. Yet, interviews suggest they have three reasons for being reticent about sharing information: first, they are concerned about revealing gaps in security; second, they do not want proprietary information to leak to competitors; and, third, passing information risks that they will become liable for other shortcomings (e.g., environmental violations).

Table 7.8 lists types of intelligence that, *were they available*, would be of interest to state and local authorities and the private sector. Evidence from foiled attacks is underscored as perhaps of special interest,

Table 7.8. *Intelligence of Interest to State and Local Authorities and the
Private Sector*

Examples of State-Local-Private Sector Questions	Examples of Possibly Valuable Intelligence Information – Indicators of Terrorist "Proclivities"
Which terrorism scenarios should be considered in risk management?	Stated interest in specific technologies
	Indications of dry runs
	Demonstrated capabilities from dry runs or analogous events
	Acquisition of training manuals
	Observation of communications between known terrorists
	Evidence from foiled attacks
Is there evidence of increased threat?	Suspicious activity reports
	Increased chatter on monitored communications channels
	Observation of communications between known terrorists

and it might be possible to do a type of tear sheet – that is, providing the attack mode without revealing exactly how it was foiled. By contrast, suspicious activity reports (SARs) have proven to be not very useful. Transmitting the reports has been an established part of efforts to counter criminality in the financial sector, and there were concerns even before September 11 that the "volume of these reports was interfering with effective law enforcement."[49] Since September 11, the range of organizations obligated to submit such reports has broadened, and there have been calls from the private sector for better guidelines on what constitutes suspicious activity.[50]

Former Secretary of Defense Rumsfeld focused attention in the intelligence war on terrorism to the "known unknowns," what we know we do not know, and especially to the "unknown unknowns," what we do not know we do not know.[51] Yet, much of the September 11 failure turned on another category, the "unknown knowns," what we did not know or had forgotten we knew. One of the striking findings from the surveys and cases is the importance of more analysis across all of Rumsfeld's categories.

That importance derives directly from the nature of the counterterrorism task. A traditional law enforcement investigation seeks to reconstruct the single trail from crime back to perpetrator. By contrast, the counterterrorism task, especially prevention, needs to look at a number of paths, assembling enough information about each to know when patterns are changing or something suspicious is afoot along a path. It is not only an intelligence-rich task; it is also a task rich in intelligence analysis.

Ideally, the analysis function would be split among the levels of government. The federal level has a comparative advantage in special sources, especially sources abroad. Its analysis will naturally concentrate on those and on the broad "connect-the-dots" function. Sometimes, those sources and that analysis will provide warning sufficiently specific to alert particular local authorities. In other cases, however, it will remain general and will serve mostly to alert local officials about what they might look for – for example, a string of apparently unrelated crimes involving false identities.

The federal government is struggling, through the NCTC and the DHS as well as a greatly expanded FBI intelligence function, to do better at its part of the ideal. Yet, what is even more striking is how limited the analytic capacity is at the local level. Only the largest police departments have much of any capacity at all, with New York in a class by itself. Yet, the local role in the division of analytic labor would be to take the general guidance provided by the federal agencies and relate it to local-domain awareness. What does new federal information or analysis add to that understanding of local circumstances?

The ideal and shortfalls against it suggest an agenda for doing better. The obvious first need is more training for more intelligence capacity, especially in analysis, at the state and local levels. The training would include techniques for increasing domain awareness and for undertaking local threat assessments. Yet, so far, federal-assistance programs emphasize equipment for consequence management, not training for intelligence – although that state of affairs is changing.

Moreover, training might also address the other visible concern – the varied and ad hoc nature of guidelines for counterterrorism intelligence. The federal government might regulate through training. It could require training to specified standards if a jurisdiction is to receive funding from the DHS. More generally, greater and more explicit federal funding for state and local intelligence agencies would permit the federal authorities a greater regulatory role over what is currently a fairly loose and ad hoc process. It would encourage local police to develop internal guidelines (including mandate) and external oversight by tying them to funding.

More generally, although law enforcement throughout the United States is fundamentally local in its structure, there is no reason that law enforcement intelligence needs to be. A program like Community Oriented Policing Services (COPS), under which the federal government supported additional law enforcement officers for a specified period, could be modified to significantly boost local intelligence capabilities. A federal program on intelligence could operate similarly, with the federal government paying the cost of an intelligence "supervisor" for eligible LEAs. The supervisor could be selected by national authorities (e.g., the FBI) and trained to national-intelligence standards. This federal–state link would embed federal capacity in state organizations. It might increase the flow of intelligence from the local level to the national level as well as help standardize the flow of information.

While the DHS has a legal mandate to take the lead in sharing intelligence, as a practical matter, the lead in sharing is likely to continue to remain with the FBI through the JTTFs – although with the fusion centers playing a more significant role. The federal, state, and local LEAs need to jointly develop a definition of terrorism and apply it by requiring that terrorism cases, including surveillance, be processed through the JTTF. In any case, it would help if *some agency* were in the lead, which is consistent with the recommendations of the DHS and the Justice Department in their recent National Criminal Intelligence Sharing Plan, which defines several recommendations regarding law enforcement's intelligence role in this area and how it could be improved.[52] It is a role that the DNI could play, as an honest broker without a direct bureaucratic stake. The DNI could develop both lanes in the road for the different agencies, and standards for both producing intelligence and sharing it – in short, for coproducing intelligence in the fight against terrorism.

It will be up to the courts, the federal courts in particular, to continue assessing how the relaxed procedures in the intelligence war on terrorism are striking the balance between privacy and civil liberties on the one hand and security on the other. What is hinted at in our survey and cases is much more explicit when talking with federal homeland-security intelligence officials. They believe that they are without much guidance in deciding, especially what they should do with information they collect that happens to be about Americans. Can they keep it in databases? For how long and on what basis? It will be the responsibility of the courts to enforce guidelines when constitutional or statutory standards apply and to put pressure on the executive branch to issue clear guidelines when such standards do not apply.

Finally, *coproduction must be a two-way street.* Local authorities, especially the private sector, will not sustain the process, given their reasons for reticence, if the information they supply does not go anywhere and if they do not see value in the information they receive. Ultimately, expectations are critical. While the larger firms know the federal government and many of their security managers come from careers in law enforcement and intelligence, some of the smaller local authorities still harbor grand hopes that the federal agencies can produce information magic from behind the green door of classification – if only they will open it.

8

Covert Action: Forward to the Past?

Intelligence, like all professions, has its own vocabulary. For most of us, *covert* and *clandestine* are synonyms meaning "secret." Not so for intelligence. There, clandestine does, indeed, mean secret. CIA spymasters are the clandestine service; their relationship to the spies they recruit is meant to remain secret. (A former father-in-law of mine, a CIA veteran, relished pronouncing *clandestine* as "candle-stine," perhaps in ironic reference to what was not.) By contrast, for intelligence operations, *covert* means "unacknowledged" or "deniable"; it is defined in the law as "intended that the role of the United States Government will not be apparent or acknowledged publicly."[1]

My introduction to covert action was a fascinating one, moving as a not-yet-minted, then freshly minted Ph.D. to Washington for the first time to work for the original Senate Select Committee on Intelligence – often called the "Church Committee" after its chair, Senator Frank Church (D-ID).[2] The investigations, hard on the heels of Watergate and allegations of covert U.S. intervention in Chile, were the nation's first-ever look behind the green curtain of intelligence. I had written about presidential decision making and so expected to work on the role of intelligence analysis in those decisions.

In fact, I spent virtually all of my time on covert action – and much of that on Chile.[3] That stint in Washington was exhilarating and frustrating, and it produced one of few "aha" moments I have had researching in deeply classified documents. Press accounts had attributed to Henry Kissinger, then the national security advisor, the statement: "I don't see why the United States should stand by and watch Chile go communist merely due to the stupidity of the Chilean people." The line rang true enough, but I did not expect to and had not seen a source. Then, we received a tranche of highly classified documents, which included minutes from the "40 Committee," the administration's interagency committee for reviewing covert actions.[4]

Kissinger, a scholar, had changed the committee's recordkeeping from the terse notations of previous administrations – "CIA project 123 is approved," with no mention of operation or country – to those of a recording secretary. So there it was at the end of the notes on one meeting: "The chairman [that is, Kissinger] closed the meeting by observing that he didn't see why...."

When I reflected some years later on covert action at book length, what struck me was how much the targets of U.S. covert action had changed from the 1940s to the 1990s and beyond.[5] Many of the CIA's early postwar targets, such as Iran's Mossadeq and Guatemala's Arbenz, sought and almost pleaded not to be regarded as enemies of the United States. However, for later targets, such as Nicaragua's Sandinistas and Iran's Khomeini – not to mention Al Qaeda's bin Laden – the United States was more useful as an enemy than a friend. Cuba's Castro bridged the two periods, with America-as-foe becoming the best thing he had going for him.

By the end of the 1990s, a second theme was also apparent: major American "secret" operations, from Nicaragua to Angola to Cambodia to Afghanistan, were not very secret and they were not even covert. They had become "overt" covert action, in that actions became public not just when their results were known but also while they were in progress. Support for the Nicaraguan rebels, or Contras – the most controversial example – was openly debated and openly funded. Neither opponents nor supporters had reason to keep it secret; for its part, the Reagan administration regarded "covert" action as good policy and good domestic politics – a key element of the Reagan Doctrine, which was intended to challenge Marxist–Leninist states around the world. Indeed, when the Reagan administration decided to sell arms to Iran and keep the operation secret, it turned inward, to the White House staff.[6] In embroidering that operation to divert money for the Contras, White House aides apparently kept the president ignorant in order to protect him – providing him with "plausible denial" of the type we were concerned about on the Church Committee and that the CIA had long since abandoned.

Now, the United States has come full circle. Not only are most covert actions not very secret, they are mostly paramilitary actions in support of broader, primarily military counterterrorism operations in an age of terror. The campaign against terrorism has thrown CIA covert operators and Pentagon Special Operations Forces together in new ways. The successes of that cooperation in Afghanistan and Iraq have been impressive. Because the operations are not very secret and because they are part of the broader campaign against a fearsome foe – transnational terrorism – the questions of how to square them with America's values are less evident. Yet, the process is making for less clarity about who does what and why. More important, it is complicating who *authorizes* lethal force and on what basis.

This chapter first reviews the early history that set the pattern for U.S. covert action in the half-century after World War II and makes inquiries into how the success or failure of covert actions should be judged. The chapter then looks at the circumstances, both at home and abroad, that changed covert action to "overt covert," and it argues for a bias toward acting openly, not covertly. If covert action is to be employed, what lessons emerge from the history? The chapter then asks how those lessons apply in current circumstances, and it concludes with a coda on how the oversight of intelligence by Congress, especially covert action, has functioned.

EARLY "SUCCESSES" SET THE PATTERN

Spying may be the world's second oldest profession, but for the United States it was only the Cold War – coming on the heels of America's wartime experience with secret operations conducted by the Office of Strategic Services – that led to the creation of an intelligence service in peacetime and to covert operations. Spying – HUMINT in the jargon of the trade – and covert action are superficially similar but, in fact, quite different, beyond the fact that the first is meant to be clandestine and the second merely covert. Both involve secret relationships between U.S. intelligence officers and foreigners. However, the point of spying is information, the U.S. officer is relatively passive, and the process is designed to protect the foreign spy's link to the United States. For covert action, by contrast, the purpose is to do something, the U.S. officer is active, and the process inherently risks being blown – the more ambitious the action, the riskier it is.

Wartime success and postwar threat: these comprised the backdrop for the creation of the CIA. In a few years, America plunged from the euphoria of victory in World War II to the confrontation with a looming Soviet threat, when Western Europe seemed to teeter in the balance. The first line of American response to the onset of the Cold War was overt: the surge of assistance to Europe through the Truman Doctrine and the Marshall Plan. However, the second line of response was renewed interest in what was then called covert *psychological warfare* – what we could now call *propaganda* – as a way to respond to the Soviet Union by means that were less than war but more than nothing.

In this atmosphere, the NSC in June 1948 approved NSC 1012, a plan that had originated with George Kennan, then-director of the State Department's Policy Planning Staff and the author of the famous "X" article outlining the policy of containment of the Soviet Union. NSC 1012 was the turning point for covert action, expanding it from propaganda to direct intervention. In the words of the document, covert action consisted of

... propaganda, economic warfare; preventive direct action, including sabotage, anti-sabotage, demolition and evacuation measures; subversion against hostile states, including assistance to underground resistance movements, guerrillas and refugee liberation groups, and support of indigenous anticommunist elements.[7]

NSC 1012 also codified the notion of plausible denial: operations were to be "so planned and executed that any U.S. Government responsibility for them is not evident to unauthorized persons and that if uncovered the U.S. Government can plausibly disclaim any responsibility for them."

The fledgling CIA's first success came that same year when its covert support to the Italian Christian Democrats helped them beat back an electoral challenge from the Italian Communist Party. By 1950, the United States had succeeded in the covert struggle in Western Europe and in Eastern Europe, its covert operations wound down to propaganda and intelligence-gathering. The center of the battle against communism, as official Washington saw the world, moved away from Europe to small, weak countries. Europe had put the CIA into the business of covert political action, but it was Asia that got the agency into secret paramilitary operations in the Korean War – a pattern repeated a decade later in another Asian war, Vietnam.

The incoming Eisenhower administration called for a more active response to the Soviet threat than the passive containment of the Truman administration. CIA operators soon registered two successes that set the pattern for the next two decades. On August 21, 1953, after a week of turmoil in the streets of Tehran, the Iranian prime minister, Mohammed Mossadeq – who had nationalized that country's oil industry – surrendered. Three days later, the Shah, who had fled Iran the previous week with his queen, returned to the capital. At his palace a few days later, he offered a toast to Kermit "Kim" Roosevelt, the chief of the CIA's Near East and Africa Division and the man who had improvised Mossadeq's downfall: "I owe my throne to God, my people, my army – and you!"[8]

The next year, on June 16, 1954, Guatemalan Colonel Carlos Castillo Armas crossed the border into his country from Honduras with a few hundred men trained and armed by the CIA. Pilots under CIA contract flew air cover. The president of Guatemala, Jacobo Arbenz Guzman, was deserted by his air force and his army, which refused his order to arm workers and peasants. The American ambassador hastily arranged a transfer of power to the chief of the armed forces. (In a moment of tragicomedy, that man immediately pledged that he would continue the struggle against Castillo Armas, America's designated successor to Arbenz. Only after complicated negotiations led by the ambassador did Castillo Armas emerge as president.[9])

The Iran and Guatemala operations – code-named TPAJAX and PBSUCCESS, respectively – coming within a few years of the CIA's success in Western Europe, made the agency's reputation and set the pattern for covert action in the years ahead. Small, cheap, fast, and tolerably secret, the operations encouraged Washington to think that other covert actions could be likewise. When the next administration decided to confront revolution in Cuba, its covert response was the same as in Guatemala; so were the CIA officers who carried it out.

The blush of short-term success amid the Cold War obscured several cautions. In the early 1950s, both Iran and Guatemala were eminently vulnerable to manipulation by an outside power, particularly the United States. In both, contending political forces were in close balance. Those balances might have tipped against Mossadeq and Arbenz even had the CIA not intervened. As a result, it appeared that relatively small operations were enough to tip the balance. Yet, in both cases, those limited interventions might have failed. In fact, Roosevelt's first plot did fail; CIA Director Allen Dulles was ready to roll up the operation and bring the troops home. The CIA officers who ran PBSUCCESS were under no illusions: if their deceptions failed and Arbenz was able to get his military into combat, the invaders would be overwhelmed.

Thus, success was purchased at the price of enlarging the intervention. American purposes did not change but the operational requirements of achieving them did. Once the United States was committed, in secret and in a small way, its stakes increased, and the CIA took the next step. The effort to intimidate Arbenz became a paramilitary campaign, if a small one. In the process, plausible deniability became increasingly tenuous.

Six years later at the Bay of Pigs, deniability evaporated entirely. "How could I have been so stupid, to let them go ahead?"[10] The words were John Kennedy's. When the CIA-trained invasion force of Cuban exiles hit the beach in the early dawn hours of April 17, 1961, everything went wrong: the lives of brave Cubans were spent, the United States was seen to be intervening, and the intervention failed. Once the plan had changed (without anyone outside of the CIA noticing it) from a guerrilla operation into a full-fledged amphibious invasion, the chance of keeping it tolerably secret diminished to the vanishing point.

JUDGING SUCCESS

Evaluating covert action in retrospect is speculative, for it is bedeviled by the imponderable of what might have been; history permits no reruns. Failures such as the Bay of Pigs are apparent, but successes are more difficult to judge. Consider the CIA intervention in the Angolan civil war of 1975. On the surface, it was a failure: the Cuban- and Soviet-supported faction, the Popular Movement for the Liberation of Angola (MPLA), was installed while the American role in trying to prevent that outcome was being exposed. If, however, the initial purpose was more limited – for instance, to raise the price of victory for the MPLA and its Soviet and Cuban backers – then Angola might be counted a short-term success. Yet, American officials did not convey the impression that their aims actually were so limited, either at the time or later.

When covert actions succeeded in their short-term purposes, it may be that the action, although marginal, was just the bit of "support for our friends" that tipped the balance in the internal politics of a foreign country. Conversely, it may be that the American support was entirely superfluous, that the same successful outcome would have ensued without U.S. involvement. If this is true, then the only accomplishment of the covert action was to implicate the United States and tarnish the success by labeling it "made in America" when its existence became known.

A case in point was covert American support to opposition political parties and media in Chile during the presidential tenure (1970–73) of Salvador Allende, a self-proclaimed Marxist. There is no question that those parties and media *were* under pressure from the Allende government.[11] The opposition forces survived to fight another day, but there is no telling whether CIA support for them was decisive or irrelevant.

What *is* clear is the signal conveyed to history by the revelations of American covert action. In retrospect, most reasonably objective observers conclude that Salvador Allende's experiment in Chile would have failed on its own terms.[12] Yet, history's lesson is not that Allende fell of his own accord; history's lesson is that the United States overthrew him in 1973. That is the public perception even though this lesson is untrue in the narrow sense: Washington did not engineer his coup, nor did the CIA or the American military participate in it. The very fact of American covert action meant that, at a minimum, "it is fair to say that the United States cannot escape some responsibility for [Allende's] downfall."[13]

By the same token, in 1975, when South Africa intervened to back the U.S.–supported Angolan factions, the National Front for the Liberation of Angola (FNLA) and the National Union for the Total Independence of Angola (UNITA), a covert action originally intended to counter the Soviet Union and Cuba then signaled something else: an alliance with the apartheid regime in Pretoria. When in December 1975, the American Congress reacted by cutting off the CIA operation, the cutoff only ratified what was seen as the inevitable result – defeat – in the eyes of both Washington policy makers and the rest of the world.

In a longer perspective, neither the Iran nor Guatemala operations can fairly be given too much credit – or too much blame – for what happened afterward in those countries. On the one hand, TPAJAX restored the Shah of Iran to his throne where he remained for nearly a quarter-century, a pro-Western bastion in a turbulent region. Twenty-five years of relative stability is no mean feat in international affairs. On the other hand, American covert action identified the Shah's Iran more closely with the United States than was good for either the Shah or the United States.

In any case, however, the aspects of American policy that loomed so large in the Shah's downfall in 1979 were overt, not covert. They comprised his image as an American client, the waste and corruption associated with his massive U.S. arms purchases, and his own dependence on the United States. Those factors owed much more to American policy during the 1970s than to the event of 1953.

A similar conclusion also applies to Guatemala in 1953. If, in retrospect, the "success" of PBSUCCESS also looks more ambiguous than it seemed at the time, most of the blame or credit lies with American foreign policy, not with covert action. PBSUCCESS did not make it inevitable that Washington would then forget about Guatemala; it only made it possible. David Phillips, a CIA officer who worked on PBSUCCESS, the Bay of Pigs, and Chile, lamented that "Castillo Armas was a bad president, tolerating corruption throughout his government and kowtowing to the United Fruit Company more than his own people." However, he argued that the United States:

... could have prevented this with the vigorous exercise of diplomatic pressure ... to assure that he pursued social reform for the many rather than venal satisfaction for a few. Instead, Washington breathed a collective sigh of relief and turned to other international problems.[14]

Several covert operations of the 1950s remained secret for a long time: the CIA's assistance to Tibetans resisting the domination of their land by the People's Republic of China – regarded in intelligence lore as a successful holding action – is still a little-discussed operation, especially because it is an embarrassment now that Sino–American relations have thawed. The effort to unseat President Sukarno of Indonesia, who had earned Washington's opposition for his espousal of nonalignment, ranged from covert political action to a paramilitary operation; it is not much better known than the Tibetan operation.[15]

Even in the 1960s, several brief and limited interventions – small in terms of numbers of people involved although not in terms of purpose – remained secret for some time. The so-called Track II – a secret effort to touch off a military coup in 1970 to prevent Allende from being seated as Chile's president, an operation run without the knowledge of the state or defense departments – was not revealed until five years after it happened. The sad plots in the early 1960s to assassinate Fidel Castro stayed buried for ten years.[16]

CHANGING TARGETS, CHANGING TIMES

Yet, times changed. Major covert actions were likely to become public knowledge – sooner rather than later, perhaps before the operation was over. In 1986, the arms sales to Iran became public even though the leak did not initially come from Washington but rather from an article published in Beirut and in Arabic. Americans became more skeptical of their government, of its information and its capacity – a skepticism that was a legacy of the long history beginning with the label "Watergate." By 1986, when Ronald Reagan, the most popular president in a long time, first denied that his administration had traded arms sales to Iran for the release of American hostages in Lebanon, most Americans did not believe him – just as most Americans in 2006 did not believe President George W. Bush when he talked about success in Iraq.

This skepticism was reinforced by the prominence of investigative journalism; every cub reporter aspired to be Woodward or Bernstein of Watergate fame. The media had more people asking hard questions, even of secret operations, and probing for leaks; fewer are prepared to take the government at its word. If reporters were more likely to seek information on "secret" operations, so were they more likely to find it. "Leaking," always present, had become routine in Washington; it was almost acceptable. Officials sometimes leaked information merely for the gratification of being pandered to by journalists more famous than themselves. More often, they leaked information to rally opposition to or, more rarely, support for a given policy. Administration after administration, regardless of its political persuasion, declares war on leakers. Those wars always fail and they fail for a simple reason: the ship of state is like no other, for it leaks from the top.

Officials at the top of government are precisely those who know of covert actions and thus are most likely to take their opposition to particular programs into the open. This is true of the executive branch and even more so of Congress, where this tendency is reinforced by institutional pride and, often, by the partisan politics of divided government. On the whole, the intelligence committees of the House and Senate have kept secrets at least as well as the executive branch. Yet, their role in overseeing covert action means that those who might oppose a particular project are more likely to know of it. The process creates a set of frustrated opponents who, on occasion, will go public with their frustration.

Not every exposé, however, has created a controversy. Even now, not every covert action is controversial. For instance, of the forty or so covert actions underway in the mid-1980s, at least half were the subject of some press account.[17] Yet, only several were controversial enough that the original leaks developed into continuing stories. Most of the other leaks were open secrets, more unacknowledged than unknown, because most members of Congress thought they made sense, as did most Americans who knew or thought about them – and, undoubtedly, most of the journalists who reported them.

Before September 11, 2001, the biggest open secret, or "overt covert" operation, was U.S. aid to those in Afghanistan who were resisting Soviet occupation of their country. Former CIA Director William Colby characterized the reaction to revelations of American assistance to the resistance in Afghanistan as follows: "Afghanistan was a two-column headline in *The Washington Post* for one day, then almost nothing."[18] Americans, in and out of Congress, broadly supported the cause of the rebels, or *mujahideen* (often called freedom fighters at the time, which became a cruel irony on September 11), and the aid was a way to increase the cost of the Soviet occupation. American assistance, reportedly begun in a small way in the last year of the Carter administration, escalated sharply to reach as much as $500 million a year by the late 1980s.[19]

The secret was an open one; the American role was not so much covert as – by tacit agreement – unacknowledged. The reason for circumspection was the delicate position of the Pakistani government, which was the conduit for the American supplies to the rebels. Pakistan was prepared to support the rebels but was unwilling to be too visible in doing so lest it antagonize its powerful neighbor, the Soviet Union. In those circumstances, resorting to the CIA rather than the American military was more a matter of being discreet than of keeping the whole affair secret. The fact that for its own reasons, Pakistan's Inter-Service Intelligence (ISI) favored the radical *mujahideen* was instrumental in the takeover of Afghanistan by the Taliban.

Certainly, there will be cycles in American attitudes, as there have been before. In the early 1980s, most Americans evidently shared their president's concern with the Soviet threat, and their congressional representatives went along with huge increases in defense spending – and in covert action. Ronald Reagan was able to rebuild considerable authority and discretion in the American presidency, the Iran–Contra debacle notwithstanding. After September 11, George W. Bush had at least as much of both support and authority in taking on the war against terrorism. Most Americans enthusiastically supported the war in Afghanistan, and they were prepared, initially at least, to support the Iraq war as a front in the longer fight against terrorism.

Still, if the changes in American domestic politics since the mid-1970s have made it more difficult for the United States to achieve its purposes *secretly*, other changes make it more difficult now than in the 1950s for the United States to intervene successfully at all, covertly or openly. Despite the controversy and mystique that surrounded covert action, and to some extent still do, history suggests that there is no magic to it. It means providing foreigners, secretly, with money, weapons, or training as tokens of American support.

With the passage of time, however, a little money here, a few weapons there became less likely to achieve grand foreign-policy purposes. Castro was a target of a different order than Arbenz. To think in 1975 that a few million dollars might alter the fate of Angola was a faint hope at best and an illusion at worst, especially given that the CIA recognized that the Soviet Union and other external actors might counter American support with more assistance of their own. Even the CIA officials who planned the Bay of Pigs knew that to delay the invasion until Cuba had received deliveries of advanced Soviet fighter planes would be to condemn the plan to certain failure.

Also, there is the contrast between two Central American cases three decades apart: Guatemala and Nicaragua. Castillo Armas's liberators numbered no more than several hundred. Their "invasion" was more conjured than real. Yet, they had control of the air, in large part because Arbenz, unsure of the loyalty of his air force, was unwilling to risk putting his own pilots in the air. *Sulfatos* – Spanish for "laxatives," the name Guatemalans gave to the invaders' bombs – plus rumors exaggerating the size of the invasion were enough to induce Arbenz to capitulate. In the case of Nicaragua, the Contras numbered about ten thousand by the mid-1980s, yet not even the most ardent advocates of American assistance to them argued that they were about to induce the Sandinistas to "say uncle," much less that they posed a threat sufficient to overthrow the regime by sheer force of arms.

The makers of revolutions learned their own lessons from history, including the history of American covert action. They determined not to repeat the mistakes of Arbenz and Mossadeq. They sought to assure themselves of the loyalty of the army or to build revolutionary cadres of their own. Before the fall of communism, they also learned that if the United States threatened them, there were other sources of support to which they could turn – and, unlike Arbenz or Mossadeq, they turned to those sources sooner rather than later.

Moreover, they learned that the United States could be useful as an enemy. Arbenz and Mossadeq and even Allende sought Washington's approval or, at least, its acquiescence. By contrast, if the United States was of use to Castro, the Sandinistas, and the Ayatollah Ruhollah Khomeini, it was primarily as a foreign demon against which their revolutions could rally – even though the Sandinistas were prepared to accept American aid as long as it was forthcoming, and the revolutionary Iranians were not above seeking American spare parts for their military. In 1979, Iranians took Americans hostage and released them only when they ceased to be useful counters in the bargaining within the revolution. Suffice it to say that no one learned the value of America-as-enemy better than Osama bin Laden.

VALUES AND INSTRUMENTS

In all likelihood, the record shows, covert operations *will* become known, and America *will* be judged for having undertaken them. Thus, the practical lessons lead into moral issues, which are muted now by the fearsomeness of the terrorist threat. They are hardly unique to covert intervention, although they are powerfully present there, and they risked – and may still risk – being obscured in policy making by the presumption that covert actions will remain secret. Overt interventions – such as the American invasion of Panama in 1989, Afghanistan in 2001, and Iraq in 2003 – or military attacks – such as the bombing of Libya in 1986 or Sudan and Afghanistan in 1998 – raise similar moral and instrumental concerns. These concerns are not absolute; they must be considered against the gravity of the threat and the adequacy of other available responses.

In December 1976, when I was in Washington working with several old friends who were making arrangements for the transition between the Ford NSC and the Carter NSC, we had decided to retain the basic structure of the Ford administration's operation, with its network of subcabinet committees for particular purposes. Yet, of course, as a new administration, it was necessary to change the names of those committees, and so we joked about names. The 40 Committee, the Ford administration's group for discussing covert action, would become the "If They Can Do It, So Can We" Committee.

Yet, the attitude of "if they can do it, so can we" did not seem, even then, an unacceptable rationale on either moral or instrumental grounds. What the Soviet Union or other nations did could not settle the issue, neither can how terrorists act. We consider ourselves different from them and imagine that the difference is not only basic to what we are as a people, but also is a source of American influence in the world, part of this country's moral armor.

We also believe that the example of democracy is powerful, one toward which people all over the world will gravitate if given the chance. Believing that, we must also believe that the example is a powerful part of our external behavior, not only our internal arrangements. If people choose democracy when given the chance, then democracy is demeaned, perhaps doomed to fail, if it is imposed from the outside. There is something incongruous about helping to overthrow governments – especially those that come to power through elections that we would define as tolerably fair (e.g., Chile in 1970) – in the name of democracy.

In this view, some of the "successes" of covert action seem ambiguous or transient in retrospect, accomplished at significant cost to what we hold dear as a people and to America's image in the world.

However, the world is a nasty, complicated place and the war against terrorism has driven home that lesson. In that regard, Americans' historical ambivalence between the high moral view and the belief that international politics is a dirty business is understandable.

Terrorism aside, nations affect one another's politics in so many ways that any too-tidy definition of *intervention* is suspect. In all the examples cited, covert action formed only part of American policy. The United States decided whether to grant economic aid to Cuba or Chile or Angola and whether to release Iranian assets held in the United States. Most of those decisions were based on explicitly political criteria. Even if similar decisions toward other countries are not so explicitly political, the decisions in any case have political effects on the country in question; of that fact, foreign political leaders have no doubt.

The same is true of actions by private American actors. U.S.–based businesses either invest or not in a country, and that decision has not only an economic effect but also a political effect – which is the case even if the decision is not political in any narrow sense of the term. Most of the businesses or banks that chose not to invest in Chile under Allende probably did not make that choice for any specific political reason, despite Washington's pressure. Rather, it was a business decision based on the climate in Chile. They saw that judgment as an economic judgment, although political instability surely was a factor in their decision.

In this context, if a unilateral self-denying ordinance against all intervention – open or covert – seemed too restrictive when the Soviet threat existed, it surely does now in an age of terror. Some threats to American national security require responses; some American friends deserve support. What is imperative is to remember the long-term costs of intervention for a government that is not notable for attending to long-term considerations.

Given that "covert" action is not likely to remain secret, why not act openly? In the case of aid to the FNLA and the UNITA in Angola, covert rather than overt aid spared the first identification with the United States for only a few months. As for aid to the Contras in Nicaragua, the "covert" form made not one whit of difference because the operation quickly became known, and the same was true of aid to the *mujahideen* in Afghanistan. Neither is it obvious that in most of these cases, the recipients of American largesse objected to the source of the money being known. There is also the risk that covertness creates a self-fulfilling prophecy: if the United States aids its friends only secretly, then any link to the United States may seem sinister, portending more than is the fact.

The scope for doing openly what might earlier have been done covertly has increased dramatically since the 1970s. Sovereignty has become less absolute and international law has come to recognize people, not just nation-states. In that sense, international law has moved in a very "American" direction, even if Americans do not always like the results (e.g., the creation of the International Criminal Court). However, international practice, if not law, recognizes that some behavior by national leaders justifies external intervention, even with force of arms.

The American radio stations broadcasting into Eastern Europe and the Soviet Union from Munich – Radio Free Europe and Radio Liberty – were in form private organizations; advertisements exhorted Americans to contribute to them. In fact, they were created and financed covertly by the CIA as propaganda vehicles. When that support was disclosed in 1967, the radio stations nevertheless continued to operate; they became supervised by a board and supported openly by appropriations from the U.S. Congress.

In the 1980s, the Reagan administration created the National Endowment for Democracy (NED), on the model of the (then-West) German party foundations, such as the Konrad Adenauer Stiftung. They are instruments of the major parties but are supported openly by government money. They have openly assisted kindred parties and labor movements around the world. The endowment, whose core budget reached $40 million in 2003, channels funds to institutes of the two American political parties as well as an AFL–CIO group and a business group, which then make grants in support of democratic institutions in a number of countries around the world.[20]

So far, the record of the NED is mixed but hopeful. Its grants, and those of its four constituent institutes, began by being cautious and close to government policy. It remains an open question, given American politics, whether public funding is compatible with creative and, thus, controversial acts by private groups. The original NED budget was only an eighth of that of the German-party foundations. Over time, Congress has placed various restrictions on the endowment – for instance, in 1985, Congress halved the endowment budget and denied any funding to the Republican and Democratic institutes, although that prohibition was relaxed the next year. It may still be easier for the CIA to get money from Congress secretly than for another institution to get it openly – even if the purposes of the two are broadly similar. Funding for the CIA remains wrapped in the cloak of national security; therefore, members of Congress may be prepared to fund particular activities but prefer not to be seen voting for them openly.

Still, the endowment organizations have become more venturesome as the international – and domestic – climate has changed. More important, the endowment now works with scores of kindred organizations, from both other governments and the private sector. To illustrate the change, in the mid-1980s, the NED provided more than $400,000, over two years, to the American Friends of Afghanistan to develop educational and cultural facilities inside those portions of the country controlled by the resistance groups – activity that might in other times have been called the "civic action" component of a paramilitary covert operation.

In another example, before Slobodan Milosevic fell from power in Serbia in 2000, the NED and other U.S. government sources openly funded opposition parties and groups to the tune of $25 million.[21] Indeed, the entire operation was almost a carbon copy, done overtly, of what the United States had earlier done covertly (e.g., in Chile). In the case of Serbia, the main difference other than overtness was that U.S. government agencies had lots of company from other countries and private NGOs. In other respects, the postmortem could have been written by a CIA operative about Chile – for instance: "Foreign assistance should focus not only on political parties but should continue to support a broad range of nongovernmental organizations, labor unions, think tanks, and media."

Acting openly, however, is not always easy or a complete substitute for covert action. It requires an explicitness about influencing the politics of a foreign country that is uncomfortable for Americans and, hence, likely to be controversial. Moreover, governments that feel threatened by that open assistance can act to prevent it more easily than if it were covert. Yet, even that ability by governments is diminishing; national borders *are* more porous. Milosevic's Serbia tried to limit the assistance to opposition organizations. It had some success in keeping out foreign advisors but much less success stopping money flows and thus ended, somewhat paradoxically, with the worst of outcomes from its perspective: the antigovernment effort was well funded but more difficult to label with the epithet "foreign influence" than if scores of foreign advisors had been present. To quote the postmortem again: "While foreign assistance helped to build and sustain the broad anti-Milosevic coalition, indigenous organizations and action were mainly responsible for driving events."

A bias toward openness has it limitations, but surely if it is the right long-term direction for American policy, openness would reflect the reality that as the century begins, national boundaries are more and more permeable. Given this reality, moreover, those groups that the United States wants to support may not be so chary of accepting help, even – perhaps especially – if it is open. The United States would say to them, "We are prepared to support you but only openly. We think that is better for you. In any case, we know it is better for us."

CHOOSING THE COVERT OPTION: LESSONS FROM HISTORY

The history of covert action before September 11 suggests that in deciding whether to choose the covert option, prudent policy makers should ask themselves a careful series of "what if?" questions. That injunction applies to all policies, foreign and domestic. However, it applies with special force to covert action because of the presumption of secrecy, at least initially.

The most obvious "what if?" is "What happens if – or more likely, when – it becomes public? What if it becomes public in midstream?" This is *"The New York Times* test." Large covert actions will not remain secret – a reminder that is easy to state but difficult to embody in the making of policy when the pressures all go in the direction of wishful thinking by the policy tribe described in Chapter 7. Witness the reflections on the Bay of Pigs by Richard Bissell, then-head of the CIA's clandestine service:

… the argument was [not] made that this is now a very public business, and we'd better treat it as such, and either cancel it if we can't stand the publicity, or else do some of the things that will increase the chances of success if we are going to go forward with it.[22]

If the Iran operation of 1985–86 had remained secret for several years after all the hostages had been released, that success might have outweighed the costs of being perceived to have traded arms for hostages when the operations became public. Perhaps, but we cannot know for certain. It did not take, however, a sophisticated analysis to show that a covert policy targeted on some Iranians was vulnerable to being publicized by opposing Iranian factions if and when it suited their political purposes. It was equally likely that when the cover was blown, trading arms for hostages with a nation that the United States had denounced as terrorist would be deemed unacceptable by America's allies, much of the rest of the world, and – most important – the American people.

Of course, whether a particular covert operation can bear the test of disclosure is apparent in retrospect but often far from obvious before the fact. Prudence suggests that presidents pay careful attention to such warning signals as the review process throws out – the views of Cabinet officers, people in the White House who attend to the president's interests, and congressional overseers who are surrogates for public reaction.

One warning signal, however, is evident in advance: Does the intervention contradict overt American policy? If it does, as with arms sales to Iran, it is especially improbable that the operation will withstand the test of disclosure. The arms sales were exactly the opposite of the administration's public policies, which had coerced America's allies not to sell arms to Iran, had sought an end to the Iran–Iraq war with neither a victor nor a vanquished, and had pledged not to bargain with terrorists over hostages, much less to sell arms to them.

A second "what if?" is "What if the first intervention does not succeed? What then?" If covert action is to remain covert, most of the time it will have to be small. Small operations often begin with grand purposes, objectives incommensurate with the instrument. When the goals could not be achieved, leaders were tempted to take the next step and the next. This happened in the Bay of Pigs and Angola and Iran in the mid-1980s. Sometimes a limited objective can be achieved, but its achievement makes it appealing to hope for more; witness Angola and perhaps Nicaragua, where the United States seemed to achieve its initial aim of cutting weapons supplies from Nicaragua to the antigovernment rebels in El Salvador. Answering this "what if?"

suggests, at a minimum, careful attention to the CIA's covert operators themselves for signs of skepticism about whether operations as initially conceived can achieve their purposes. Such signs were there between the lines of Track II and Angola and Nicaragua. Some risks are worth running, but few are worth running in ignorance.

A third set of "what if?" questions includes "What signal will be received, by whom, and with what result?" – judgments that are also easier with the benefit of hindsight because they involve calculations of threat and American interests. Intelligence assessments, by the CIA or the State Department, provide one set of indicators. In 1985–86, for example, American intelligence on Iran was weak, but what there was offered precious little ground for believing that there were "moderates" who might be detached from their revolutionary colleagues. Later U.S. intelligence cast doubt on the imminence of a Soviet threat to Iran, an original premise of the operation. These were cautions that the intended signals might go awry.

The nature of those who are to receive secret American assistance can provide another warning signal. Because their relationship to the United States is meant to be clandestine, the CIA is often in a weak position to compel the recipients to act to suit American purposes. Yet, the United States inevitably will become associated with "their" actions, like it or not, if and when the fact of support becomes known. Aid to the Contras was dogged by its origins in Somoza's hated National Guard and by continuing charges of human-rights violations. Similarly, support for resistance forces in Afghanistan could have been justified as a way to put strategic pressure on Soviet occupation of that country. However, given the character of the resistance forces, it was hardly a way to bring "democracy" to Afghanistan – far from it.

The regional context, particularly the attitude of American friends in the region, is another source of guidance. In the case of Afghanistan, American assistance to the resistance was supported – although with varying degrees of publicity – by nations ranging from Pakistan to Egypt to Saudi Arabia to China. In Central America, this indicator was more ambiguous because most of the nations of the region publicly expressed qualms about the aid to the Contras while privately hoping the Sandinistas could be made to go away.

The second round of covert action in Angola raised these questions of signals given versus those intended, questions for which the 1975 episode provided guidance. In early 1986, the CIA was authorized to provide $15 million in weaponry to Jonas Savimbi's UNITA. For the Reagan administration, the intended signal was anticommunism. For the administration, there was nothing incompatible about supporting anticommunism in Angola and anti-apartheid in South Africa. Alas, the reality of South Africa frustrated that conception in the mind of Washington policy makers. Whatever his attractions, Savimbi had one flaw, a fatal one: he was almost completely dependent on South Africa, his army almost a unit of South Africa's. To support him was to signal to Africans that the United States was throwing its lot in with South Africa in 1986 as in 1975.

These rules of thumb amount to establishing a presumption against covert action. The guidance is mostly negative, a series of cautions. It is unwelcome to officials who are looking for something to do rather than something to avoid – a trait that runs deep in the American character and is reinforced by the circumstances in which covert action becomes an option. Yet, given how both America and the world have changed during the postwar period, the circumstances in which major covert action makes sense as policy are sharply limited.

Guidelines akin to these were articulated in the 1970s by Cyrus Vance, later secretary of state. For Vance, the criterion for covert action in the National Security Act of 1947 – "affecting the national security" – was too loose. Instead, he recommended covert intervention only as an exceptional measure, when it was "absolutely essential to the national security" and when no other means would do.[23] Decisions would still be matters of judgment under this more restrictive guide, but no one has improved on the Vance standard.

COVERT ACTION SINCE SEPTEMBER 11

How has covert action changed since September 11? How do those changes bear on the lessons from earlier operations? Most striking, September 11 dramatically underscored another theme from the review of earlier covert actions – the problem of control. The very fact that the interventions are meant to be covert gives rise to special problems of control. The link between U.S. intentions and the actions of those foreigners is tenuous at best. They are acting; the United States is only helping. "Their" purposes may not be "ours." They have every incentive to hear from their CIA liaisons what they want to hear or construe it to their own purposes. In the details of earlier operations, this meant that covertly supported groups sometimes engaged in a little unsanctioned drug-dealing or killing along the way or tried to overturn regimes when the United States thought it was only keeping opposition forces alive.

In supporting the anti-Soviet *mujahideen* in Afghanistan, however, the problem of control was strategic. To minimize the American role, the CIA provided mostly money. Most of the contact in Afghanistan with the *mujahideen* was made by Pakistan's ISI. For its own and Pakistani reasons, ISI gave preference to the radical Islamists among the *mujahideen*, thus sowing the seeds for the takeover of Pakistan by the Taliban and the formation of Al Qaeda as a unified fighting force. "Their" purposes were manifestly not "ours." The two sets of purposes converged only as long as both wanted to expel the Soviet Union from Afghanistan.

In that sense, the problem of control merges with the more general problem of longer term, unintended side effects, a problem that afflicts not only foreign policy but also all of human action. In this case, however, as in most others, it seems unlikely that any amount of asking "what if?" could have changed the decisions in the 1970s and 1980s; the "what if?" was simply too iffy. The Soviet Union was there in Afghanistan; getting it out, somehow, was more than U.S. policy makers could hope for at the time. No story about the trail from ISI support to the Taliban to Al Qaeda to collapsing towers could have been made vivid enough, then, to change the decision.

The most that might have been accomplished would have echoed David Phillips's comment, quoted earlier in this chapter, about Guatemala a half-century earlier: support for the *mujahideen* did not have to entail that the United States, not to mention the rest of the world, would forget about Afghanistan after the Soviet Union departed in 1989. In 1994, while serving in government, I stopped in Geneva en route home from a trying visit to wartime Sarajevo. I did the rounds of the international relief and humanitarian organizations. The conversations were fascinating in many respects but depressing in this: we all agreed that times were dire, a breeding ground for extremists, in Afghanistan. Yet, what was true for government policy was also true for their donors of assistance: Afghanistan had been "solved" with the Soviet withdrawal. The world's attention had turned else-where and Afghanistan was forgotten.

A major part of the change in covert action happened before September 11, as Serbia illustrated. Given the end of the Cold War and the changing currents in international law and attitudes, the CIA seems all but out of the business of Chile-style political actions to sus-tain opposition forces or overturn regimes. In 2006, the Bush admin-istration proposed major funding in support of Iranian opposition groups; however, it did so openly, through the State Department. There may arise cases in which covert funding seems imperative – for example, it is difficult to imagine supporting North Korean opposition elements at all but surely impossible openly – but they should be rare. In promoting democracy, or even regime change, the world has trans-formed sufficiently to allow the bias toward openness to prevail, along with the bias toward company.

To that extent, covert action has become – post–September 11 – primarily paramilitary, with the CIA operating either independently or, more often, with military Special Operations Forces. Certainly, the CIA's performance as the first Americans in Afghanistan was impressive.[24] Its operations were secret only in the tactical details and thus met *The New York Times* test. The national investigation of September 11 lauded that CIA role and the Afghanistan prece-dent of joint CIA–military teams. It recommended, however, that the CIA cede responsibility for directing and executing operations to the military, with CIA officers and capabilities integrated into military-directed teams, giving both the CIA and the Special Opera-tions Forces the opportunity to do what each does best.[25] The Decem-ber 2004 intelligence-reform bill was silent on this issue, and the CIA and the military decided that both would remain in the paramilitary-operations business.

Which agency is responsible for conducting paramilitary opera-tions had been at issue well before September 11, driven by Vietnam and other conflicts. The arguments for giving the military control historically were those that the 9/11 Commission cited: the requisite capabilities are military, the task has not been a continuous priority for the CIA, and it makes no sense for the nation to build two parallel capacities. Operations by the military would give those carrying them out the status of combatants under international law, at least if they were visibly soldiers. On the other side is the concern that the military was never agile or discreet, much less covert. That concern may have diminished, but it has not disappeared, as the Special Operations Forces developed a wide variety of units and types of operations.

What is notable is the increase in military covert operations and, with it, the challenges to oversight and authorization. During his tenure as secretary of defense, a key part of Donald Rumsfeld's drive to reshape the U.S. military into a leaner, more agile force was increasing the Pentagon's Special Operations Forces under the U.S. Special Operations Command (SOCOM). By all accounts, the emphasis on special operations was only reinforced by Rumsfeld's frustration that the military had to rely on CIA operatives at the beginning of the conflict in Afghanistan in order to establish links to the Northern Alliance fighters.[26] Special Operations Forces were to be increased from about fifty thousand at the beginning of 2006 to sixty-four thousand by 2011. (The numbers are less impressive than they look because, of the fifty thousand, only about a fourth or a fifth are "trigger pullers." Of those, only about two thousand are "black" – that is, conducting covert or clandestine operations. By comparison, CIA covert operatives number seven hundred to eight hundred.)

Rumsfeld also shook up SOCOM leadership, seeking more aggressive action in the war against terrorism, and he converted it from a supporting command (which meant it could only act in support of the regional commands) to a supported command. SOCOM could now plan and execute its own operations, with the approval of the secretary and, if necessary, the president. In May 2004, Rumsfeld succeeded in making SOCOM the lead command in the war against terrorism. SOCOM became even more independent in October 2004 when Congress, for the first time, granted it the authority to spend money to pay informants, recruit foreign fighters, and buy weaponry for them. Until then, only the CIA had such authority, which had rendered SOCOM dependent on CIA funding for military operations.

The military's increased independence in covert operations was underscored by revelations in 2006 of military liaison elements (MLEs) – that is, small detachments of special operators deployed in embassies around the world, including friendly countries.[27] Their mission, reportedly, was to gather intelligence and to disrupt, capture, or kill terrorists. According the press accounts, some of the MLEs had operated, at least initially, without the knowledge of the U.S. ambassador and the country team.

Both CIA and especially SOCOM operations raise thorny questions of authorization and accountability. In 2002, CIA operatives killed five suspected Al Qaeda operatives in Yemen with a *Predator* missile fired from a UAV. One of the five killed was an American citizen.[28] This was only the first of a series of similar CIA attacks along the border between Pakistan and Afghanistan.

CIA covert operations require a presidential finding, one transferred in secret to the relevant committees of Congress.[29] Existing findings apparently provided authorization for the CIA to conduct both *Predator* attacks. The term *finding* comes from the Hughes Ryan Act of 1974, which required the president to "find" a particular operation necessary to U.S. national security. Turned into a noun, that became a "finding" delivered in secret to Congress. After the Iran–Contra Affair of the 1980s, Congress tightened the rules for covert action in several ways in the 1991 Intelligence Authorization Act.[30] Findings are to be transmitted to the relevant committees as soon as possible after they are signed and, in any event, before the operation begins. Only "extraordinary circumstances" can alter that requirement; then, the committees are to be informed "in a timely fashion" – a phrase that reflected artful dodging after a long argument over specific periods.

Moreover, after the involvement of NSC staffers in the Iran–Contra Affair, Congress extended the finding process to "any department, agency, or entity of the United States Government." Gone was the presumption that only the CIA would conduct covert actions, and Congress expressed its determination to oversee them no matter who conducted them.

By contrast, an operation similar to the *Predator* attacks conducted by the military Special Operations Forces could be set in motion simply by the chain of command from the president as commander in chief. The 1991 Act created what turned out to be a loophole by exempting from the definition of covert action "traditional military activities or routine support to such activities." The Act did not define what *traditional* meant; however, the committee report indicated that it meant what is usually called "preparing the battle space" – that is, actions before and related to anticipated hostilities involving U.S. troops or when hostilities are underway, whether or not the actions are public.[31] *Anticipate* was interpreted in the report to mean that operational planning had already been approved.

By contrast, in the war against terrorism, the Pentagon and the Bush administration interpreted "traditional military activities" to include those years ahead of any hostilities and even away from where actual fighting can be imagined in continuous military operations to develop the situation in which the United States can attack global terrorist organizations. As a result, if the Pentagon conducts an unacknowledged operation in a country where U.S. troops are not present, how can the administration prove that it is in anticipation of late involvement by regular military units and not a covert action for which a finding is required?

More to the point, who will make the administration prove it? As with other covert actions, the intelligence committees cannot ask about operations of which they are unaware. They cannot ask if the operation fails because, for congressional overseers, they are in Rumsfeld's category of "unknown unknowns." Moreover, even if Congress knows about an operation, its oversight is a three-way tug of war, one that continues to rage. The House and Senate intelligence committees are responsible for the intelligence-authorization bills, but those bills go to the armed-services committees before being passed to the full chambers. Real control of the purse strings rests with the defense subcommittees of the appropriations committees. As the negotiation over the 2004 intelligence-reform bill showed, those responsible for defense on the Hill are not eager to invite their intelligence-committee colleagues to hunt in their domain.

Unfortunately, the difference between the processes for CIA and SOCOM covert operations ultimately may be less than meets the eye. If findings in the war against terrorism have become so broad as to cover almost any CIA operation – including those direct *Predator* attacks on suspected terrorists – whether the CIA or the military conducts them seems to matter little. If this is true, however, the problem lies with the breadth of the findings – if they are so broad as to cover almost anything, then the finding process has become a sham.

COVERT ACTION AND OPEN DEMOCRACY

The United States will remain in the business of covert action and thus will continue to confront the paradox of secret operations in a democracy, even if those operations are mostly paramilitary and counterterrorist in character. However, similar issues will be even sharper at home, as the age of terror requires more intelligence-gathering on inhabitants of the United States; that paradox is at the heart of Chapter 9.

Unfortunately, the process of congressional oversight of intelligence, including covert action, so carefully crafted in the 1970s, is now regarded as something of a joke in Washington. Terrorism is frightening enough to the body politic to justify almost any action in response: the controversy in 2006 over eavesdropping on Americans by the NSA in the wake of September 11 emphasized the "almost," and the eventual outcome in 2007, in which congressional Democrats all but caved in before the administration returned the emphasis to "any." The House and Senate oversight committees have not escaped the bitter partisanship that has come to afflict Congress as a whole and, for various reasons, the stature of the committee members has declined, although with several outstanding exceptions.

The 9/11 Commission suggested that if a single DNI is to oversee the entire intelligence community – as well as preside over funding for all of it – Congress also should concentrate its oversight. Accordingly, the Commission called on Congress to renew its commitments from the 1970s, having either a single joint committee to oversee intelligence (on the model of the old Joint Atomic Energy Committee) or single committees in each house. Like the House homeland-security committee after them, the intelligence committees were never given the monopoly that was intended at their creation and, through the years, even more committees have become involved.

The 9/11 Commission also sought to revamp ideas from the 1970s agreements in several other ways. To represent other committees with interests in the field, the new oversight committee or committees would revert to the practice of having a member who also serves on each of the following committees or subcommittees: Armed Services, Judiciary, Foreign Affairs, and Defense Appropriations. To promote continuity and expertise, oversight-committee members should serve indefinitely on the new intelligence committees. The new committees should be smaller – perhaps seven or nine members in each house – so that each member feels a greater sense of responsibility and accountability for the quality of the committee's work.

Here, too, the arguments are long-standing, going back to the congressional investigations of the 1970s. However, changing times reshuffle the arguments. Surely, having real focal points is the right idea. The objective was identical in the 1970s; however, it was never fully achieved and has eroded since then as more committees have gotten into the act. In those days, the model favored by the 9/11 Commission – a single committee for both houses on the Atomic Energy Committee model – was not in favor because that committee was regarded as having become the captive of the agency it oversaw. The fear that permanent committee members might become "too cozy" with the agencies they oversaw also led Congress in the 1970s to give the intelligence committees rotating memberships.

Now, however, those memories are distant and the need for focal points is more intense. To try to achieve those focal points, the 9/11 Commission also favored the 1970s practice of appointing members from other committees with stakes in intelligence to the oversight committees. By 2004, when the Commission reported, the need for experience on the oversight committees outweighed concerns about cooption; thus, the Commission favored open-ended (not rotating) assignments to the committee or committees. However, these are just details; the real challenge for Congress is to not lag too far behind the executive branch in its own reshaping for the intelligence challenges of the twenty-first century.

The Iran–Contra Affair two decades earlier showed how difficult it can be to manage the paradox of secret operations in an open society. When President Reagan finally signed the finding in January 1986 for the Iran arms-sales operation, that finding was explicit: do not tell Congress. The congressional overseers did not find out about the operation until autumn – hardly the law's requirement of "fully and currently informed" by anyone's definition. Later, the president himself apparently was not told when the Iran and Contra operations crossed, with proceeds from the arms sales to Iran being used to fund the Contras without congressional appropriation.

In another sense, however, the system worked. In deciding to sell arms to Iran, the president pursued a line of policy opposed by both his secretaries of state and defense, about which he was afraid to inform the congressional intelligence committees and which was liable to be revealed by Iranian factions as and when it suited them. It is difficult to imagine any system providing more warning signals. When most of the government's senior foreign-policy officials are opposed, it is likely that the policy, not them, is wrong. The president thus proceeded at his own peril.

Concerning the diversion of money for the Contras, the lesson is a caution for presidents and those who advise them: do not run covert operations from the White House. Before the 1970s, it would have been unthinkable for an administration to do so; at that time, the reason was that presidents wanted to stay at arms' length from such operations, even if they could not plausibly deny them in a pinch. Now, however, if covert actions are to be undertaken, they should be done by the agency of government constructed to carry them out – the CIA, which has both the expertise and the accountability.

Moreover, the history of covert action suggests that if the president's closest advisors become the operators, then the president loses them as sources of detached judgment on the operations. The president's own circle becomes advocates, as Allen Dulles did in the Bay of Pigs, rather than protectors of the president's stakes (even if he or she does not quite realize the need for protection). So it was with President Reagan's national security advisors, Robert McFarlane and John Poindexter; once committed, they had reason to overlook the warning signals thrown out by the process. Excluding the designated congressional overseers also excluded one more "political scrub," one more source of advice about what the American people would find acceptable. Thus, the chances increased that someone like Lieutenant Colonel Oliver North would misguidedly interpret the president's interest after his own fashion.

William Miller, the staff director of the first Senate Intelligence Committee, reflected as follows on the Iran–Contra Affair: "If clear lines hadn't been drawn a decade ago, there would have been no hue and cry now."[32] Now is the time to both remember those lines and draw them again, even more so as the boundary between covert action and military special operations blurs.

9

Rebuilding the Social Contract[1]

The Church Committee stated it well three decades ago: "The United States must not adapt the tactics of its enemies. Means are as important as ends. Crisis makes it tempting to ignore the wise restraints that make men free. But each time we do so, each time the means we use are wrong, our inner strength, the strength which makes us free, is lessened."[2]

Because intelligence agencies operate in secret and because they engage in activities that are sensitive or even illegal at home, they depend on public trust. I first came to know intelligence in the 1970s through the Church Committee when that trust had been broken. The social contract had been broken then by revelations about excesses, both foreign and domestic – ranging from assassination plots against foreign leaders, to the covert CIA role in Chile and other countries, to illegal spying on Americans. Poignantly for me as a young person, the trust had been broken not only with the public at large but also with some of my then-young counterparts who worked in the intelligence agencies. More than once when I was riding the famous Blue Bird buses from CIA headquarters to downtown Washington, I had occasion to chat with young CIA officers who expressed their disappointment verging on disillusion: "They told me when I joined that the CIA didn't engage in assassinations, and now I found out that it did."

The social contract between the public and intelligence had been broken. In that contract, the American people said, in effect, "We cannot know about much of what you do, but we will give you license to act in our name, even to take illegal or unsavory actions, but we count on you to understand the limits imposed by our values." For a long time after 1976, the mere mention that I had worked for the Church Committee would elicit hisses from intelligence audiences but, over time, intelligence professionals also realized that the Committee's work was an essential part of rebuilding the social contract. At the time, our colleagues in the government, then-DCI William Colby foremost among them, understood that fact even if they did not always like it or the airing of intelligence's dirty linen that it required of them. As we sought to fashion oversight arrangements, the emphasis was on devising ways – like the finding process discussed in Chapter 8 – that would be surrogates for what the American people would accept if they could know what actions were contemplated in their name.

Now, the contract is broken again, in a combination of intelligence failures and epithets. Even if the failures, like that of September 11, ensued for understandable reasons, they were still failures. Even if the epithets, like Abu Ghraib or waterboarding, are at the margins of intelligence proper, they still cast a dark shadow over it. The outrages at Abu Ghraib were committed by military-intelligence officers, and if interrogation was but a small part of Cold War strategic intelligence, it always has been a key element of police work and will continue to be important to intelligence in an age of terror, both at home and abroad. Intelligence has been deemed incompetent and worse. The contract is broken again.

At the same time and partly in result, intelligence in democracies is becoming more the subject of political debate. The change in intelligence's targets and the consequent need to expand surveillance at home is driving that debate as it stretches democratic oversight of intelligence – as the controversies over the boundaries of SIGINT in countries from the United States to Sweden testify. For oversight, too, the Cold War's solutions may no longer suffice. After the investigations of the 1970s, the U.S. Congress passed the FISA to provide some judicial oversight of domestic surveillance for national-security – as opposed to law enforcement – purposes. A secret court reviewed applications from the Justice Department and the FBI. After September 11, however, the administration argued, it could not target named individuals with specific warrants before the fact; rather, it needed to scan wide swathes of communication, searching for connections of interest. It may be that oversight will have to move from judicial approval before the fact to some form of continuing legal or congressional review as surveillance proceeds.

The change in intelligence's targets also raises ethical issues, ones that slide into prudential questions in a democracy. These also are illuminated by some comparative perspective, suggesting how different practices and experiences are reflections of the different national ways of dealing with intelligence, which in turn reflect different political cultures with different relationships between governments and people and different ways of defining power. In Europe, for instance, Britain and France still perceive themselves as global powers and are quite different from countries like Germany and the Netherlands, which do not.

The campaign against terrorism not only is mixing military force and intelligence in new ways, it is also straining the limits of both – from the limits of preemption to the use of covert action away from the battlefield. Intelligence is expanding dramatically in both expense and breadth of activity, some of which is controversial. At the same time that intelligence is seeking and being given new powers, technology is providing new opportunities to survey large quantities of information about individuals. The irony is that intelligence will be more effective the less terrorists understand of its scope and methods – which constrains the scope of the public debate.[3]

THE EPITHETS OF INTELLIGENCE

A confluence of revelations created the epithets, putting torture and the treatment of detainees at center stage, and cast a long shadow over the effort to reshape intelligence. The events included the revelation of mistreatment of prisoners, including by military intelligence, at Abu Ghraib prison outside Baghdad; the revelations of a network of so-called black sites – covert prisons for suspected terrorists run by the CIA in Eastern Europe; the continuing debate about the prisons at Guantanamo Bay – how prisoners there were treated and how they will be dealt with; and the controversy over whether waterboarding is torture, including a leaked classified report by the CIA's IG providing evidence that interrogation techniques approved by the White House might have violated international conventions against torture.[4]

Even before September 11, there were charges that the United States engaged in "renditions" – that is, the transferring of prisoners not to the United States for trial but rather to countries that may engage in torture. After September 11, the most widely known example was the case of a Canadian citizen, Maher Arar, apprehended by U.S. officials while transiting New York for having alleged connections to Al Qaeda and deported via Jordan to Syria (his birth country), where he was imprisoned and allegedly tortured. In 2007, the Canadian (but not the American) government cleared him of any connection to terrorism, apologized, and awarded him a $10.5 million settlement.

Bush administration officials argued that the government neither advocated nor ordered the use of torture, but they also argued that members of Al Qaeda, the Taliban, and other suspected terrorist groups do not qualify as lawful "enemy combatants" and therefore do not have rights under the Geneva Conventions (i.e., the internationally accepted rules on conduct during wartime that govern the treatment of detainees). By this logic, terrorists do not enjoy legal protections because they do not follow any rules of war: they fight for no nation-state, they target innocents, they wear no insignia, and they disguise themselves as civilians. Nonetheless, the Bush administration pledged that the treatment of detainees at Guantanamo Bay was consistent with the Geneva Conventions.

For Senator John McCain (R-AZ), who was tortured during his time as a prisoner of war in Vietnam, waterboarding – defined as strapping a detainee down and then pouring water on his nose to make him believe he is drowning – was "torture, no different than holding a pistol to his head and firing a blank." McCain proposed an amendment outlawing all forms of "cruel, inhuman, or degrading treatment or punishment" for U.S.–held detainees. The bill became the Detainee Treatment Act (DTA) of 2005, attached to the defense appropriations act.[5] The amendment limited interrogation techniques to those in Army Field Manual, 34–52 Intelligence Interrogation. The effect of the amendment was attenuated by simultaneous congressional actions that blocked Guantanamo prisoners from filing new petitions of habeas corpus, although they were granted limited appeal rights to the Court of Appeals in Washington.[6] Another legislative attempt to limit the CIA (and other agencies) to the interrogation practices of the military as described in the Army Field Manual was vetoed by President Bush in early 2008.

Secret prisons established in the immediate aftermath of September 11, 2001, were used to house "high-level" detainees. The existence of these CIA-run detention centers was first reported in November 2005.[7] The exact locations remain secret, although news reports suggest that they were in Romania and Poland. Similar camps in Afghanistan and Thailand were closed down. There were perhaps thirty detainees in the camps who were considered major terrorist suspects – several of whom later were transferred to Guantanamo Bay – while seventy "less important" detainees were reportedly sent to Egypt, Morocco, and other Muslim nations. The camps were established under a sweeping order signed by President Bush, in light of Congress's passage, one week after September 11, 2001, of the Authorization for Use of Military Force (AUMF). The authorization granted the president broad authority to use all necessary force "against those nations, organizations, or persons he determines planned, authorized, committed, or aided the [9/11] terrorist attacks"; this included, administration officials argued, the powers to secretly gather intelligence on Al Qaeda and associated groups as well as the authority to kill, capture, or imprison suspected members of Al Qaeda.[8]

In June 2006, the U.S. Supreme Court held that the military commission established by the Bush administration to try detainees at Guantanamo Bay lacked "the power to proceed because its structures and procedures violate both the Uniform Code of Military Justice and the four Geneva Conventions signed in 1949."[9] The defendant was Salim Ahmed Hamdan, a native of Yemen and former driver for Osama bin Laden, who was captured during the 2001 war in Afghanistan; held in Guantanamo Bay after 2002; and charged with conspiracy, murder, and acts of terrorism. The defense argued that military tribunals fail to give defendants a free and fair trial, a universally recognized right that falls under customary international law (which is binding and carries nearly the same jurisdiction as codified, or treaty, law).

In contrast, the Bush administration argued that Congress granted the president, as commander in chief, direct AUMF, which allows for the creation of military courts. The administration subsequently adjusted the procedures for the military tribunals; however, it was – in terms of international opinion, at any rate – too little, too late.

The simplest way to end the epithets and their overhang for intelligence is to end the practices that give rise to them. The CIA stated that it stopped using waterboarding in 2003.[10] According to DNI Mike McConnell, the CIA used "special methods of questioning" on about thirty people.[11] Rather than vetoes, an administration could start by stating that the United States does not engage in torture, including waterboarding, and that no techniques other than those outlined in the Army Field Manual will be employed. The administration might underscore its seriousness by seeking, not shunning, congressional action in support of that view. For me, it is not a close call: even if it was waterboarding that eventually broke several high-value detainees like Khalid Sheikh Mohammed, Abd al-Rahim al-Nashiri, and Abu Zubaida, the price was too high. The conflict with Islamic extremist terrorists is ultimately a war of ideas, and we lose the war if we stoop to their methods. On that score, the Church Committee got it right a generation ago.

Moreover, what we Americans hear in these episodes is not what is perceived abroad. We as Americans are conscious of the checks and balances in our system. If an Abu Ghraib happens, the nation will get to the bottom of it, and those responsible will be punished. If the CIA goes too far, it will be restrained. The trouble is that the rest of the world sees only the images of Abu Ghraib or hears the word *torture*. For them, that is the end of the story, not the beginning of a complicated process of investigation and correction in our system. It is the image or the epithet that lasts, not the qualifications or remediation.

For those reasons, Guantanamo was an "open sore" for the nation, including its intelligence agencies. Its existence was a visible counter to all for which we said we stood. Yet, it was not an easy problem to solve. International law permits detaining potential combatants during war, but the wars contemplated by that were limited in time. Thus, can potential combatants at Guantanamo Bay be held without trial *forever?* Surely, the answer must be no, but then what? Legal scholars have and will continue to spew megabytes on the subject, but suffice it to say that most of the current detainees could not be tried in either U.S. courts or military tribunals – about three quarters of the approximately 350 detainees being held as of late 2007.

The practical problems of trying the detainees are daunting because most of their actions were committed in far-off lands, witnesses are dead or have disappeared, and so on. However, it is the jurisdictional problem that is the showstopper because many of the acts were not crimes when and where they were committed. Simply sending the detainees home is difficult – as the years since September 11 have shown – because in many cases, their ostensible "home countries" do not want them. About a fifth of the detainees in 2007 had been cleared for release but there was no country willing to take them.

The place to start rectifying Guantanamo as an epithet would be for an administration to announce that the prison would be closed, which might put pressure on foreign countries to agree to take some of the detainees – it surely would put pressure on U.S. institutions to find ways of dealing with them. For the few detainees that still might be considered dangerous, procedures for preventive detention might be fleshed out to offer legal protection.

The "Guantanamo problem" should arise less frequently in the future, when detainees will fall into one of three categories. Those arrested here, especially in homegrown plots such as in Fort Dix, will be candidates for criminal trials – however messy or unsatisfying those trials may be. Those arrested in Europe or other industrial countries but accused of plotting against the United States will be tried where they are caught – now that the jurisdictions of virtually all industrial countries include terrorism-related offenses – or perhaps they will be extradited to the United States for trial. It is only those who might be captured in or rendered from hostile or ungoverned spaces that will invoke the Guantanamo challenges of procedure and jurisdiction.

THE IMPACT OF SEPTEMBER 11

In setting the epithets in some context, it is worth pausing over the history since September 11 because the nation is still very much in the middle of the process of striking anew the balance between liberty and security. In the phrase of one observer, the war on terrorism put "two vital, deeply grounded principles of American government on a collision course." On the one hand, the president has an unquestioned responsibility to protect the nation against foreign attacks and to prevent hostile foreign powers from conducting covert intelligence activities within our borders. On the other hand, law enforcement power, always potentially dangerous to a free society, may operate only within boundaries established by the Bill of Rights.[12] On that very argument, the nation established the "distinctions" – between law enforcement and intelligence and between foreign and domestic – that made sense during the latter years of the Cold War but set up the nation to fail on September 11, 2001.

Yet, it is worth remembering that for most people, the *liberty* in question is specific – that is, privacy – not the more general sense. As Richard Betts stated:

The most legitimate trade-off is not between security and liberty in general, but between security and privacy, the one aspect of liberty that inhibits the government's acquisition of information. There is no need to compromise the more important elements of civil liberties having to do with freedom of speech, political organization, religion, or especially the right to due process of law. ... [13]

The reminder is important because so much of the debate after September 11 was conducted in the sweeping "liberty or security" terms. It is true that a wider swath of civil liberties was affected immediately after September 11, and some of those events framed the epithets that now surround intelligence, which range from constitutional to administrative.[14]

Constitutional

American constitutional law distinguishes sharply between "U.S. persons" – that is, U.S. citizens and resident aliens – and "others"; therefore, most attention is focused on U.S. citizens. Nonetheless, the large numbers of noncitizens affected, especially in the immediate aftermath of the war in Afghanistan, raised concerns those rose almost to the level of being "constitutional":

- *Detaining foreign nationals in the United States.* In the immediate aftermath of the 9/11 attack, 1,200 foreign nationals living in the United States were arrested and detained in considerable secrecy; 460 were still in detention in January 2002, their identities and locations undisclosed. Only ninety-three who were charged with a crime were ever identified. The Justice Department's own internal report, released in June 2003, was critical of the process: bureaucratic inertia left a number of innocent people languishing in jails for months while systematic understaffing left them with little chance to prove their innocence. Often, no distinction was made between serious suspects and immigrants who had no connection to suspect groups.[15]

- *Detaining foreign nationals in Guantanamo.* Guantanamo became an epithet, and it was controversial from the beginning. At the start of 2004, 650 foreigners who had been captured in Afghanistan were still being held at the U.S. prison camp in Guantanamo Bay, Cuba. While the detaining of foreigners in the United States declined in visibility as they were released, deported, or charged, the Guantanamo prisoners were a continuing embarrassment at least and a foreign-policy nightmare at worst. Overall, 775 detainees had been brought to Guantanamo by 2007, with more than 400 released.

- *Detaining and confining American citizens without judicial review and restricting access to counsel.* This small subset of the detentions was of particular concern because of citizenship. One detainee, Yasser Esam Hamdi, had left the United States with his Saudi parents when he was less than a year old and thus may have lost his American citizenship; however, the citizenship of the other, Abdullah al Muhajir (born José Padilla) was undisputed. When Padilla was transferred to military detention, one of the justifications for doing so was to prevent him from communicating with his lawyer lest he advance terrorist activity. However, in 2006, he was transferred to a jail in Miami, tried in federal court, and found guilty of conspiring to kill people in an overseas *jihad* and funding and supporting overseas terrorism. In January 2008, he was sentenced to 208 months in prison. In 2004, Hamdi was stripped of his U.S. citizenship and released to Saudi Arabia.

- *Retaining names of U.S. persons in databases and on watch lists.* As the U.S. government tried to do better by way of keeping tabs on potential terrorists, officials in several agencies reported concern that under the pressure of acting, they are randomly collecting names of U.S. persons. So far, the government has not provided much guidance to those agencies in dealing with them – a concern echoed by a Markle Foundation task force.[16] If a U.S. person has been implicated as a suspected terrorist in an FBI investigation, he or she can be included in, for example, a database. However, what if the FBI investigation is only preliminary? Should there be restrictions on how widely the U.S. person's inclusion is shared? These issues, and many others, still remain to be settled.

• *Enhancing surveillance by expanding the FISA.* Here, the issues turned out to be two. The first issue discussed immediately after September 11 was the Patriot Act, which widened the scope for national-security eavesdropping. It was only years later when the nation learned that the administration had also authorized after September 11 a second NSA eavesdropping program, called by the administration the TSP, with no court authorization whatsoever. This section discusses the Patriot Act expansion; a subsequent section describes the controversy over the second NSA program in more detail.

Modern presidents had claimed, but the courts had called into question, warrantless searches for national-security – as opposed to law enforcement – purposes. The FISA was a compromise, establishing a special secret court to review applications for national-security search and wiretaps of both citizens and noncitizens. The Patriot Act, passed in the immediate aftermath of September 11, widened the scope for the FISA warrants.[17]

The FISA and its court, the FISC, had been the preeminent tools that the FBI and other federal agents used for pursuing the war against terrorism *in the absence of probable cause that a crime has been committed*. They or something like them probably are necessary because by the time terrorists commit a crime, it is too late. Ideally, the United States would prevent all terrorist acts and there would never be a crime to prosecute. By contrast, criminals such as drug traffickers commit a stream of crimes; thus, if they are well into that stream by the time authorities are able to apprehend and prosecute them, it is a shame but not a catastrophe.

In any case, the handling of the Moussaoui case spurred action to loosen the FISA, which the Patriot Act put into effect. Some of the Act's provisions simply corrected oversights in statutory language or updated the law to match new technology. For instance, FISA wire-taps were designed for an era of analog telephones; the Patriot Act authorized the use of "roving" or "multipoint" wiretaps, which allow monitoring of all devices that a suspect might use – a long-standing practice in criminal investigations.

Other parts of the Patriot Act were more controversial. FISA wire-taps always were permitted to be longer than law enforcement coun-terparts – 90 days versus 30 – with extensions easier to obtain. The Patriot Act extended them further, to 120 days, and it doubled from 45 to 90 days the period in which foreign agents, including U.S. citi-zens, could be subject to clandestine physical searches.

Perhaps of greater concern, the Act made an apparently small change that it was feared would have significant consequences. Before September 11, obtaining foreign-intelligence information had to be "*the* purpose" of FISA surveillance.[18] If evidence of a crime was un-covered in the course of the wiretap, that evidence was admissible in court, but the foreign-intelligence purpose was paramount. The Patriot Act loosened the requirement to "*a significant* purpose."[19] Because FISA wiretaps do not require probable cause of a crime and are longer, more flexible, and less controlled by judges than law enforcement wiretaps, there was and is concern that FISA wiretaps will be used to troll for law enforcement purposes.

The expansion of the FISA also led to tensions between the FBI and the FISC about who can approve the sharing of FISA data with FBI law enforcement agents. However, in November 2002, a federal-court ruling upheld more sharing of intelligence across the intelligence–law enforcement divide within the Bureau and, in Octo-ber 2003, new guidelines were distributed to the FBI field offices con-firming the change.[20] Before the Patriot Act, the Bureau would have had to open separate wiretaps – a criminal one based on a court order and a FISA one for intelligence purposes – and would have been sharply constrained in sharing information between the two. Under the new guidelines, it could open, for example, a single FISA surveil-lance looking at whether a suspect was part of a terrorist organiza-tion (an intelligence purpose) and whether the suspect planned to buy explosives (a law enforcement purpose). Agents working on the two aspects of the case could cooperate closely.

Legislative

Because surveillance has the potential to touch the privacy if not the lives of so many Americans, it is the core concern – even if those concerns do not always reach the constitutional:

*   *Monitoring the source and destination of e-mail and Internet traffic.* These so-called pen and trap-and-trace techniques were previously limited to telephones but were extended by the Patriot Act. They do not record content but can be put in place by a court order short of showing relevance to an investigation. They are not considered searches under the Fourth Amendment, the U.S. Supreme Court having ruled that people have no expectation of privacy about their telephone numbers, which are used by telephone companies for billing.

However, intercepted e-mail also contains a subject line, thus blurring the line between "communications attributes" and content. Content *is* protected and requires a warrant. The concern is even greater because the technology for e-mails – unlike telephone calls – also has the ability to intercept the entire message.

*   *Expanding clandestine searches.* The Patriot Act also extended the scope of these "sneak-and-peak" searches, which have little to do with terrorism because the FISA confers much broader powers.
*   *Enlarging access to transaction information in national-security investigations from communications providers, financial institutions, and credit agencies.* Before September 11, the FBI was permitted to issue National Security Letters (NSLs), seeking bank-account information without the holders' knowledge and without a court order. The Patriot Act expanded that access beyond banks and loosened the criterion to any foreign-intelligence or counterterrorism purpose.[21] Before September 11, the letter of request had to certify that the information was for foreign-intelligence purposes and that there were facts proving that the targeted customer was a foreign agent. Under the Patriot Act, it became sufficient that the request had a foreign-intelligence or counterterrorism purpose.[22] A parallel change opened access to telephone records on the same basis[23]; another change opened up access to educational records on roughly the same basis.[24]

Administrative

Some of the issues of concern reflected neither constitutional nor legislative provisions but rather administrative guidelines. In particular, Attorney General John Ashcroft relaxed guidelines issued by his predecessors, especially Edward Levy in 1976 and Benjamin Civiletti in 1980, as follows:

- *Allowing more discretion to officers in the field.* Here, Moussaoui is the celebrated case and argument for more discretion in the field. However, critics see the shadows of COINTELPRO in the prospect of giving yet more discretion to field officers who already have a great deal. On May 30, 2002, the attorney general relaxed the prevailing guidelines to permit FBI agents to search the Web, mine open data, and attend public meetings, including those of political and religious groups.[25]
- *"Connecting the dots" about individuals.* Here, the *cause célèbre* was the Pentagon's program for Total (later Terrorism) Information Awareness (TIA). It was a public-relations nightmare, seen by much of the public as "Big Brother" while still in its infancy. Its director, John Poindexter, was a lightning rod for critics because he had been convicted (later reversed on appeal) for lying to Congress during the Iran–Contra Affair of the 1980s. A research project, not an operation, it built on previous artificial intelligence and data-mining research sponsored by the DARPA.[26] It was to use modern computer power to scan public and private databases against templates of terrorist-attack scenarios.[27] More fundamentally, new technology and process raise fundamental questions about what constitutes a "search" if that process can assemble a detailed mosaic of information – about a person, for instance – that is, in principle, available publicly.[28]

Yet, if the concerns are visible, the need for domestic information also is plain. The September 11 terrorists not only trained in Afghanistan, they also used European cities such as Hamburg and Brixton as "staging" areas where they could live, train, and recruit in a protective environment. Similarly, they mixed easily in some areas of the United States, "hiding in plain sight" in South Florida and

Southern California and perhaps in Lackawanna. The need for information extends beyond simply following individuals; it also requires knowledge of what is being said on the streets and in the mosques of Brixton or Boston or New Jersey – that is, it is conducting "foreign intelligence" domestically.

In March 2003, for instance, a prominent Yemeni cleric was apprehended in Germany on charges of financing terrorism at a Brooklyn mosque used to help funnel millions of dollars to Al Qaeda and, according to federal officials, he boasted that he had personally delivered $20 million to Osama bin Laden. The cleric, Sheik Muhammad Ali Hassan al-Mouyad, told an FBI informant that he was a spiritual advisor to bin Laden and had worked for years to provide money and weapons for a terrorist *jihad*.[29] Sheik Mouyad boasted that *jihad* was his field and said he received money for *jihad* from collections at the Al Farooq mosque in Brooklyn. As NYPD Commissioner Raymond W. Kelly said, Al Qaeda operatives "did their fund-raising right here in our own backyard in Brooklyn." More recently discovered groups or cells, like the Fort Dix plotters, have been homegrown and thus do not even need to hide in plain sight.

The collision of values runs through the war against terrorism. For instance, stories abound of people continually harassed when they tried to fly because they are on one of the watch lists.[30] At the same time, Congress's General Accounting Office criticized the various agencies for not sharing their watch lists. Nine federal agencies maintained lists to spot terrorist suspects trying to get a visa, board a plane, cross a border, or engage in similar activities – the FBI, the then-INS, the DHS, the Pentagon, the State Department, and four other agencies.

All kept such lists and shared information from them with other federal officials, as well as local and state police officials as needed. However, the congressional study found that some agencies did not even have policies for sharing watch-list information with other agencies, and that those that did often required complex, labor-intensive methods to cull information. Agencies often had different types of databases and software that make sharing information next to impossible. As a result, sharing of information was often fractured, "inconsistent and limited," the study reported.[31]

Beneath the heat of the political controversy surrounding the second NSA program for wiretapping of U.S. citizens in connection with suspected terrorists abroad lay the same issue of where to strike the balance between privacy and security in the context of a changed threat and changing technology. President Bush described the domestic-surveillance program as vital to protecting the United States from terrorist attacks. "If Al Qaeda is calling someone in America, we want to know what they're saying on that call," he said.[32] Yet, critics charged that the program violated the U.S. Constitution's separation of powers, its Fourth Amendment protections from illegal search and seizure, as well as circumventing – thus violating – the FISA.

It is intriguing that in the late 2000s, Sweden grappled with similar issues that evoked clear echoes of the arguments heard in the United States. Sweden's Defence Radio Establishment (FRA), the nation's SIGINT service, argued – much like supporters of the NSA program – that it must have access to major communications lines passing through Sweden. It argued that it would filter out Swedish calls and focus on its targets. For its part, the Swedish Security Service opposed the expansion. Committed to wiretapping only with court involvement, the Service argued that the FRA would necessarily intercept Swedish calls – who knows where "Swedish" calls are routed – and that its work would intrude on nonmilitary responsibilities such as counterterrorism and organized crime.

The expanded authority was finally approved by the Swedish Parliament in June 2008 after an intense public and parliamentary debate in which a number of lawmakers from the governing coalition threatened to vote with the opposition and reject the bill.[33] As a concession to the internal and external opposition, the government promised to tighten the process of authorization and control, and limit the number of agencies permitted to make requests for tapping. One agency excluded from access was the Security Service, an exclusion that means the Service will not have access to any communications that do no pass over purely domestic phone lines – a reflection of the political fear of a public outcry against "free-for-all" wiretapping.

In the immediate aftermath of September 11, the Bush administration opted in secret not to seek court approval before conducting wiretaps on the communications of terrorism suspects to and from the United States. Former Attorney General Alberto R. Gonzales argued that the president's authority to spy on U.S. "persons" communicating with suspected terrorists abroad was granted by Congress through the AUMF. Although the authorization did not specifically mention wiretapping, its powers were very broad and included, administration officials argued, the powers to secretly gather intelligence on Al Qaeda and associated groups. The administration notified the so-called Gang of Eight – the leaders of each of the two parties, and the chairs and ranking members of the intelligence committees from each of the two houses of Congress.

Once the program spilled into the public, it was opposed on a number of grounds. First, not only did it seem to many people a violation of privacy – although the administration was careful to emphasize that unless a U.S. citizen was communicating with a suspected terrorist overseas, the communication would not be monitored – it also seemed of dubious legality. After all, the AUMF did not explicitly authorize "warrantless" wiretapping on U.S. citizens, and the program violated the FISA, which was established expressly for the purpose of this type of covert surveillance. In its history, the FISA process has rarely denied the executive branch a wiretapping warrant and even allows federal agencies to request "after-the-fact" warrants for up to seventy-two hours.

How effective the program has been was also debated, although the issue is difficult to settle, given its secrecy. According to press reporting, most of the tips by the wiretaps led to "dead ends" and swamped the FBI.[34] Administration officials, however, asserted that the wiretaps saved lives. In January 2006, General Michael V. Hayden, then-principal DDNI and later CIA director, said, "Had this program been in effect prior to 9/11, it is my professional judgment that we would have detected some of the 9/11 Al Qaeda operatives in the United States, and we would have identified them as such."[35] Vice President Cheney, in a speech in January 2008, said "the program has uncovered a wealth of information that has foiled attacks against the United States; information that has saved countless innocent lives."[36]

The Bush administration's arguments for the program were something of a moving target, and it turned out that there had been internal divisions over the program. Attorney General Gonzales suggested that the White House originally considered legislation to legalize its secret wiretaps but thought it would not pass Congress. He and other officials later backtracked and said a bill to reform the FISA was not sought because the program's details would be made public, thus endangering its effectiveness. Critics also pointed to earlier contradictory statements made by administration officials denying the existence of the domestic-spying program. "When we're talking about chasing down terrorists, we're talking about getting a court order before we do so," President Bush said in an April 2004 speech in Buffalo. "Nothing has changed."[37]

Finally, most on Capitol Hill outside of the Gang of Eight were kept out of the loop on the domestic-spying program. "What is unique about this one particular program among all the other sensitive NSA programs that justifies keeping Congress in the dark?," asked Senator Jay Rockefeller (D-WV), a member of the Gang of Eight as chairman of the Senate Intelligence Committee. Attorney General Gonzales said that notifying all congressional members was unnecessary because of the AUMF granted by Congress after September 11. Those informed who, like Senator Rockefeller, had doubts about the program were in the uncomfortable dilemma faced by overseers of secret programs: their choice was stark – either acquiesce in secret or risk blowing the program in open opposition.

Administration officials maintained that the FISA is an outdated law enforcement mechanism that is too time-consuming and not conducive to current intelligence-gathering demands. The concerns certainly are relevant. The FISA presumes that the government knows who it wants to wiretap, a reasonable assumption for the era of white-collar spies. Now, however, the government may not know whose communications it wants to monitor. Rather, it seeks to troll for suspicious conversations – for instance, from the Pakistan–Afghanistan border region. As DNI McConnell stated in a June 2007 interview, "The threat has increased, the intent is stated, and the way the wording in the current law is captured inhibits or prevents us from being successful."[38]

Under political pressure, Attorney General Gonzales announced in January 2007 a plan to end the program, ceding oversight to the FISA. However, questions about the legality of the program lingered in Congress. In May 2007, congressional hearings revealed that top

Justice Department officials, including then–Attorney General John Ashcroft, had expressed reservations about the program back in 2004, prompting the White House to push the program forward without the Justice Department's consent.[39] In August 2007, Gonzales resigned, at a time of constant congressional questioning over his role in overseeing domestic surveillance.

The Bush administration's vow to seek FISA approval for domestic surveillance was short-lived. In July 2007, weeks before Gonzales stepped down, intelligence officials approached lawmakers seeking emergency legislation to broaden their wiretapping authority. The request came on the heels of a ruling by the FISC, the court overseeing the FISA – a ruling that impacted the government's ability to intercept foreign communications passing through telecommunications "switches" on U.S. soil. According to a report of the Senate Intelligence Committee, the DNI reported that the FISC's decision "led to degraded capabilities in the face of a heightened terrorist threat environment."[40] Congress responded, giving the attorney general and the DNI stopgap power to approve international surveillance, bypassing the FISA. The legislation also deemed warrants unnecessary for surveillance of a person "reasonably believed" to be located overseas. Yet, Democrats let the measure expire on February 1, 2008.

There is merit to the argument that oversight will have to move from judicial approval before the fact to some form of continuing legal or congressional review as surveillance proceeds. However, by overreaching and simply bypassing the FISA, rather than working with Congress to try to fix it in the first years after September 11, the Bush administration discredited good arguments. In frustration, congressional Democrats made an inane argument of their own, refusing to grant immunity from lawsuits to companies that had cooperated with the warrantless NSA program. That issue was a sideshow because if people opposed the program, the right destination for protest was the government, not the companies. "The intelligence community doesn't have the facilities to carry out the kind of international surveillance needed to defend this country since 9/11," Vice President Cheney said in the speech quoted previously. "In some situations there is no alternative to seeking assistance from the private sector." It certainly would make no sense to encourage private entities not to cooperate with the government when the government asked.

Yet, what was and is important is putting the NSA programs in some legal framework, and the FISA provided such a framework. Shunning it was a mistake and a shame because it created a needless argument over the past when the discussion should be about what our security requires in the future and how that is balanced with civil liberties. The Bush administration's answer – that the FISA was too cumbersome – rings hollow in light of the changes in the FISA to which Congress agreed after September 11. For instance, Congress loosened the standard for FISA wiretaps in terrorism cases, and it extended from one day to three the emergency period during which an administration could start wiretaps before getting retroactive FISA authorization. If the NSA had needed still more flexibility, it is difficult to believe that Congress would not have granted it, especially in those fearful days after September 11.

If the threats posed by changing technology mean that administrations have to be given latitude to troll through communications, then the counterpart should be requiring them to come back to the FISA or a similar body to justify continued surveillance. Indeed, precisely because intelligence tools of the war against terrorism cannot be entirely transparent – lest the nation's enemies adapt their operations to circumvent them – the social contract requires *some* processes of secret oversight. The public does not need to know the details of what is being done in its name; it does need to know that a body independent of an administration knows and approves. What is critical is the process before the fact and oversight afterward, if not before. If, in the famous phrase, the constitution is not a suicide pact, neither is war a blank check.[41]

In his confirmation hearings, U.S. Supreme Court Judge Samuel Alito gave new salience to U.S. Supreme Court Justice Robert Jackson's distinction of a half-century ago: the president's power is greatest if his action is consistent with what Congress has done, less if Congress has been silent, and least if the action is contrary to the will of Congress.[42] In passing the FISA, Congress could hardly have been clearer. Not only did it make the FISA "the exclusive means by which electronic surveillance...may be conducted" for national-security purposes, it also explicitly rejected proposed language from the Ford administration that would have left open the possibility that a president could continue warrantless wiretaps.

In that light, the July 2008 law that resolved the issue falls short of what the public deserves and thus is unlikely to be the last word on the subject. Under the law, the NSA would be allowed to seek FISC orders for broad groups of foreign targets. The law created a new seven-day period for directing wiretaps at foreigners without a court order in "exigent" circumstances if government officials assert that important national-security information would be lost. The law also expanded the period for emergency wiretaps on Americans without a court order from three days to seven if the attorney general certifies that there is probable cause to believe the target is linked to terrorism. The law makes the FISA the "exclusive" means of conducting intelligence eavesdropping.

By all accounts, the FISA process is detailed and scrupulous – indeed, perhaps too scrupulous in the case of Zacarias Moussaoui, the famous "twentieth hijacker" of September 11. The FISA requests are almost never formally rejected, but that is because they are carefully crafted and sometimes withdrawn during the process. The problem is that the process is not and probably cannot be transparent. It will all depend on how broadly groups of targets are defined. The 2008 law includes no explicit requirement that the NSA return to the court to justify continuing surveillance, perhaps on just a subset of the original group, which is sad; rebuilding the social contract requires better.

LEARNING THE RIGHT LESSONS

As the nation restrikes the balance between security and privacy, the first lesson is that the more intrusive surveillance is at home, then the more important is process for oversight and accountability. The second lesson is the need to carefully assess any proposed measure. In the fearful days after September 11, the American people and their Congress were prepared to accept almost anything that boded to make them more secure – and so it would be in the aftermath of another major attack. That makes it even more important to assess any proposed measure for indications that it might be pain for no gain. That is, will it cause citizens inconvenience – if not damage to their privacy – for scant or no gain in the war on terrorism?

Most of the financial-reporting requirements expanded under the Patriot Act fall into that category. Before September 11, financial institutions had been required to submit a Currency Transaction Report (CTR) for any cash transaction more than $10,000 and a SAR when they "had reason to suspect" that a transaction was "not the sort in which the particular consumer would be expected to engage."[43] Already before September 11, there were concerns about the sheer volume of such reports. However, the Patriot Act increased that flow by expanding the requirements – from financial institutions to securities brokers and dealers in the case of SARs, and from financial institutions to any business or trade in the case of CTRs.

Those financial-reporting requirements may have value for other threats, such as drug trafficking. However, they are pain for no gain in the war on terrorism because, alas, terrorism is not expensive. Estimates for the total cost of the September 11 attacks are in the thousands, not millions, of dollars.

By the same token, questions have been raised about the value of SARs regarding both financial transactions and other individual behaviors for detecting terrorist activities. In the financial arena, where SARs have been an established part of efforts to counter criminal activity, even before September 11 there were concerns that the "volume of these reports was interfering with effective law enforcement."[44] After September 11, the range of organizations obligated to submit such reports was broadened, prompting calls from the private sector for better guidelines on what constitutes suspicious activity and laments from federal officials that what is reported has little value.[45] An NCTC official was quoted in the press observing, "In many instances, the threshold for reporting is low, which makes it extremely difficult to evaluate some of this information."[46] In January 2008, the DNI issued standards for SARs.[47]

Similarly, the FBI's use of National Security Letters (NSLs) after the expansion of authority in the Patriot Act became controversial. From calendar years 2003 through 2005, the FBI issued approximately 44,000 NSLs containing 143,074 requests. In one investigation, it issued nine NSLs requesting information relating to eleven thousand telephone numbers.[48] It issued another 49,425 requests in 2006 for a total of 192,499 requests during the four-year period from 2003 through 2006.[49] It also turned out that procedures for both authorizing NSLs within the Bureau and recordkeeping about them had been haphazard. A report by the Department of Justice's IG found that the

FBI had "used NSLs in violation of applicable NSL statutes, Attorney General Guidelines, and internal FBI policies" but that no criminal laws had been broken. A year later, a second IG report confirmed the findings of the first, and noted what the FBI had done to correct the shortcomings.

Moreover, if we are honest, many of the airport-safety measures are in the pain-for-little-gain category. In any case, it is not obvious that airport security is worth the almost $6 billion the nation is now spending on it.[50] That amounts to one FBI for airport security; if the cost to private citizens of increased inconvenience and delay were added, the number could amount to two FBIs.[51] Indeed, one of the real failures is that while the strategic warning that existed well before September 11 pointed to one fairly inexpensive fix – reinforced airplane cockpit doors – even that was judged too expensive before September 11. To be sure, the intended purpose of many airport-security measures is public confidence as much as real security; ultimately, however, measures that do not add much to security will not build confidence either.

Part of the reason for the striking cleavage between security and liberty in the public debate over domestic intelligence is the absence of any "Compared to what? And for what gain?" questions. It is imperative to begin to develop a systematic framework for assessing the value of particular intelligence-gathering measures, the civil liberties involved in them, and the costs that arise from the measures. That obstinate assessment is all the more necessary the sharper is the clash of values; the assessment will not settle the argument over values but can at least put it in a clearer focus.

The issue of profiling is a good example: on the one hand, it is offensive to our values; on the other, it seems common sense. So far – although surely not forever – the terrorists of most threat to the nation have come from or had roots in one part of the world. Not giving special concern to the people (so far, men) who fit that description seems simply ignorant. Worse than ignorant, it seems to impose gratuitous costs on all those light-skinned grandmothers who are searched at airports as potential terrorists. There is a considerable cost, including in privacy if not liberty, to *not* profiling. In fact, it turns out that most broad profiling – singling out Middle Easterners, for instance – is ineffective because it overwhelms the system with false positives. As a result, airport screening has turned to *behavioral* profiling, endeavoring to screen people on the basis of visible behavior.[52]

It is imperative to be more open about costs and benefits. The civil-liberties costs are usually argued in terms of individual cases, and those are provocative. However, any system will make mistakes, and while it is a shame that those errors will fall disproportionately on one set of people, that shame does not eliminate the need to assess carefully the overall costs. The same is true of benefits. As with profiling, more sophisticated watch lists are better than less sophisticated. Searching every dark-skinned young male airline traveler is both offensive and wasteful. Making watch lists more discriminating by noting those who bought one-way tickets, paid in cash, and other relevant indicators can reduce the numbers who are singled out.

To be sure, collecting the information to make still more discriminating watch lists – for instance, by identifying people who had been associated with one another before but who made entirely separate arrangements to travel on the same flight – can itself invoke privacy concerns. Yet, if the information is public in any case – as is true of most business and other associations – the value of permitting watch lists to assemble it probably outweighs the cost.

In September 2003, Homeland Security Presidential Directive 6 (HSPD-6) established a Terrorist Screening Center (TSC) to consolidate the U.S. government's approach to terrorist screening.[53] It was meant to consolidate more than a dozen previous lists, including the State Department's TIPOFF database of more than 110,000 known and suspected terrorists. To this end, TIPOFF, which had been maintained by the State Department's INR, and other watch-list functions were transferred to the newly established TSC and the TTIC (now the NCTC). Originally based largely on TIPOFF, the NCTC maintains a Terrorist Identities Datamart Environment (TIDE), which reportedly contains more than 325,000 terrorist-related records.[54]

For its part, the TSC is an interagency effort administered by the FBI. The NCTC shares international-terrorist identities data, which is TIDE-generated, with the TSC. Combining these data with other government watch lists, the TSC maintains a consolidated Terrorist Screening Database (TSDB), which included 238,000 records as of January 2005, according to the Justice Department.[55] The TSC, in turn, distributes TSDB-generated international-terrorist alert records – along with domestic-terrorist alert records generated by the FBI – to frontline screening agencies. The TSC, for example, supports the terrorist-screening activities of the DHS's TSA and the Customs and Border Protection (CBP), as well as State's Bureau of Consular Affairs.

Coordination between the Justice Department and the DHS, not surprisingly, proved to be challenging. Also not surprising, misidentifications, especially false positives, continued to be controversial. Moreover, in the aftermath of the August 2006 plot to bomb airliners bound for the United States from Britain, the DHS sought passenger name records (PNRs) *before* flights, rather than 15 minutes after the flight's departure, as required previously. The United States and the European Union negotiated over these issues, reaching a temporary agreement in October 2006 and a permanent agreement in June 2007. In both negotiations and in separate U.S. legislation, a central issue was procedures for redress if travelers felt they had been wrongly included on a watch list.

The TSA "No Fly" and "Automatic Selectee" watch lists are a much smaller subset of the watch lists. As the names imply, the No Fly list means potential passengers departing from U.S. airports are barred from boarding and passed to law enforcement, while Automatic Selectees are selected for secondary security screening before being cleared to board. The No Fly list reportedly contained twenty thousand names at the end of 2004. False positives, however, included some prominent politicians, such as Senator Edward Kennedy (D-MA).

These issues are not precisely about intelligence but they are intelligence-driven. Thus, they also raise the question about how intelligence relates to new needs and new mechanisms in an age of terror. They also drive home the lesson that if new processes will impose some pain, their gain needs to be clearly assessed and understood. Another example is the Computer-Assisted Passenger Prescreening System II (CAPPS II). Prompted in part by the 9/11 Commission's recommendations, the TSA decided to stop developing the system. It was originally designed to use sophisticated algorithms to search both government and commercial databases to acquire limited background information on ticket-buyers to authenticate their identity and look for irregularities in behavior patterns that might suggest potential risks. Critics, however, decried the mask of secrecy under which CAPPS II was developed and argued that the potential loss of privacy would not be counterbalanced by a corresponding increase in security.[56] The pain, they argued, was not worth the gain. However, the successor program, dubbed "Secure Flight," also was beset by problems and repeatedly delayed.

A third lesson is that some caution, and some slowness, is not a bad policy as the nation rethinks the "oppositions" on which Cold War institutions and processes were based. The values at stake are powerful and we have yet to calibrate the terrorist threat. Indeed, we still do not understand what happened to the nation on September 11, 2001. We are learning, but there are still large unknowns about the terrorists' logistics, their own intelligence, and other concerns. We sense but do not yet know that terrorism against the homeland will be serious for the United States but not in a class with the threat faced by Israel. Thus, we suspect but do not yet know that the nation will not be forced to shift the balance as far toward security as Israel has had to do.[57]

Because of the controversy surrounding them, many (but not all) provisions of the Patriot Act were "sunset" powers that expired in 2005 if they were not specifically reauthorized in subsequent legislation (which most were). It seems wise to continue sunset measures, especially controversial ones, in the war against terrorism, given that the terrorist threat is yet to be calibrated and the costs and benefits of particular measures are yet to be assessed seriously. It seems wiser given that with the benefit of some hindsight, for example, some of the first Patriot Act's provisions seem only tangentially connected to the war on terrorism. The need to reauthorize antiterror measures can be an opportunity to rejudge the threat and to sense again how willing the American people are to take particular pains in confronting it.

By the same token, although it makes sense for the nation to think seriously about the prospect of creating a domestic-intelligence service separate from law enforcement, it is probably not yet time – for all the reasons outlined in Chapter 5 – to actually create such a service. At the federal level, much is in motion but not much is settled. FBI Director Mueller is determined to turn the mission of the Bureau from law enforcement to prevention and intelligence, but doing so runs against the powerful organizational culture. The DHS has been endowed with an intelligence unit, but it has been slow to find both its footing and its place among the established agencies.[58]

The DHS was also to have the mission of "connecting the dots," but that mission passed to the NCTC, which seems to serve senior officials well but finds it difficult to move information downward to state and local officials and the private sector. What its "strategic operational planning" mission is in the war against terrorism or how effective it can be at that mission also remain in question.

Perhaps the slowly turning wheels of bureaucracy can provide time for reflection on the threats and values at stake. The "oppositions" are not to be discarded lightly. We do not yet have consensus on where to strike the balance between security and liberty, so we are still near the beginning of rethinking and reshaping as we calibrate the terrorist threat against the homeland. As with fighting the Cold War, we probably will come to settled new arrangements for fighting terrorism just as the threat moves on to something else!

A FINAL WORD

For guidance about intelligence in a democracy, no one has improved on Stansfield Turner's advice, which turns *The New York Times* test for covert action into a more general prescription: "There is one overall test of the ethics of human intelligence activities. That is whether those approving them feel they could defend their decisions before the public if their actions became public."[59]

Yet, it is difficult for me not to end this book in a wistful tone. One of the benefits of comparisons across countries is that is does make you clearly see your own arrangements and your own country. In this case, the experience has been watching our British colleagues – from "the land of official secrets" – put in place what seem to me to be sensible arrangements for expanded intelligence and its oversight. In that work, they take considerable pride and justifiably so.[60] For me, their experience harkened back to how we felt after the Church Committee and the FISA and the oversight committees: like we had fashioned sturdy approaches to difficult dilemmas. It has not worked all that badly, but it has not worked all that well either – hence, wistfulness. Mostly, no arrangements in the political arena can fail to be affected by the increasingly bitter partisanship that has afflicted the American system during the past generation. The quality of the members of the intelligence oversight committees also has diminished as the work has gotten more difficult and less "sexy" – however, that may be mostly an artifact of the partisanship.

Yet, the larger reason for my wistfulness is that important figures in American politics do not seem to understand the point that I and my British colleagues hold central: to do more intelligence, you have to be more transparent and accountable. It is not just right ethically; it is practically necessary. In the Bush administration, Vice President Cheney in particular seemed to believe that either the threat is self-evidently so great that Americans (and their allies) should tolerate almost anything or simply that recent presidents had conceded too much power. On that score, no one has improved on Jackson's argument that presidents are least powerful when they act against the expressed spirit of Congress. In that sense, the way to maximize presidential power is not simply to assert it.

Yet, I confess that I hear the Cheney-esque view from other Americans as well. At a luncheon, a member of the Los Angeles County Sheriff's Advisory Committee on Homeland Security said he regarded the terrorist threat as a war to the finish, one in which no holds were barred. When I demurred, saying that if in the end this was a fight to the finish, it still was a fight over ideas, my interlocutor listened to the point but did not really take it. He did not understand that more terrorist attacks, even several more on the scale of September 11, will not destroy America. What might destroy us is our own reaction.

In this grander way as well, we determine the threat to ourselves in this age of terror. My friend and colleague, Brian Jenkins, stated it plainly:

> The terrorist threats we confront today will continue for many years. We are still closer to the beginning than the end of what is likely to be a very long campaign.... America will be judged not just by what we say but by what we do. We cannot claim to be a nation of laws, a champion of democracy, when we too easily accept a disturbing pattern of ignoring inconvenient rules, justifying our actions by extraordinary circumstances, readily resorting to extrajudicial action based upon broad assertions of unlimited executive authority, and espousing public arguments against any constraints on how we treat those in our custody. The defense of democracy requires the defense of democracy's ideals.[61]

Or, as I would say it less gracefully: I do not fear the terrorists. I do sometimes fear us.

Notes

Chapter 1: Introduction

1. The two most detailed in the United States are those of the 9/11 Commission and the WMD Commission. Formally, they are (respectively) the National Commission on Terrorist Attacks Upon the United States, *The 9/11 Commission Report* (Washington, DC, 2004), available at http://www.9-11commission.gov/; and *Final Report of the Commission on the Intelligence Capabilities of the United States Regarding Weapons of Mass Destruction* (Washington, DC, 2005), available at http://www.wmd.gov/report/. Britain's inquiry into pre–Iraq War intelligence, the Butler report, is *Review of Intelligence on Weapons of Mass Destruction* (London, 2004), available at http://www.butlerreview.org.uk/index.asp.

2. As quoted in Peter Taylor, *Brits* (London: Bloomsbury Publishing, 2001), p. 265.

3. On the distinction between puzzles and mysteries, see Gregory F. Treverton, "Estimating Beyond the Cold War," *Defense Intelligence Journal, 3*, 2 (Fall 1994); and Joseph S. Nye, Jr., "Peering into the Future," *Foreign Affairs, 77*, 4 (July/August 1994), 82–93.

4. From Suzy Platt (ed.), *Respectfully Quoted: A Dictionary of Quotations Requested from the Congressional Research Service* (Washington, DC: Library of Congress, 1989), p. 80.

5. *WMD Commission Report*, p. 3.

6. *Report on the U.S. Intelligence Community's Prewar Intelligence Assessments on Iraq*, June 2004, available online at http://www.fas.org/irp/congress/2004_rpt/index.html.

7. Some of that flavor runs through even the best of the outside reports on the issue, *Creating a Trusted Network for Homeland Security*, Second Report of the Markle Foundation Task Force, December 2003,

available at http://www.markletaskforce.org/markle_programs/policy_
for_a_networked_society/national_security/projects/taskforce_national_
security.php (as of September 2005).

8. "Season of inquiry" is a compliment to my friend and colleague's book
about the Church Committee investigations. See Loch K. Johnson, *A Season of Inquiry: The Senate Intelligence Investigation* (Lexington, KY: University Press of Kentucky, 1985).

Chapter 2: The Changed Target

1. Dave Snowden, "Complex Acts of Knowing: Paradox and Descriptive
Self-Awareness," *Journal of Knowledge Management*, Special Issue,
September 2002, available at http://www.kwork.org/Resources/snowden.
pdf (last visited December 17, 2003).

2. This is also the conclusion of Richard Betts, a distinguished student of
intelligence and analysis. See his *Enemies of Intelligence: Knowledge and
Power in American National Security* (Columbia University Press, 2007),
pp. 115–16.

3. It should be said, however, that the most venturesome act by the Soviet
Union – installing nuclear missiles in Cuba in 1962 – was a "whopper."
Even with all the benefit of hindsight, it still seems stunningly reckless
on the part of a usually conservative Soviet leadership. See Alexander
Fursenko and Timothy Naftali, *"One Hell of a Gamble": Khrushchev,
Kennedy, Castro and the Cuban Missile Crisis, 1958–1964* (London: John
Murray, 1997).

4. In fact, there was disagreement about whether "wiped off the map" was
a correct translation of the Persian, with other scholars translating it as
"wiped away from the pages of time [or history]." Other Iranian officials
insisted that his reference was to the regime, not the state, although a
summary on the official Iranian Web site stated that he has said that
"the new wave of confrontations generated in Palestine and the growing turmoil in the Islamic world would in no time wipe Israel away."
For various sources on the dispute, see http://en.wikipedia.org/wiki/
Mahmoud_Ahmadinejad_and_Israel#2005_22World_Without_Zionism.22_
speech.

5. I spell out this distinction in my *Rethinking National Intelligence for
an Age of Information* (Cambridge: Cambridge University Press, 2001),
pp. 43–6.

6. For a compilation of polls, see *AEI Studies in Public Opinion*, "America after 9/11: Public Opinion on the War on Terrorism, the War with
Iraq, and America's Place in the World," March 26, 2004, available at
http.www.aei.org/publications/pubID.16974/pub_detail.asp.

7. See *Country Reports on Terrorism*, released by the U.S. State Department Office of the Coordinator for Counterterrorism, April 28, 2006, available at http://www.state.gov/s/ct/rls/crt/2005/65970.htm.
8. See Paul Slovic, "Perceptions of Risk," *Science, 236* (April 17, 1987), 281.
9. The studies suggest that people are much more willing to accept "voluntary" risks, like skiing, than "involuntary" and "controllable" risks than "uncontrollable" risks. Slovic, cited previously, 282.
10. James Fallows interviewed a number of terrorism experts five years after September 11. What he found was near consensus on a high degree of optimism about America's situation with respect to Al Qaeda, "better than many Americans believe, and better than nearly all political rhetoric asserts." See his "Declaring Victory," *The Atlantic*, September 1, 2006.
11. For a provocative analysis of the political and social impacts, see Nils Gilman, Peter Schwartz, and Doug Randall, *Impacts of Climate Change: A System Vulnerability Approach to Consider the Potential Impacts to 2050 of a Mid-upper Greenhouse Gas Emissions Scenario* (San Francisco, CA: Global Business Network, March 2007), available at http://www.gbn.com/ArticleDisplayServlet.srv?aid=39932.
12. The DHS-sponsored fusion centers interviewed by the Congressional Research Service averaged one SCI-cleared person in an average staff of twenty-seven. See Todd Masse and others, *Fusion Centers: Issues and Opportunities for Congress* (Washington, DC: Congressional Research Service, July 6, 2007), p. 26.
13. James N. Rosenau, "Patterned Chaos in Global Life: Structure and Process in the Two Worlds of World Politics," *International Political Science Review, 9,* 4 (1988), 327–64.
14. For a readable discussion of networked phenomena, see Albert-Laszlo Barabasi, *Linked: How Everything Is Connected to Everything Else and What It Means* (New York: Plume, 2003).
15. Testimony in the Oversight Hearing on the Constitutional Limitations on Domestic Surveillance before the Subcommittee on the Constitution, Civil Rights, and Civil Liberties, Committee on the Judiciary, U.S. House of Representatives, June 7, 2007, http://judiciary.house.gov/Oversight.aspx?ID=335; "Legal Authorities Supporting the Activities of the National Security Agency Described by the President," U.S. Department of Justice (2006), http://www.usdoj.gov/opa/whitepaperonnsalegal authorities.pdf; John Yoo, "The Terrorist Surveillance Program and the Constitution," *George Mason Law Review, 14,* 3 (Spring 2007), http://www.gmu.edu/departments/law/gmulawreview/issues/14-3/ Volume14Issue3.php.

16. The Fort Dix plot, discussed in more detail later, allegedly involved six individuals who planned to attack the base using a variety of military-style assault weapons. It was first noticed by a clerk at a local video store who saw a video one of the men brought in to be duplicated that contained footage of weapons training and other suspicious activity; the clerk notified the police.

17. These techniques, being developed at RAND and elsewhere, are called robust decision making (RDM). To make decisions, analysts and policy makers would look for strategies that seem robust across many scenarios. For intelligence analysis, the aim might be to identify outcomes that seem robust across variables.

18. See his *Sensemaking in Organizations* (London: Sage Publications, 1995).

19. *National Security Strategy of the United States of America* (Washington, DC: September 2002), pp. 14–15, available at http://www.whitehouse.gov/nsc/nss.pdf.

20. Available at http://www.whitehouse.gov/infocus/iraq/iraq_archive.html.

21. Available at http://www.whitehouse.gov/news/releases/2002/06/20020601-3.html.

22. It also consumed much of my intellectual attention during the Cold War. See, for instance, *Nuclear Weapons in Europe*, Adelphi Paper No. 168 (London: International Institute for Strategic Studies, 1981).

23. Among other sources, this episode is discussed in Richard L. Russell, *Sharpening Strategic Intelligence: Why the CIA Gets It Wrong and What Needs to Be Done to Get It Right* (Cambridge University Press, 2007), pp. 47–8.

24. At a U.S. Department of Defense news briefing, February 12, 2002, available at http://www.defenselink.mil/Transcripts/Transcript.aspx?TranscriptID=2636.

25. This approach draws on conversations with and work – as yet unpublished – done by my RAND colleagues, Lynn Davis and David Howell.

26. See, for instance, U.S. Department of Health and Human Services, Center for Disease Control and Prevention, "Bioterrorism Agents/Diseases," n.d., available at http://www.bt.cdc.gov/agent/agentlist-category.asp.

27. See Judea Pearl, *Probabilistic Reasoning in Intelligent Systems: Networks of Plausible Inference* (San Mateo, CA: Morgan Kaufmann Publishers, 1991).

Chapter 3: The Cold War Legacy

1. For a recent litany of failures, see Richard L. Russell, *Sharpening Strategic Intelligence: Why the CIA Gets It Wrong and What Needs to Be Done to Get It Right* (Cambridge: Cambridge University Press, 2007).

2. See Amy Zegart, *Flawed by Design: The Evolution of the CIA, JCS, and NSC* (Stanford, CA: Stanford University Press, 1999). Her perceptive analysis is, in this view, exaggerated and deterministic. To be sure, the bureaucratic interests she emphasizes played a role in how institutions and processes developed. However, so too did the broader currents of domestic politics and national values – a point that she acknowledges. However, she treats politics mostly as a negative, a constraint on ideal outcomes; for me, as this instance suggests, it is simply a fact and sometimes a positive one.

3. In the spirit of full disclosure, I was a staff member of the Senate Select Committee, chaired by Senator Frank Church (D-ID). It was my first job in government, a fascinating introduction and the beginning of my abiding interest in intelligence.

4. See *Final Report of the Select Committee to Study Governmental Operations with Respect to Intelligence Activities of the United States Senate*, 94th Congress, 2nd Session, 1976; Book II, *Intelligence Activities and the Rights of Americans*; and Book III, *Supplementary Detailed Staff Reports on Intelligence Activities and the Rights of Americans*. For links to these reports, as well as to a rich range of other documents, both historical and contemporary, see http://www.icdc.com/~paulwolf/cointelpro/cointel.htm.

5. The act is the Foreign Intelligence Surveillance Act of 1978, Pub. L. No. 95-511, 92 Stat. 1783 (codified as amended at 50 U.S.C. §§ 1801–1811, 1821–1829, 1841–1846, 1861–1862).

6. The idea that the president, given his inherent powers, could not be constrained by law during wartime is often called the "unitary executive theory." The argument, made often by Vice President Dick Cheney, had its intellectual godfather in John Yoo, the Berkeley law professor who served in the Justice Department's Office of Legal Counsel, where he wrote or contributed to a number of the memoranda about interrogation. See his *The Powers of War and Peace: The Constitution and Foreign Affairs After 9/11* (Chicago: University of Chicago Press, 2005).

7. John le Carré, *The Night Manager* (New York: Knopf, 1993), p. 42.

8. See, for example, David Weisburd and Anthony A. Braga (eds.), *Police Innovation: Contrasting Perspectives* (Cambridge: Cambridge University Press, 2006); Darric Milligan et al., *Intelligence-Led Policing Tool: Intelligence-Led Policing Technology for State and Local Law Enforcement Agencies* (Bedford, MA: Mitretek Corporation, MTR-2006-016, 2006); and Jerry H. Ratcliffe, "Intelligence-Led Policing and the Problems of Turning Rhetoric into Practice," *Policing and Society*, *12*, 1 (2002), 53–66.

9. See my *Reshaping National Intelligence for an Age of Information* (Cambridge: Cambridge University Press, 2001), pp. 139ff.

10. National Security Act of 1947, 50 U.S.C. 403, Sec. 102 (e).

11. For this case, see Kristen Lundberg, *The SS-9 Controversy: Intelligence as Political Football* (Harvard University, Kennedy School of Government, 1989), C16-89-884.0. See also Lawrence Friedman, *U.S. Intelligence and the Soviet Strategic Threat* (Princeton, NJ: Princeton University Press, 1986), p. 139.

12. This episode is also discussed in the joint congressional investigation *Final Report*, and in Shelby's *Additional Views*, p. 18, both cited previously.

13. A heavily redacted version of the memorandum is available at http://www.thememoryhole.org/911/phoenix-memo/01.htm.

14. The distinctions were not new with Rumsfeld, but he used them, famously, in a Pentagon press briefing, December 12, 2002. For the transcript, see http://www.defenselink.mil/transcripts/transcript.aspx?transcriptid=2636.

15. See http://fly.hiwaay.net/~pspoole/fiscshort.html. See also Ronald Kessler, *The Bureau: The Secret History of the FBI* (New York: St. Martin's Press, 2002), pp. 438–43.

16. The attorney general's letter-report is posted at http://www.fas.org/irp/agency/doj/fisa/2002rept.html.

17. This account derives from *Interim Report on FBI Oversight in the 107th Congress by the Senate Judiciary Committee: FISA Implementation Failures* (February 2003), pp. 14ff, posted at http://www.fas.org/irp/congress/2003_rpt/fisa.html.

18. 50 U.S.C. Section 1805 and Section 1824, and 50 U.S.C. App. Section 1801 (b).

19. A sanitized version of the letter was released to the Senate Judiciary Committee by the Justice Department on June 6, 2002. The quote is from pp. 7–8, fn. 7.

20. See his *Additional Views*, cited previously, p. 36.

21. Ibid., p. 37.

22. Shelby, *Additional Views*, cited previously, p. 37.

23. This discussion and chapter are enriched by that RAND project for the Security Division of the FBI. The final report of that project, *Reinforcing Security at the FBI*, DRR-2930-FBI (Santa Monica, CA: RAND, January 2003), has been briefed to the FBI and to Congress but has not yet been publicly released.

24. Quoted from the panel investigating the Hanssen spy case, chaired by former FBI (and CIA) Director Judge William Webster. Its report, *A Review of FBI Security Programs* (Washington, DC: Commission for Review of FBI Security Programs, March 2002), is available at http://www.usdoj.gov/05publications/websterreport.pdf. Hereafter referred to as the "Webster report."

25. This account draws heavily on Amanda Ripley, "The Fort Dix Conspiracy," *Time*, December 6, 2007. The quotes are from that article.

Chapter 4: The Imperative of Change

1. The most complete account of these events is the 9/11 Commission report, formally the "National Commission on Terrorist Attacks Upon the United States," *The 9/11 Commission Report* (Washington, DC, 2004), available at http://www.9-11commission.gov/ (last visited August 2, 2004). Hereafter referred to as the "9/11 Commission" and the "9/11 Commission report."

2. The findings of the joint House–Senate investigation of September 11 outlined the basic story. It is *Final Report*, Part I, The Joint Inquiry, December 10, 2002. A fuller account is contained in Senator Richard Shelby's long supplementary document, *September 11 and the Imperative of Reform in the Intelligence Community, Additional Views*, December 10, 2002. Both are available at http://news.findlaw.com/hdocs/docs/911rpt/. See, in particular, Shelby's report, pp. 15ff. The definitive account is that of the 9/11 Commission, formally, the "National Commission on Terrorist Attacks Upon the United States," *The 9/11 Commission Report* (Washington, DC, 2004), available at http://www.9-11commission.gov/ (last visited August 2, 2004).

3. See Walter Pincus and Don Eggen, "CIA Gave FBI Warning on Hijacker," *Washington Post*, June 4, 2002, p. A1.

4. 9/11 Commission report, pp. 268–72.

5. Ibid., p. 271.

6. Bob Drogin, Eric Lichtblau, and Greg Krikorian, "CIA, FBI Disagree on Urgency of Warning," *Los Angeles Times*, October 18, 2001, p. A1, available at http://articles.latimes.com/2001/oct/18/news/mn-58738.

7. Ibid.

8. Joe Klein, "Closework: Why We Couldn't See What Was Right in Front of Us," *The New Yorker*, October 1, 2001, pp. 44–9.

9. Available at http://specials.ft.com/attackonterrorism/index.html.

10. The conference report and therefore the text of the final bill are available at http://www.fas.org/irp/congress/2004_rpt/h108-796.html (last visited January 4, 2005).

11. In fact, the law restricts the DNI from transferring more than 5 percent or $150 million, whichever is smaller, from one agency in one year.

12. This provision echoed the blue-ribbon intelligence panels of the 1990s. For instance, the Aspin–Brown panel – formally, the Commission on the Roles and Capabilities of the United States Intelligence Community – had called for two assistant DCIs, one for the intelligence community and one for the CIA. Congress passed this into law, then later

approved giving the DCI two more deputies, for analysis and collection. The Commission report is titled *Preparing for the 21st Century: An Appraisal of U.S. Intelligence* (Washington, DC, 1996), available at http://www.access.gpo.gov/int/report.html (last visited April 25, 2005).

13. This transformation is discussed at length in Chapter 4 of Gregory F. Treverton, *Reshaping National Intelligence for an Age of Information* (Cambridge: Cambridge University Press, 2001).

14. See Alfred Cumming, *The Position of Director of National Intelligence: Issues for Congress* (Washington, DC: Congressional Research Service, July 29, 2004), available at http://www.fas.org/irp/crs/RL32506.pdf (last visited August 5, 2004).

15. Todd Stiefler, *Intelligence Restructuring: Patterns and Pitfalls*, RAND Corporation (forthcoming). See also Richard A. Best, Jr., *Proposals for Intelligence Reorganization, 1949–2004* (Washington, DC: Congressional Research Service, July 29, 2004), available at http://www.fas.org/irp/crs/RL32500.pdf (last visited August 3, 2004).

16. WMD Commission, cited previously, p. 5.

17. As elsewhere in life, the devil is in the details and, intriguingly, the purpose of the 9/11 Commission and Senate legislators was only partly public accountability. Part of their purpose was procedural: if the top-line budget were public, it could be appropriated directly and publicly to the DNI. The DNI would be in visible charge. If, however, the top line remained secret – as it did in the final bill – then the budget would still have to be "laundered" through the Pentagon. Even if the DNIs had full control in principle (which the final bill did not give them), their control still might have been diluted by the pass-through in the Pentagon.

18. See http://www.fas.org/sgp/news/2007/10/dni103007.pdf.

19. President Truman and his confidants wanted a more powerful DCI in the late 1940s but retreated in the face of Pentagon and State Department opposition, especially so because the administration's eyes were fixed on the main prize, a more centralized Pentagon. See Loch K. Johnson, "A Centralized Intelligence System: Truman's Dream Deferred," *American Intelligence Journal*, 23 (Autumn/Winter 2005), 6–15.

20. Walter Pincus, "Military Espionage Cuts Eyed," *Washington Post*, March 17, 1995, p. A1.

21. The model is explicitly that of military joint staffs, and the Center would play the roles of both J-2 (intelligence) and J-3 (operational planning).

22. The 9/11 Commission suggested that the existing Homeland Security Council should be merged into the NSC – a recommendation also made in a RAND Corporation study. Lynn Davis et al., *Coordinating the War on Terrorism*, OP-110-RC (Santa Monica, CA: RAND Corporation, 2004). The bill did not do so.

23. See Chapter 7 of Treverton, *Reshaping National Intelligence*, on the need for such a structural reorganization.

24. That resistance came through loud and clear in interviews throughout the analytic elements of the intelligence community in 2004. See Gregory F. Treverton and C. Bryan Gabbard, *Assessing the Tradecraft of Intelligence Analysis*, TR-293 (Santa Monica, CA: RAND Corporation, 2008). The bias toward current intelligence was even more marked, which is a central theme of the WMD Commission report.

25. See William Colby, with Peter Forbath, *Honorable Men: My Life in the CIA* (New York: Simon and Schuster, 1978), pp. 352–3.

26. This language is akin to my own in *Reshaping National Intelligence for an Age of Information*, p. 235.

27. For instance, existing findings apparently provided authorization for the CIA to fire a missile from a Predator drone over Yemen in November 2002. The attack killed six people, including one American. For a newspaper account, see Walter Pincus, "U.S. Strike Kills Six in Al Qaeda: Missile Fired by Predator Drone; Key Figure in Yemen Among Dead," *Washington Post*, November 5, 2002, p. A01, available at http://www.washingtonpost.com/ac2/wp-dyn?pagename=article&contentId=A5126-2002Nov4 (last visited November 26, 2008).

28. WMD Commission, p. 30.

Chapter 5: The Agenda Ahead

1. I should say that the best and most interesting group of people I have had the pleasure of working with in my career was President Carter's NSC staff. In earlier years, teaching bright graduate students whose deformation was the belief that the problem of government was that its officials were not as smart as those graduate students, I would end that comment by saying, "And look where that got the Carter administration!"

2. See U.S. Intelligence Community, *500 Day Plan: Integration and Collaboration*, October 10, 2007, available at http://www.dni.gov/500-day-plan/500-day-plan.pdf.

3. For the order, promulgated in December 1981, see http://www.fas.org/irp/offdocs/eo12333.htm. It was amended by Executive Order 13355, August 27, 2004. For the 2008 amendments, see http://www.whitehouse.gov/news/releases/2008/07/print/20080731-2.html.

4. For a detailed journalistic account of the FIA fiasco, see Philip Taubman, "Failure to Launch: In Death of Spy Satellite Program, Lofty Plans and Unrealistic Bids, *New York Times*, November 11, 2007, available at http://www.nytimes.com/2007/11/11/washington/11satellite.html?scp=1&sq=&st=nyt#step1. Quotations in the following paragraphs are from that article.

5. See Richard A. Best, Jr., *Intelligence Issues and the 104th Congress*, CRS Issues Brief 95018, updated September 26, 1996, available at http://www.fas.org/irp/crs/95-018.htm.

6. The quotations in this paragraph and the next are from pp. 3 and 21, respectively.

7. For an intriguing set of recommendations by a former CIA spymaster, see Robert Baer, "Wanted: Spies Unlike Us," *Foreign Policy* (March–April 2005).

8. I elaborated on this point in *The Need to Know, Report of the Twentieth Century Fund Task Force on Covert Action and American Democracy* (New York: Twentieth Century Fund, 1992), pp. 23–4.

9. On the mismatch between take and processing capacity, see Mark M. Lowenthal, *Intelligence: From Secrets to Policy*, 3rd ed. (Washington, DC: CG Press, 2003), pp. 45–7.

10. George Cahink, "National Security: Breaking the Code," *Government Executive*, September 1, 2001, available at http://www.govexec.com/story_page.cfm?filepath=/features/0901/0901s6.htm.

11. For a good discussion, see Chapter 7 of the WMD Commission report.

12. Treverton, *Reshaping National Intelligence*, cited previously, p. 88.

13. In his speech to the UN in early 2003, however, Secretary Colin Powell did play the transcript of a recorded conversation between an Iraqi general and colonel in the Republican Guard. The transcript of the speech is available at http://www.whitehouse.gov/news/releases/2003/02/20030205-1.html (last visited April 29, 2005).

14. On individuals learning from experience, see the work of K. A. Ericsson on acquiring expertise. Ericsson's research is also relevant to "what makes an exceptional analyst." See, for instance, *The Cambridge Handbook of Expertise and Expert Performance* or *The Road to Excellence: The Acquisition of Expert Performance in the Arts and Sciences, Sports, and Games*.

15. For instance, *The Fifth Discipline, 1992*.

16. V. Friedman, L. Lipschitz, and M. Popper, "The Mystification of Organizational Learning," *Journal of Management Inquiry*, *14*, 1 (2005), 19–30.

17. See, for instance, General Accounting Office, *Forum: High-Performing Organizations – Metrics, Means and Mechanisms for Achieving High Performance in the 21st Century Public Management Environment*, GAO-04-343SP (Washington, DC, February 2004), available at http://www.gao.gov/cgi-bin/getrpt?GAO-04-343SP.

18. To mitigate the limits of purely financial metrics, the private sector has turned to techniques such as the balanced scorecard – a management system (not only a measurement system) that enables organizations to clarify their vision and strategy and translate them into action. It

provides feedback around both the internal business processes and external outcomes in order to continuously improve strategic performance and results. Public-sector organizations (e.g., the FBI) have begun to employ variants of this approach.

19. The report of the Commission, formally the National Commission on the Public Service, is at http://www.brook.edu/gs/cps/volcker/urgentbusiness report.htm. However, one of the Commission's examples of clarity in mission was the DHS, perhaps not quite what the commissioners had in mind.

20. Gregory F. Treverton, "The State of Federal Management," *Government Executive*, January 2004.

21. Gregory F. Treverton and C. Bryan Gabbard, *Assessing the Tradecraft of Intelligence Analysis*, TR-293 (Santa Monica, CA: RAND Corporation, 2008).

22. Gregory F. Treverton and Tora K. Bikson, *New Challenges for International Leadership: Positioning the United States for the 21st Century*, Issue Paper IP-233-IP (Santa Monica, CA: RAND Corporation, 2003).

23. A recent RAND study did extensive sampling across the range of analytic products of the various intelligence agencies; among other analyses, it compared the subjects of the products with the NIPF categories. The study is classified but, perhaps not surprisingly, the correspondence between products and NIPF priorities was closest for agencies farthest from customers: the NSA and the NGA. The correspondence was much less for agencies such as State's INR or the NIC, which had relatively intense, ongoing interactions with actual customers; they both needed and heeded NIPF much less.

24. See Gregory F. Treverton and Tora K. Bikson, *New Challenges for International Leadership: Positioning the United States for the 21st Century*, RAND, IP-233-IP, 2002.

25. These conclusions derive from Treverton and Gabbard, cited previously. They echo those of a fascinating assessment by an anthropologist of intelligence's analytic processes; see Rob Johnston, *The Culture of Analytic Tradecraft: An Ethnography of the IC* (Washington, DC: Center for the Study of Intelligence, Central Intelligence Agency, 2005).

26. See *The U.S. Intelligence Community's Five-Year Strategic Human Capital Plan*, October 18, 2006, available at http://www.dni.gov/publications/DNIHumanCapitalStrategicPlan18October2006.pdf.

27. See Nancy Bernkopf Tucker, "The Cultural Revolution in Intelligence: Interim Report," *The Washington Quarterly, 31*, 2 (Spring 2008), 52.

28. See, for instance, National Academy of Public Administration, *Transforming the FBI: Roadmap to an Effective Human Capital Program* (Washington, DC, September 2005).

29. This is the conclusion of a RAND assessment of the training of analysts, done in parallel with the analysis of analytic products cited previously.

30. The classic article from a business perspective is Steven Kerr, "On the Folly of Rewarding A, While Hoping for B," *The Academy of Management Journal, 18*, 4 (December 1975), 769–83.

31. This discussion draws on work, as yet unpublished, by my colleagues Bruce Don and David Frelinger.

32. The observations are echoed by Johnston, cited previously.

33. For an assessment of the proposed CIA plan, see Business Executives for National Security, *Pay for Performance at the CIA: Restoring Equity, Transparency and Accountability: The Assessment of the Independent Panel on the Central Intelligence Agency's Compensation Reform Proposals* (Washington, DC, January 2004).

34. As quoted in Thomas Frank, "Push Is on to Overhaul FBI," *Newsday*, December 29, 2002.

35. See the *Final Report*, cited previously, "Recommendations."

36. 9/11 Commission report, Staff Statement No. 9, "Law Enforcement, Counterterrorism, and Intelligence Collection in the United States Prior to 9/11," pp. 1, 3.

37. This is the central argument of the most detailed critique. See Judge Richard A. Posner, *Uncertain Shield: The U.S. Intelligence System in the Throes of Reform* (Lanham, MD: Rowman & Littlefield Publishers, Inc., 2006).

38. Quoted in Jan W. Rivkin and Michael A. Roberto, *Federal Bureau of Investigation (A)* (Boston, MA: Harvard Business School, 2007), p. 3.

39. WMD Commission, p. 30.

40. This process has not been without its challenges. See Office of the Inspector General, Department of Justice, "Follow-Up Audit of the Federal Bureau of Investigation's Efforts to Hire, Train, and Retain Intelligence Analysts," Audit Report 07-30, April 2007.

41. Both the Mudd and Ford quotes are from Rivkin and Roberto (B), cited previously, p. 7.

42. Scott Shane and Lowell Bergman, "FBI Struggling to Reinvent Itself," *New York Times*, October 9, 2006.

43. This draws on my *Reorganizing U.S. Domestic Intelligence: Assessing the Options*, MG-767 (Santa Monica, CA: RAND Corporation, 2008), available at http://www.rand.org/pubs/monographs/MG767/.

44. An earlier RAND study investigated domestic intelligence arrangements in four countries. See Chalk and Rosenau, cited previously. More recently, RAND was asked by Congress to examine the entire issue of creating a separate domestic intelligence service, one focused on counterterrorism, although not to make a recommendation. As part of

that assessment, RAND studies domestic intelligence arrangements in Britain, France, Germany, Canada, Australia, and Sweden. See *Reorganizing U.S. Domestic Intelligence: Assessing the Options*, cited previously.

45. James Burch, "A Domestic Intelligence Agency for the United States? A Comparative Analysis of Domestic Intelligence Agencies and Their Implications for Homeland Security," *Homeland Security Affairs* III/2 (June 2007), 3. See also Harvey Rishikof, "The Role of the Federal Bureau of Investigation in National Security," in Roger George and Robert Kline (eds.), *Intelligence and National Security Strategist: Enduring Issues and Challenges* (New York: Rowman and Littlefield Publishers, 2006), p. 126; and the Markel Foundation, *Protecting America's Freedom in the Information Age: A Report of the Markle Foundation Task Force* (New York: Markle Foundation, 2002), p. 21.

46. See, for example, General Accounting Office, *Combating Terrorism: How Five Countries Are Organized to Combat Terrorism* (Washington, DC: GAO, April 2002), p. 8.

47. See *Looking Back: The Case for Security Intelligence Review in Canada*, 1981, available at http://www.sirc-csars.gc.ca/reflections/sec2a_e.html#13a.

48. In one sense, DHS's growing pains could be seen as an argument for a separate service with a clear and singular mission because the root of the challenge for DHS is that its 180,000 officials and twenty-two constituent agencies do *not* share a single mission.

49. Terry Moe, "The Politics of Bureaucratic Structure," in John E. Chubb and Paul E. Peterson (eds.), *Can the Government Govern?* (Washington, DC: The Brookings Institution, 1989), p. 267.

50. See *Reorganizing U.S. Domestic Intelligence: Assessing the Options*, cited previously.

51. One of few to suggest such an initiative is Morton Halperin. See his "Safe at Home," *The American Prospect*, November 1, 2003, available at http://www.prospect.org/cs/articles?article=safe_at_home.

52. The Service Web site is http://www.aivd.nl.

Chapter 6: The Special Challenge of Analysis

1. The two most detailed are those of the 9/11 Commission and the WMD Commission, cited previously. The first, formally, is the National Commission on Terrorist Attacks Upon the United States, *The 9/11 Commission Report* (Washington, DC, 2004), available at http://www.9-11commission.gov/.

2. Formally, the Intelligence Reform and Terrorism Prevention Act of 2004, available at http://www.nctc.gov/docs/pl108_458.pdf.

3. The complete quote from which the saying derives is pertinent: "Great cases, like hard cases, make bad law. For great cases are called great, not by reason of their importance in shaping the law of the future, but because of some accident of immediate overwhelming interest which appeals to the feelings and distorts the judgment. These immediate interests exercise a kind of hydraulic pressure which makes what previously was clear seem doubtful, and before which even well settled principles of law will bend." Oliver Wendell Holmes, dissenting. *Northern Securities Co. v. United States*, 193 U.S. 197, 400–411 (1904).

4. The signature reports on 9/11 and the WMD issue are cited previously. For Iran, one readable account is Gregory F. Treverton, "Iran, 1978–1979: Coping with the Unthinkable," in Ernest R. May and Philip Zelikow (eds.), *Dealing with Dictators: Dilemmas of U.S. Diplomacy and Intelligence Analysis, 1945–1990* (MIT Press, 2006). See also Gary Sick, *All Fall Down: America's Tragic Encounter with Iran* (New York: Random House, 1985). Robert Jervis's classified postmortem, conducted soon after the case, has been declassified although heavily redacted. See Jervis, "Analysis of NFAC's Performance on Iran's Domestic Crisis," National Archives and Records Administration, CIA CREST system, CIA-RDP86B00269R00110110003-4. (NFAC was the National Foreign Assessment Center, which at the time combined the CIA DI and the NIC.) The India postmortem was chaired by former vice chairman of the Joint Chiefs of Staff, Admiral David Jeremiah. The report itself has not been declassified. For reportage on the case and report, see *The Washington Post*, June 3, 1998, p. A18, and *The New York Times*, same date.

5. Among many good discussions of this issue, see Stephen Marrin, "Preventing Intelligence Failures by Learning from the Past," *International Journal of Intelligence and Counterintelligence, 17* (2004), 657 ff.

6. The estimate has been declassified. See *Yugoslavia Transformed*, NIE 15–90 (October 1990), available at http://www.foia.cia.gov/browse_docs.asp.

7. The concept was popularized in Masaaki Imai, *Kaizen: The Key to Japan's Competitive Success* (New York: McGraw-Hill/Irwin, 1986). The Japanese concept of *kaizen* is directly derived from the principles of designed-in (versus fixed-after-production) quality, customer-centrism, and continuous improvement brought to Japan after World War II by Edwards Deming, an American who worked with the Japanese to recover their industrial capacity. His work did not get traction in the United States until *kaizen* was promoted here in the 1980s as a Japanese management practice known as Total Quality Management. Deming's approach was to examine and improve the system in which operations take place and not simply

to reorganize structure or blame the person. A modern incarnation of this thinking is in Six Sigma programs to reduce product flaws as applied at Motorola and GE. For example, see http://www.deming.org/ regarding Deming's work and some current resources; and http://www.isixsigma. com/me/six_sigma/ regarding Six Sigma methods. It is also relevant to service and intellectual processes, such as intelligence, in its reliance on three concepts: (1) products alone are not as important as the process that creates them; (2) the interdependent nature of systems is more important than any one isolated problem, cause, or point solution; and (3) nonjudgmental regard for people in that people usually execute as the system directs or allows, people are not sufficient explanation for a problem (or a success), and blaming violates an associated principle against waste.

8. For instance, the Dempster–Shafer theory is a generalization of Bayesian logic that allows analysts to derive degrees of belief in one question from probabilities for a related question – for example, information provided by an observer or informant whose reliability is subjectively assessed. For a description, see http://www.glennshafer.com/assets/downloads/article48.pdf.

9. See, for instance, James Dewar et al., *Assumption-Based Planning: A Planning Tool for Very Uncertain Times* (Santa Monica, CA: RAND Corporation, 1993).

10. I am grateful to David Moore for suggestions about and embellishments to an earlier version of this table.

11. Some of these issues relate to organization and workflow as well, and the issues bring in train a set of psychological questions, which are outlined later in this chapter.

12. Elaine C. Kamarck emphasizes uncertainty and information overload. See her *Transforming the Intelligence Community: Improving the Collection and Management of Information* (Washington, DC: IBM Center for the Business of Government, October 2005), p. 9.

13. Dave Snowden, "Complex Acts of Knowing: Paradox and Descriptive Self-Awareness," *Journal of Knowledge Management*, Special Issue, September 2002, available at http://www.kwork.org/Resources/snowden.pdf (last visited December 17, 2003).

14. See Johnston, cited previously. Dennis M. Gormley speaks in similar ways about intelligence's lack of rigor, and he makes a number of thoughtful suggestions. See his "The Limits of Intelligence: Iraq's Lessons," *Survival, 46*, 3 (Autumn 2004), 15ff.

15. These techniques, being developed at RAND and elsewhere, are called robust decision-making (RDM). To make decisions, analysts and policy makers would look for strategies that seem robust across many

scenarios. For intelligence analysis, the aim might be to identify outcomes that seem robust across variables.

16. This list is adapted from Kamarck, cited previously.

17. Malcolm Gladwell's popular account weaves together stories of such tacit knowledge across a range of fields. See *Blink: The Power of Thinking Without Thinking* (New York: Little Brown, 2005). See also Gary Klein, *Intuition at Work: Why Developing Your Gut Instinct Will Make You Better at What You Do* (New York: Doubleday, 2002). The idea of unconscious knowledge in psychological inquiry, however, goes back to the nineteenth century: Helmholz in psychophysiology and vision and Freud in psychology. Current usage derives from Michael Polanyi's 1950s writings on science (see, e.g., http://www.infed.org/thinkers/polanyi.htm). Psychologist Robert Sternberg has popularized three kinds of intelligence: creative or experiential, analytical or componential, and practical or contextual, the last of which features tacit knowledge. See R. J. Sternberg, *Beyond IQ: A Triarchic Theory of Human Intelligence* (New York: Cambridge University Press, 1985) and http://www.yale.edu/rjsternberg/). For an introduction to knowledge management in business, see Tim Ray and Stephen Little, *Managing Knowledge: An Essential Reader* (London: Sage Publications, 2005). The military has also sponsored research on the role of tacit knowledge in military leadership; for example, Cynthia T. Matthew, Ann T. Cianciolo, and Robert J. Sternberg, *Developing Effective Military Leaders: Facilitating the Acquisition of Experience-Based Tacit Knowledge* (Technical Report 1161), Army Research Institute for the Behavioral and Social Sciences (2005), available at http://www.hqda.army.mil/ari/pdf/TR1161.pdf.

18. Some critics fault Sternberg's underlying research, claiming that the ideas are more theory than empirical fact. See Linda Gottfredson, "Dissecting Practical Intelligence Theory: Its Claims and Evidence," *Intelligence, 31,* 4 (2003), 343–97, 415–24.

19. For example, see his *Expert Political Judgment: How Good Is It? How Can We Know?* (Princeton, NJ: Princeton University Press, 2005).

20. See N. Dalkey, B. Brown, and S. Cochran, *The Delphi Method, III: Use of Self Ratings to Improve Group Estimates* (Santa Monica, CA: The RAND Corporation, 1969).

21. Bruce Bueno de Mesquita is the creator of this line of approach, along with Jacek Kugler. For the basic logic, see Bueno de Mesquita, *Forecasting Political Events: The Future of Hong Kong* (New Haven, CT: Yale University Press, 1985), pp. 11–54; with David Newman and Alvin Rabushka, *Red Flag Over Hong Kong* (Chatham, NJ: Chatham House, 1996), pp. 165–86; with Frans N. Stokman, *European Community Decision Making: Models Applications, and Comparisons* (New Haven, CT:

Yale University Press, 1994, pp. 71–104; "A Decision Making Model: Its Structure and Form," *International Interactions*, 23 (1997), 235–66; *Predicting Politics* (Columbus: Ohio State University Press, 2002).

22. Quoted in "Amid Furor, Pentagon Kills Terrorism Futures Market," *CNN.com/Inside Politics*, July 30, 2003, available at http://edition. cnn.com/2003/ALLPOLITICS/07/29/terror.market/index.html. For an example of the analysts' reaction, see William Jackson, "Consultant: Good Theory Behind DARPA's 'Terrorism Futures'," *Government Computer News*, August 6, 2003, available at http://www.gcn.com/online/vol1_no1/23051-1.html.

23. The classic work is Richards S. Heuer, Jr., *The Psychology of Intelligence Analysis* (Washington, DC: Center for the Study of Intelligence, 1999).

24. Collection management officers play the first of these roles. Although CMOs are collections officers, they add analytic value to raw intelligence before the reports get to the analysts. See https://www.cia. gov/careers/jobs/collection_manage_off.html.

25. The classic work is Irving L. Janis, *Victims of Groupthink: Psychological Study of Foreign-Policy Decisions and Fiascos* (Boston, MA: Houghton Mifflin, 1972). See also Cass R. Sunstein, *Infotopia: How Many Minds Produce Knowledge* (New York: Oxford University Press, 2006).

26. See https://www.cia.gov/cia/information/eo12333.html. Competition is cited in Part 1, 1,1a.

27. See J. Scott Armstrong (ed.), *Principles of Forecasting: A Handbook for Researchers and Practitioners* (Norwell, MA: Kluwer Academic, 2001).

28. For an exploration from a sensemaking perspective of how creativity unfolds in large, complex organizations of long standing, see R. Drazin, M. A. Glynn, and R. K. Kazanjian, "Multilevel Theorizing About Creativity in Organizations: A Sensemaking Perspective," *Academy of Management Review*, 24, 2 (1999), 286–307. Oldham and Cummings found that employees were most creative when they worked on complex, challenging problems under supportive, not controlling, supervision. See G. R. Oldham and Anne Cummings, "Employee Creativity: Personal and Contextual Factors at Work," *The Academy of Management Journal*, 39, 3 (June 1996), 607–34.

29. Red-teaming seeks to get inside the minds of adversaries, not asking what we would do if we were them but creatively trying to ask what they might do given their own goals, culture, organization, and the like. Red-teaming in its various forms is really only one, albeit an important one, among a family of "what-if?" techniques under the label *alternative analysis*. For more, see Warren Fishbein and Gregory F. Treverton, *Making Sense of Transnational Threats*, Central Intelligence Agency, Kent Center for Analytic Tradecraft, Occasional Papers, 3, 1 (October 2004), available

at https://www.cia.gov/cia/publications/Kent_Papers/pdf/OPV3No1.pdf. Fulfilling the latter directive, the DNI established the Office of Analytic Integrity and Standards under the Deputy Director for National Intelligence for Analysis.

30. For an overview of alternative analysis techniques, see Roger George, "Fixing the Mindset Problem: Alternative Analysis," in *International Journal of Intelligence and Counterintelligence, 17,* 3 (Fall 2004), 385–405. On devil's advocacy, see Charlane Nemeth, Keith Brown, and John Rogers, "Devil's Advocate vs. Authentic Dissent: Stimulating Quantity and Quality," *European Journal of Social Psychology, 31* (2001), 707–20. On scenarios, see Philip Tetlock's experiments in Chapter 7 of his book, cited previously.

31. The WMD Commission makes a parallel plea; see p. 20. The CIA's Center for the Study of Intelligence, which published the Johnston book cited herein, would seem to be such a focal point, at least for the CIA, and it does a number of histories. Yet, its bias is that of historians and of covert operators, which tends to focus on the particularities of cases, not their possible lessons for the future.

32. Karl Weick, *Sensemaking in Organizations* (London: Sage Publications, 1995).

33. See, for example, Karl Weick and K. M. Sutcliffe, *Managing the Unexpected: Assuring High Performance in an Age of Complexity* (San Francisco, CA: Jossey-Bass, 2001).

34. See Weick, *Sensemaking in Organizations.* See also Karl E. Weick, "Leadership When Events Don't Play by the Rules," available at http://www.bus.umich.edu/FacultyResearch/Research/TryingTimes/Rules.htm. The watchwords are from the latter, as are the paraphrases of the descriptions.

35. Enabled by increasingly sophisticated spreadsheet-based programs, these would allow consumers to manipulate variables to generate alternative outcomes. Decision makers could quickly and easily explore a range of possibilities in a way that is more likely to be retained than if presented in a long and dry formal tome. See https://www.cia.gov/cia/publications/Kent_Papers/vol3no2.htm.

36. For more detail, see Loch K. Johnson, *Bombs, Bugs, Drugs and Thugs: Intelligence and America's Quest for Security* (New York: New York University Press, 2000), especially Chapter 6.

Chapter 7: Many Customers, Too Many Secrets

1. Some of that flavor runs through even the best of the outside reports on the issue, *Creating a Trusted Network for Homeland Security,* Second Report of the Markle Foundation Task Force, December 2003,

available at http://www.markletaskforce.org/markle_programs/policy_ for_a_networked_society/national_security/projects/taskforce_national_ security.php (as of September 2005).

2. John Gannon, "Managing Analysis in the Information Age," in Roger Z. George and James B. Bruce (eds.), *Analyzing Intelligence: Origins, Obstacles and Innovation* (Washington, DC: Georgetown University Press, 2008), pp. 221–2.

3. Formally, the *Final Report of the Commission on the Intelligence Capabilities of the United States Regarding Weapons of Mass Destruction* (Washington, DC, 2005), available at http://www.wmd.gov.

4. Paul Pillar makes this point in his discussion of intelligence and the Iraq war. See his "Intelligence, Policy, and the War in Iraq," *Foreign Affairs*, *85*, 2 (March/April 2006), 15–28.

5. See Pilar, cited previously.

6. See Kenneth M. Pollack, "Spies, Lies, and Weapons: What Went Wrong," *The Atlantic Monthly*, Januay/February 2004; and, especially, Seymour Hersh, "Selective Intelligence," *New Yorker*, May 12, 2003.

7. Ernest R. May, *Strange Victory: Hitler's Conquest of France* (New York: Farrar, Straus and Giroux, 2000).

8. On the 1973 war, see, for instance, William B. Quandt, *Peace Process: American Diplomacy and the Arab–Israeli Conflict Since 1967* (Washington, DC: Brookings Institution Press, 1990).

9. The postmortem was chaired by former vice chairman of the Joint Chiefs of Staff, Admiral David Jeremiah. The report was never made public; however, for reportage on it, see *The Washington Post*, June 3, 1998, p. A18, and *The New York Times*, same date. For the transcript of Jeremiah's briefing on the report, see http://www.fas.org/irp/cia/product/jeremiah.html (last visited December 16, 2003).

10. Peter Schwartz, *The Art of the Long View* (New York: Doubleday, 1991), p. 220.

11. See *Prewar Assessments of Postwar Iraq*, Report of the Senate Select Committee on Intelligence, July 9, 2004, p. 259, available at http://intelligence.senate.gov/prewar.pdf.

12. Dennis M. Gormley, "The Limits of Intelligence: Iraq's Lessons," *Survival, 46*, 3 (Autumn 2004), 10.

13. See Jennifer Sims (ed.), "Mission-Based Counterintelligence: An Approach to Counterintelligence and Homeland Defense," Jennifer Sims and Burton Gerber, *Vaults, Mirrors and Masks: The Future of US Counterintelligence* (Washington DC: Georgetown University Press, 2008).

14. *Bayesian*, from Bayes' theorem, describes a process of updating subjective probabilities in light of new evidence. See Chapter 3.

15. See the *Comprehensive Report of the Special Advisor to the DCI on Iraq's WMD* (the "Duelfer report"), posted on the CIA Web

site October 6, 2004. An easier-to-download version is available at http://www.lib.umich.edu/govdocs/duelfer.html.

16. The full estimate has not yet been declassified. The Key Judgments are at http://www.ceip.org/files/projects/npp/pdf/Iraq/declassifiedintellreport. pdf. See also Joseph Cirincione et al., *WMD in Iraq: Evidence and Implications* (Washington, DC: Carnegie Endowment, January 2004), available at http://www.ceip.org/files/projects/npp/resources/iraqintell/home. htm.

17. *Report on the U.S. Intelligence Community's Prewar Intelligence Assessments on Iraq*, June 2004, available online at http://www.fas.org/irp/ congress/2004_rpt/index.html.

18. The key judgments were declassified and are available at http://www. fas.org/irp/dni/iran120307.pdf. All quotations are from that citation.

19. See the interview with CIA Director Michael Hayden in Lawrence Wright, "The Spymaster," *The New Yorker*, January 21, 2008, p. 59.

20. See Mark D. Mandeles et al., *Managing Command and Control in the Persian Gulf War* (Westport, CT: Greenwood, 1996), pp. 91ff.

21. See James Worthen, "The Gates Hearings: Politicization and Soviet Analysis at the CIA," *Studies in Intelligence* (Spring 1994).

22. See Lawrence Freedman, *U.S. Intelligence and the Soviet Strategic Threat*, 2nd ed. (Princeton, NJ: Princeton University Press, 1986); and John Prados, *The Soviet Estimate: U.S. Intelligence Analysis and Russian Military Strength* (New York: Dial Press, 1982).

23. See Gregory F. Treverton, "Intelligence: Welcome to the American Government," in Thomas E. Mann (ed.), *A Question of Balance: The President, the Congress and Foreign Policy* (Washington, DC: The Brookings Institution, 1990).

24. The setting was a conference at Princeton in New Jersey in 2006, and the rendition of Shultz's views is that of the author.

25. See GAO, *Rail Safety and Security: Some Actions Already Taken to Enhance Rail Security, but Risk-Based Plan Needed*, GAO-03-43 (Washington, DC, April 2003), available at http://www.gao.gov/new.items/ d03435.pdf.

26. For my assessment, see my "Intelligence Gathering, Sharing and Analysis," in Donald Kettle (ed.), *The Department of Homeland Security's First Year: A Report Card* (The Century Foundation, March 2004), available at http://www.tcf.org/Publications/HomelandSecurity/2.intelligence.pdf.

27. For a recommendation for a fleshed-out structure for sharing, one that resonates with many of the ideas in this book, see *Creating a Trusted Network for Homeland Security*, cited previously, p. 8.

28. Formally, the National Commission on Terrorist Attacks Upon the United States, *The 9/11 Commission Report* (Washington, DC, 2004),

available at http://www.9-11commission.gov/; and *Final Report of the Commission on the Intelligence Capabilities of the United States Regarding Weapons of Mass Destruction* (Washington, DC, 2005), available at http://www.wmd.gov/report/. The WMD Commission recommends jettisoning that language, not least because it implies that agencies, not the government, own information (p. 29).

29. Gregory F. Treverton and C. Bryan Gabbard, *Assessing the Tradecraft of Intelligence Analysis* (Santa Monica, CA: The RAND Corporation, 2008).

30. Program Manager, Information Sharing Environment, "Information Sharing Environment Implementation Plan," November 2006, p. xiii.

31. I owe the term *coproduction* to my friend and colleague, Lt. John Sullivan of the Los Angeles County Sheriff's Office.

32. Lawrence Wright, "The Spymaster," *The New Yorker*, January 21, 2008, p. 57.

33. "Intelligence Community Classification Guidance: Findings and Recommendations Report," January 2008, available at http://www.fas.org/sgp/othergov/intel/class.pdf.

34. Some examples that address domestic and foreign intelligence issues include *Countering the Changing Threat of Terrorism* (National Commission on Terrorism, June 2000); the first through fifth reports from the *Advisory Panel to Assess Domestic Response Capabilities for Terrorism Involving Weapons of Mass Destruction* (Gilmore Commission), 1999–2004; and *Final Report of the National Commission on Terrorist Attacks Upon the United States* (9/11 Commission report), July 2004.

35. This discussion is drawn from K. Jack Riley et al., *State and Local Intelligence in the War on Terrorism* MG-394-RC (Santa Monica, CA: RAND Corporation, 2005). I thank my colleagues in that venture, Lois Davis, Jack Riley, Jeremy Wilson, and Gregory Ridgway. This draws on a 2002 survey of all fifty states and two hundred local authorities, and on detailed interviews with eight local authorities around the country. The 2002 survey results are published in more detail in Lois M. Davis et al., *When Terrorism Hits Home: How Prepared Are State and Local Law Enforcement?* MG-104-MIPT (Santa Monica, CA: RAND Corporation, 2004).

36. "Title III" refers to Title III of the Omnibus Crime Control and Safe Streets Act of 1968. For a discussion of the Patriot Act's relationship to Title III issues, see Testimony of Robert S. Mueller, III, Director, Federal Bureau of Investigation Before the United States Senate Committee on the Judiciary, Sunset Provisions of the USA Patriot Act, April 5, 2005, available at http://www.fbi.gov/congress/congress05/mueller040505.htm (last visited May 23, 2005).

37. The JTTFs vary in size and structure relative to the terrorist threat dealt with by each FBI field office. On average, forty to fifty people are assigned full-time to the JTTFs; however, some task forces such as New York City can have as many as 550 personnel and a number of part-time personnel can also be assigned to the JTTFs.

38. Lois M. Davis et al., *Summary of Selected Survey Results*, Appendix D, in the report, "The Advisory Panel to Assess Domestic Response Capabilities for Terrorism Involving Weapons of Mass Destruction," Fifth Annual Report to the President and Congress, "V. Forging America's New Normalcy: Securing Our Homeland, Protecting Our Liberty," December 15, 2003.

39. *Seattle Post-Intelligencer*, "Portland Becomes First to Pull Out of FBI-Led Anti-Terror Team," April 29, 2005, available at http://seattlepi. nwsource.com/local/222207_fbi29.html (last visited May 23, 2005).

40. See, for example, *Information Week*, "Two More States Withdraw From Database Program," March 12, 2004, available at http://www. informationweek.com/story/showArticle.jhtml?articleID=18312112 (last visited June 10, 2005).

41. That is the conclusion of one study that is an exception to that conclusion. Charles H. Kennedy and Peter P. Swire, "State Wiretaps and Electronic Surveillance after September 11," *Hastings Law Journal, 54* (2003).

42. The Web site of the Constitution Project Initiative on Liberty and Security provides information on the status of each state's wiretap legislation, along with an overview across states. See http://www.ncsl.org/logic. htm?returnpage=http://www.ncsl.org/programs/lis/CIP/surveillance.htm.

43. *Berger v. New York*, 388 U.S. 42, 54–55, 58–59 (1967); and Electronic Communication Privacy Act of 1986, Pub.L. No. 99-508, 100 Stat. 1848 (1986).

44. Kennedy and Swire, cited previously, p. 982.

45. This and the next paragraph draw on Todd Masse, Siobhan O'Neil, and John Rollins, *Fusion Centers: Issues and Options for Congress*, CRS Report for Congress, July 6, 2007, p. 11, 29–30.

46. For more, see http://www.dhs.gov/xnews/releases/press_release_0616. shtm.

47. The site is at https://www.it-isac.org/membership.php.

48. Masse et al., cited previously, p. 29.

49. Stephen J. Schulhofer, *The Enemy Within: Intelligence Gathering, Law Enforcement, and Civil Liberties in the Wake of September 11* (New York: Century Foundation Press, 2002), p. 52.

50. Business Executives for National Security, "Recommendations for Improving the Suspicious Activity Report (SAR)," April 11, 2003.

51. The distinctions were not new with Rumsfeld, but he used them, famously, in a Pentagon press briefing on December 12, 2002. For the transcript, see http://www.defenselink.mil/transcripts/transcript.aspx? transcriptid=2636.

52. The Global Justice Information Sharing Initiative Intelligence Working Group, which is a national criminal intelligence council, developed the National Criminal Intelligence Sharing Plan. This plan is available at http://it.ojp.gov/documents/National_Criminal_Intelligence Sharing_Plan.pdf.

Chapter 8: Convert Action: Forward to the Past?

1. 50 U.S.C., sec. 413(b)(c). For more detail, see Jennifer D. Kibbe, "Covert Action and the Pentagon," *Intelligence and National Security, 22,* 1 (February 2007), 57.

2. For an assessment by a fellow staffer, see Loch K. Johnson, "Congressional Supervision of America's Secret Agencies: The Experience and Legacy of the Church Committee," *Public Administration Review, 64* (January 2004), 3–14.

3. See *Final Report of the Select Committee to Study Governmental Operations with Respect to Intelligence Activities of the United States Senate,* 94th Congress, 2nd Session, 1976. For links to these reports, as well as to a rich range of other documents, both historical and contemporary, see www.icdc.com/~paulwolf/cointelpro/cointel.htm.

4. The "40" merely referred to the directive that had created the committee. At other times, in modest attempts at discretion, the committees had been named for the room in which they met.

5. Gregory F. Treverton, *Covert Action: The Limits of Intervention in the Postwar World* (New York: Basic Books, 1987). This chapter draws on an article produced from the book by Gregory F. Treverton, "Covert Action and Open Society," *Foreign Affairs, 65,* 5 (Summer 1987).

6. For an authoritative account of the affair, see *Report of the President's Special Review Board* (the Tower Commission), Washington, DC: U.S. Government Printing Office, 1987. The *Final Report of the Independent Counsel for Iran–Contra Matters,* 1993, is available at http://www.fas.org/irp/offdocs/walsh/.

7. Reprinted in William M. Leary (ed.), *The Central Intelligence Agency: History and Documents* (Tuscaloosa, AL: University of Alabama Press, 1984), pp. 131–3.

8. Cited in Kermit Roosevelt, *Countercoup: The Struggle for the Control of Iran* (New York: McGraw-Hill, 1979), p. 199. Because Roosevelt's account is not independently documented, his recollections should be taken as evocative, not gospel.

9. The most authoritative account of the Guatemala intervention is Richard H. Immerman, *The CIA in Guatemala: The Foreign Policy of Intervention* (Austin, TX: University of Texas Press, 1982), although additional details have been declassified more recently.

10. Quoted in Theodore C. Sorensen, *Kennedy* (New York: Harper & Row, 1965), p. 309.

11. The best account of covert action during this period is *Covert Action in Chile*, staff report to the Senate Select Committee to Study Governmental Operations with Respect to Intelligence Activities, 94th Congress, 1st Session, December 1975.

12. See, for example, Conor Cruise O'Brien, "How Hot Was Chile?" in *The New Republic*, August 26, 1985, p. 37.

13. Author's press briefing on behalf of the Church Committee, in Washington, DC, December 4, 1975.

14. David Atlee Phillips, *The Night Watch* (New York: Atheneum, 1977), p. 53.

15. For accounts of both, see Chapters 8 and 9 of John Prados, *Presidents' Secret Wars: CIA and Pentagon Covert Operations Since World War II* (New York: Morrow, 1986).

16. Both Track II and the anti-Castro plots are detailed in *Alleged Assassination Plots Involving Foreign Leaders*, an interim report of the Senate Select Committee to Study Governmental Operations with Respect to Intelligence Activities, 94th Congress, 1st Session, November 20, 1975.

17. This number is rough, based on my interviews at the time and on press accounts. In any case, the precise number does not mean much because operations vary widely in cost, not to mention risk and degree of controversy.

18. Interview, January 9, 1986.

19. See Steve Coll, *Ghost Wars: The Secret History of the CIA, Afghanistan, and Bin Laden, from the Soviet Invasion to September 10, 2001* (New York: Penguin Press, 2004).

20. NED's Web site contains a careful history of the idea and organization, one that is self-aware of the constraints on NED's operations. See http://www.ned.org/about/nedhistory.html.

21. For this figure, the following quotes, and a good summary of the Serbian case, see United States Institute of Peace, *Whither the Bulldozer: Nonviolent Revolution and the Transition to Democracy in Serbia*, Special Report 72, 6 August 2001, available at http://www.usip.org/pubs/specialreports/sr72.html.

22. Interview, Columbia University Oral History Research Office, 1967, p. 25.

23. Testimony before the Senate Select Committee to Study Governmental Operations with Respect to Intelligence Activities, December 5, 1975.
24. As usual in Washington, if success did not have a thousand fathers, it surely did have a thousand chroniclers. Among many accounts of the CIA role, see Gary C. Schroen, *First In: How the CIA Spearheaded the War on Terror in Afghanistan* (New York: Random House, 2005).
25. Formally, the National Commission on Terrorist Attacks Upon the United States, *The 9/11 Commission Report* (Washington, DC, 2004), available at http://www.9-11commission.gov/ (last visited August 2, 2004). The specific recommendations are summarized in the Executive Summary and spelled out in more detail in Chapter 13, "How to Do It?: A Different Way of Organizing the Government." Hereafter referred to as "9/11 Commission" and "9/11 Commission Report."
26. See Kibbe, "Covert Action and the Pentagon," cited previously, p. 60. The numbers in the next paragraph are also from the same source, pp. 60, 68.
27. See Kibbe, cited previously, p. 70.
28. See Dana Priest, "U.S. Citizen Among Those Killed in Yemen Predator Missile Strike," *The Washington Post*, November 8, 2002, available at http://www-tech.mit.edu/V122/N54/long4-54.54w.html; and Walter Pincus, "U.S. Strike Kills Six in Al Qaeda: Missile Fired by Predator Drone; Key Figure in Yemen Among Dead," *The Washington Post*, November 5, 2002, p. A01, available at http://www.washingtonpost.com/ac2/wp-dyn?pagename=article&contentId=A5126-2002Nov4.
29. For a careful parsing of the authority for covert action and the debate about it when done by the military, see Jennifer D. Kibbe, "The Rise of the Shadow Warriors," *Foreign Affairs* (March/April 2004).
30. The governing legislation is still the Intelligence Authorization Act of 1991. The quoted phrases are from that Act. For more details, see Kibbe, "Covert Action and the Pentagon," cited previously, pp. 62–3.
31. See Kibbe, cited previously, p. 63.
32. Interview, January 16, 1987.

Chapter 9: Rebuilding the Social Contract

1. I owe this title to Philip Zelikow.
2. *Alleged Assassination Plots Involving Foreign Leaders*, An Interim Report of the Select Committee to Study Governmental Operations with Respect to Intelligence Activities of the United States Senate, 94th Congress, 1st session, 1976, p. 285, available at http://www.aarclibrary.org/publib/church/reports/ir/html/ChurchIR_0150a.htm.

3. This is a theme of David Omand in "The Limits of Avowal: Secret Intelligence in an Age of Public Scrutiny," in Gregory F. Treverton and Wilhelm Agrell (eds.), *National Intelligence Services: Current Research and Future Prospects*, forthcoming from Cambridge University Press.
4. For background, see http://www.humanrightsfirst.org/us_law/etn/misc/backgrounder-hayden.html.
5. Officially, Public Law 109-148, div. A, title X, §§ 1001–1006, 119 Stat. 2680, 2739–44 (2005).
6. Officially, Military Commissions Act, Public Law 109-366, 120 Stat. 2600 (2006).
7. Dana Priest, "CIA Holds Terror Suspect in Secret Prisons," *The Washington Post*, November 2, 2005; p. A01, available at http://www.washington post.com/wp-dyn/content/article/2005/11/01/AR2005110101644.html.
8. Officially, Public Law 107-40 [S. J. RES. 23], September 18, 2001.
9. *Hamdan v. Rumsfeld*, 126 S. Ct. 2749 (2006), p. 4, point 4.
10. CIA Director Michael Hayden provided the most explicit public statement about the Agency's use of waterboarding to the Senate Intelligence Committee in February 2008. He confirmed that it had been used on the three suspects mentioned herein. See Mark Mazzetti, "Intelligence Chief Cites Qaeda Threat to U.S.," *The New York Times*, February 6, 2008, p. A1, available at http://www.nytimes.com/2008/02/06/washington/06intel.html?_r=1&th&emc=th&oref=slogin.
11. Lawrence Wright, "The Spymaster," *The New Yorker*, January 21, 2008, p. 52.
12. See Stephen J. Schulhofer, *The Enemy Within: Intelligence Gathering, Law Enforcement and Civil Liberties in the Wake of September 11* (New York: The Century Foundation, 2002), p. 46.
13. Richard K. Betts, *Enemies of Intelligence: Knowledge and Power in American National Security* (New York: Columbia University Press, 2007), p. 163.
14. Schulhofer, cited previously, provides a very good, readable discussion of many of these categories.
15. Department of Justice Inspector General, "The September 11 Detainees: A Review of the Treatment of Aliens Held on Immigration Charges in Connection with the Investigation of the September 11 Attacks," April 2003, available at www.usdoc.gov/oig/special/0603/full.pdf.
16. See *Creating a Trusted Network for Homeland Security*, Second Report of the Markle Foundation Task Force, December 2003, available at http://www.markletaskforce.org (last visited December 5, 2003).
17. *Uniting and Strengthening America by Providing Appropriate Tools Required to Intercept and Obstruct Terrorism Act* (hereafter referred to as the Patriot Act), Pub. L. No. 107-56, 115 Stat. 272 (2001).

18. 50 U.S.C., section 1804 (a)(7)(b), emphasis added.

19. Ibid., as amended by the Patriot Act, section 218, emphasis added.

20. For background, see "FBI Pairs Criminal and Intelligence Cases," *CNN.com*, December 13, 2003, available at http://www.cnn.com/2003/LAW/12/13/fbi.terrorism.ap/index.html (last visited December 23, 2003).

21. See Dan Eggen and Robert O'Harrow, Jr., "U.S. Steps Up Secret Surveillance," *The Washington Post*, March 23, 2003, at http://www.washingtonpost.com/wp-dyn/articles/A16287-2003Mar23.html.

22. 12 U.S.C., section 3414(a)(1)(C); 3414(a)(5)(A) (2001).

23. 18 U.S.C., section 2709 (b) (2001), as amended by the Patriot Act, section 505 (a) (2001).

24. 20 U.S.C., section 11232g (j) (1)&(2) (2001), as amended by the Patriot Act, section 507 (2001).

25. Officially, the "Attorney General's Guidelines on General Crimes, Racketeering Enterprise and Terrorism Enterprise Investigations" (May 30, 2002). A sanitized version of the partly classified "Attorney General's Guidelines for FBI Foreign Intelligence Collection and Foreign Counterintelligence Investigations" is available at http://www.usdoj.gov/ag/readingroom/terrorismintel12.pdf.

26. See Shane Harris, "Total Information Awareness Official Responds to Criticism," *Government Executive*, Daily Briefing, January 31, 2003, http://goveexec.com/daily/fed/0103/013103h.1.htm.

27. For a summary of the privacy issues involved by TIA, see Gina Marie Stevens, *Privacy: Total Information Awareness Programs and Related Information Access, Collection and Protection Laws* (Washington, DC: Congressional Research Service, March 21, 2003).

28. See, for example, the report of the Department of Defense Technology and Privacy Advisory Committee, "Safeguarding Privacy in the Fight Against Terrorism," March 2004, and the Electronic Privacy Information Center Web page presenting a variety of descriptive material on the TIA program from both open sources and as a result of Freedom of Information Act requests (http://www.epic.org/privacy/profiling/tia/).

29. Eric Lichtblau and William Glaberson, "Millions Raised for Qaeda in Brooklyn, U.S. Says," *New York Times*, March 5, 2003, www.nytimes.com/2003/03/05/international/europe/05TERR.html?ex=1047.

30. See, for example, "The System That Doesn't Safeguard Travel," *Business Week Online*, at http://uk.biz.yahoo.com/030417/244/dxz9z.html.

31. General Accounting Office, *Information Technology: Terrorist Watch Lists Should Be Consolidated to Promote Better Integration and Sharing*, GAO-03-322 (Washington, DC: April 15, 2003). http://www.nytimes.com/2003/04/30/international/worldspecial/30TERR.html.

32. In a speech in Washington, in September 2006. Available at http://www.whitehouse.gov/news/releases/2006/09/20060905-4.html.
33. Lag (2008:717) om signalspaning i försvarsunderrättelseverksamhet, SFS 2008:717, Sveriges riksdag, Stockholm (Law on signals intelligence in defence intelligence operations). I thank my Swedish colleague and friend, Wilhelm Agrell, for comments and the citation on this issue.
34. For further details, see Eric Lichtblau and David Johnston, "Court to Oversee U.S. Wiretapping in Terror Cases," *The New York Times*, January 18, 2007; "A Spy Program in from the Cold," Editorial, *The New York Times*, January 18, 2007; James Risen, "Administration Pulls Back on Surveillance Agreement," *The New York Times*, May 2, 2007; and "Spying on Americans," Editorial, *The New York Times*, May 2, 2007.
35. Speech to the National Press Club, January 23, 2006, available at http://www.fas.org/irp/news/2006/01/hayden012306.html.
36. Available at http://www.whitehouse.gov/news/releases/2008/01/print/20080123-2.html.
37. In a conversation in Buffalo, April 2004, available at http://www.whitehouse.gov/news/releases/2004/04/20040420-2.html.
38. Interview with the Council on Foreign Relations, June 28, 2007, available at http://www.cfr.org/publication/13692/.
39. Dan Eggens and Paul Kane, "Gonzalez Hospital Episode Detailed," *The Washington Post*, May 16, 2007; p. A01, available at http://www.washingtonpost.com/wp-dyn/content/article/2007/05/15/AR2007051500864.html.
40. Senate Select Committee on Intelligence, *Foreign Intelligence Surveillance Act of 1978 – Amendments Act 2007: Report*, 110 Cong., 2nd sess. (Washington, DC: October 26, 2007), p. 5.
41. As with many famous lines, the parentage of the "suicide pact" is complicated. In the sense used here, that liberties may have to bend in the face of emergencies, it probably derives from Justice Jackson, "There is danger that, if the court does not temper its doctrinaire logic with a little practical wisdom, it will convert the constitutional Bill of Rights into a suicide pact." *Terminiello v. City of Chicago*, 337 U.S. 1 (1949).
42. *Youngstown Sheet & Tube Co. v. Sawyer*, 343 U.S. 579 (1952).
43. *Annunzio-Wylie Act of 1992*, P.L. 91-508, 32 U.S.C., section 531 (g); 31 C.F.R, sections 103.18(a)(2) and 108.19(a) (2) (ii).
44. Stephen J. Schulhofer, *The Enemy Within: Intelligence Gathering, Law Enforcement, and Civil Liberties in the Wake of September 11* (New York: Century Foundation Press, 2002), p. 52.
45. Business Executives for National Security, "Recommendations for Improving the Suspicious Activity Report (SAR)," April 11, 2003; and discussions with federal officials.

46. Walter Pincus, "Corralling Domestic Intelligence: Standards in the Works for Reports of Suspicious Activity," *The Washington Post*, January 13, 2006, p. A5.

47. See Ben Bain, "ODNI Releases Standards for Suspicious-Activity Reporting," *FCW.COM*, available at http://www.fcw.com/online/news/ 151462-1.html.

48. See Department of Justice, Office of the Inspector General, *A Review of the Federal Bureau of Investigation's Use of National Security Letters (IG Report I)*, March 2007, pp. xviii–xix, available at http://www. usdoj.gov/oig/special/s0703b/final.pdf.

49. See Department of Justice, Office of the Inspector General, *A Review of the Federal Bureau of Investigation's Use of National Security Letters (IG Report II)*, March 2008, p. 9, available at http://www.usdoj.gov/ oig/special/s0803b/final.pdf.

50. Of the TSA's $7.1 billion budget for 2003, $6.1 billion was for aviation security. See E. Marla Felcher, "Aviation Security," in *The Department of Homeland Security's First Year: A Report Card* (New York: The Century Foundation, 2004).

51. See Gregory F. Treverton et al., "The Costs of Responding to the Terrorist Threats: The U.S. Case," in Philip Keefer and Norman Loayza (eds.), *Terrorism, Economic Development, and Political Openness* (New York, Cambridge: Cambridge University Press, 2008).

52. For instance, the TSA's Screening Passengers by Observation Techniques (SPOT) was designed to train screeners to notice involuntary physical and physiological reactions that people exhibit in response to a fear of being discovered. See http://www.tsa.gov/what_we_do/layers/ spot/index.shtm.

53. The White House, *Homeland Security Presidential Directive/HSPD-6, Subject: Integration and Use of Screening Information* (Washington, DC, September 16, 2003), available at http://www.whitehouse.gov/ news/releases/2003/09/20030916-5.html.

54. See William J. Krouse and Bart Elias, *Terrorist Watchlist Check and Air Passenger Prescreening*, CRS Report RL33645, updated March 1, 2007, p. 4.

55. U.S. Department of Justice, Officer of the Inspector General, Audit Division, *Review of the Terrorist Screening Center*, Audit Report 05-27, June 2005, p. 49.

56. See Jill D. Rhodes, "CAPPS II: Red Light, Green Light, or 'Mother, May I?'," *The Homeland Security Journal*, March 2004, p. 1. For further discussion of CAPPS II and other aspects of air passenger prescreening, see CRS Report RL32802, *Homeland Security: Air Passenger Prescreening and Counterterrorism*.

57. Extrapolating from the Israeli experience in the first years of this century, an "Israel-sized" terrorist threat to the United States would imply about 10,000 deaths and 100,000 casualties per year.

58. For an argument for such a capability, along with the formidable obstacles to creating it, see my "Intelligence, Law Enforcement and Homeland Security," Twentieth Century Fund, August 2002, at http://www.homelandsec.org. For my more recent assessment, see "Intelligence," in *The Department of Homeland Security's First Year: A Report Card*, cited previously.

59. Admiral Stansfield Turner, *Secrecy and Democracy* (London: Sidgwick and Jackson, 1986), p. 178.

60. See, for instance, Omand, cited previously.

61. *Unconquerable Nation: Knowing Our Enemy, Strengthening Ourselves* (Santa Monica, CA: RAND Corporation, 2006), p. 176.

Index

293